Consciousness Reconsidered

Consciousness Reconsidered

Owen Flanagan

A Bradford Book
The MIT Press
Cambridge, Massachusetts
London, England

This book was set in Palatino by Asco Trade Typesetting Ltd., Hong Kong, and was printed and bound in the United States of America.

First printing.

Library of Congress Cataloging-in-Publication Data
Flanagan, Owen J.
  Consciousness reconsidered / Owen Flanagan.
        p.   cm.
  Includes bibliographical references.
  ISBN 0-262-06148-1
  1. Consciousness. 2. Mind and body. I. Title.
B808.9.F57   1992
126—dc20
                                                      92-10057
                                                          CIP

To my sisters—Virginia, Kathleen, and Nancy—my brother Mark, and the memory of our brother Peter

Contents

Preface

Naturalism is the view that the mind-brain relation is a natural one. Mental processes just are brain processes. This idea has increased in credibility as the picture of the mind as a sophisticated information processor has become more widely accepted and as neuroscience has shown that the brain possesses both the complexity and the power to do the information processing human minds in fact do.

But there is a gnawing suspicion that the picture of persons as sophisticated information processors leaves something out. And indeed, it does. We are *conscious creatures*. Perhaps we are information processors, but if we are, we are *conscious* information processors. Our mental life has a phenomenal side, a subjective side, that the most sophisticated information processor might lack.

Whereas the brain seems suited to processing information, it is harder to imagine the brain's giving rise to consciousness. The very idea of consciousness materializing, of subjectivity being realized in the activity of a physical organism, is puzzling. The rich phenomenology of the conscious stream and complex neural activity appear to belong to two entirely different orders: the subjective and the objective. This book is an attempt to make less puzzling the idea that consciousness is a natural phenomenon. I present a view of consciousness that I call "constructive naturalism." Consciousness is a natural phenomenon, and we can construct a theory about its nature, forms, roles, and origins by blending insights from phenomenology, psychology, cognitive science, neuroscience, and evolutionary biology. Consciousness is neither miraculous nor terminally mysterious.

The origins of this book date back to the seminar "Consciousness" that I taught in the spring of 1989. Thanks to a grant from the Alfred P. Sloan Foundation, I was able to invite as visitors Daniel Dennett, Michael Gazzaniga, Patricia Kitcher, Carolyn Ristau, Georges Rey, David Rosenthal, and Robert Van Gulick. Two colleagues from Wellesley's psychology department and fellow members of our cognitive science group, Margery Lucas and Larry Rosenblum (now at the University of California, Riverside), and my colleague from philosophy, Ken Winkler, also participated in the seminar. The seminar was a source of great intellectual stimulation to me, thanks to these individuals and to the wonderful group of students who were involved in the exploration.

In the summer of 1989, as I was gathering my thoughts from the seminar, Colin McGinn's important paper "Can We Solve the Mind-Body Problem?" appeared in *Mind*. McGinn argued that the consciousness-brain problem could never be solved by creatures with our kind of minds. McGinn's argument was imaginative, forceful, and complex—as I discovered when he was kind enough to send me several chapters of his then forthcoming book, *The Problem of Consciousness* (1991). If McGinn was right, then my whole approach to the problem of consciousness was just plain wrong. So McGinn's work inspired me. I first presented a response to his argument to my department's faculty seminar in the fall of 1989. Then during the winter and spring of 1990, I sketched out my view on the problem of consciousness and offered a reply to McGinn's 1989 paper. I published this material as the chapter "Consciousness" in the second edition of *The Science of the Mind* (1991). Writing that chapter was a good first start, but when I finished it, I found that I had a good deal more to say about consciousness. *Consciousness Reconsidered* was conceived at that time. Part of the unfinished work involved providing a more complete response to McGinn's arguments against the possibility of constructive naturalism. Chapter 6 below is specifically devoted to this task. But the book as a whole is the real response to McGinn's anticonstructive naturalism. For its overall goal is to show that a constructive theory of consciousness is not merely possible; in certain respects it is already actual.

During the fall term of the 1990/1991 academic year, Daniel Dennett invited me to participate in his seminar "Consciousness" at Tufts. Weekly conversations with Dan about his almost completed book *Consciousness Explained* (1991a) and with Ned Block and Andrew Woodfield were especially helpful in sharpening my views and giving me the courage of my convictions.

I started to write again during the spring term of 1991, when I taught a new version of my "Consciousness" seminar. This time no foundation paid for visitors, so I forged ahead with a new group of students, as intelligent and conscientious as the first group had been. I thank them for helping me get clearer on many of the issues discussed in these pages. My students and Hu-Min Ji, a visiting philosopher from Beijing, forced me to explain how, where, and why my views differ from those of other naturalists like Daniel Dennett, Robert Van Gulick, Paul Churchland, Patricia Churchland, and Colin McGinn. And they pressed me hard to respond to challenges to naturalism itself, in particular, to the challenges of Thomas Nagel and Frank Jackson.

I am indebted to a great many people. Over the past few years, I have had the good fortune to talk extensively about the problem of consciousness with Robert Van Gulick. Bob's excellent work on consciousness increased my confidence in the idea that insights from the phenomenological, psychological, and neuroscientific levels can be blended profitably in seeking to understand the nature and function of consciousness. In addition to Bob Van Gulick, I also had help from Ned Block, Robert McCauley, Daniel Dennett, George Graham, Paul Churchland, Patricia Churchland, and Jonathan Cheek, who gave me encouragement, good leads, helpful preprints and reprints, and sage advice. A visit to Saint Louis came at just the right time. There Roger Gibson introduced me to Marc Raichle, from whom I received an immensely helpful tutorial on the latest in brain-imaging research over the course of a most pleasant dinner.

David Galloway read the first draft and made many helpful comments. Ned Block made me think extra hard about epiphenomenalism and the problem of the function of consciousness by letting me read some of his unpublished work on the topic and with his written comments on chapter 7. George Graham read and commented on the entire manuscript. George pressed me to provide a clear map of the various philosophical positions on the problem of consciousness. George described his own impression of the live positions in a most helpful manner. His map helped me immensely in drawing my own map of "philosophical space" in the second section of chapter 1. That section is dedicated to George. Ken Winkler and Jerry Samet read the manuscript, sometimes successive versions, with the utmost care. Both wrote me pages and pages of comments and spent many hours talking the project over with me. I feel most fortunate to have two such excellent and tireless critics as friends. I am eternally grateful to both of them for helping me make this book far better than it would otherwise have been.

Joyce Knowlton Walworth and our children, Ben and Kate, helped make writing this book an especially pleasant experience. Writing is an activity I do at home in the presence of my family. Ben and Kate always ask me what I am working on, and as things that I work on go, they found this topic unusually fun and interesting. Ben specializes in the area of consciousness and sports. Apparently, when a Little League pitcher stares at his catcher, there is heightened awareness as the next pitch is planned. Once the plan is firmed up, automaticity takes hold, and a split-finger fastball or change-up is thrown. If consciousness kicks in at the wrong point, it is called a "wild pitch." Things are somewhat different for a second baseman or shortstop. An infielder has clear awareness of the sound of the ball coming off the bat; there is a vivid visual lock onto the ball as it heads in his direction, but there is only dim awareness of what his body is doing as it moves to make the catch. If body awareness is heightened, it is called an "error." Soccer and basketball have their own distinctive phenomenology. Whereas Ben works primarily in phenomenology and on the connection between types of consciousness and behavior, Kate is a neurophilosopher, with expertise on the sensory nerves. Consciousness is in the brain. You feel the pain in your toe not because the pain is in the toe but because the nerves in the toe tell the brain to tell you that something is wrong in your toe. They don't teach this in second grade. But Kate knows it, and she hasn't even read *Neurophilosophy* or *Consciousness Explained*.

This book is dedicated to my brothers and sisters. They each in their own way command my deep love, respect, and admiration. This book is a small token of appreciation for all they mean to me individually and collectively.

Consciousness Reconsidered

Chapter 1
Subjectivity and the Natural Order

1 Subjectivity

Three of the greatest perplexities are these. Why is there something rather than nothing? How did some of the stuff there is come to be alive? How did some of the living stuff come to be conscious? Alongside and intimately related to the questions of how and why matter, life, and consciousness came into being are questions about the nature of matter, life, and consciousness.

Here I take on the third perplexity and sketch a naturalistic theory of consciousness. My aim is to say something illuminating about the nature, function, and origin of consciousness. Subjectivity has emerged so far only in certain biological systems. It makes sense, therefore, to seek a theory of consciousness with the guidance of the neo-Darwinian theory of evolution and the best current brain science.

2 Philosophical Space

There are several main philosophical positions on the problem of consciousness. First, there is *nonnaturalism*, the view that consciousness is not a natural phenomenon and therefore cannot be understood in naturalistic terms. Some nonnaturalists think that consciousness can be made intelligible if it is understood as a power of a nonphysical substance or as composed of nonphysical properties (Popper and Eccles 1977). Others think that we need to invoke a supernatural cause to explain why phenomenal qualia, the sensation of red or the scent of a rose, are correlated with specific types of brain states (Adams 1987, Swinburne 1984). Still others think that consciousness is miraculous. Like transubstantiation and the Trinity, it is not for us to fathom.

Second, there is *principled agnosticism* (Nagel 1974, 1986). Naturalism is a position we do not understand, because we do not understand (at least at present) how the relation of consciousness and the brain can be made intelligible in naturalistic terms. We don't understand what it would mean to give an objective account of subjectivity. Since one should not believe a theory one does not even understand, agnosticism is the best policy.

Third, there is *anticonstructive naturalism*, noumenal naturalism, or the *new mysterianism*, as I will also call it (McGinn 1991). This is the view that naturalism is true. There are in fact properties of the brain that account naturalistically for consciousness. But we cannot grasp these properties or explain how consciousness depends on them. Consciousness is terminally mysterious to our minds but possibly not to minds of greater intelligence. It is terminally mysterious not because it is a nonnatural phenomenon, not because it is a miracle, but because an understanding of its nature is "cognitively closed" to us. The problem of consciousness is a case where we know how to ask the question but lack the mental powers to find the answer.

Fourth, there is *eliminativist naturalism* (P. M. Churchland 1981, P. S. Churchland 1983). According to the eliminativist, naturalism is true. The complete story of our brain will tell the complete story of our mental life. But there is a sense in which consciousness cannot be explained. Consciousness is a concept that is simultaneously too simplistic, too vague, and too historically embedded in false and confused theory to perspicuously denote a phenomenon or set of phenomena in need of explanation. Concepts like consciousness, qualia, and subjectivity are unhelpful in setting out the explanatory agenda for a naturalistic theory of mind. Whatever genuine phenomena these concepts inchoately gesture toward will be explained by the science of the mind. But the explanation will proceed best if we eliminate these concepts from the explanatory platter and seek more perspicuous and credible replacements undergirded by a rich neuroscientific theory.

Finally, there is *constructive naturalism*. This is the position I aim to defend. Like the anticonstructivist and the eliminativist, I think that naturalism is true. Against the anticonstructivist and principled agnostic, I maintain that there is reason for optimism about our ability to understand the relation between consciousness and the brain. We can make intelligible the existence of consciousness in the natural world. Against the eliminativist, I maintain that the concept of consciousness, despite its shortcomings, is needed, at least at the beginning of inquiry, to mark what is in need of explanation. Phenomenal, qualitative consciousness is what needs to be explained. Indeed, the method I propose for attacking the problem of consciousness requires that we use, but treat as revisable, our ordinary first-person modes for taxonomizing subjectivity.

Even at this early stage in the development of the science of the mind, there are deep differences of opinion among naturalists about whether the mystery of consciousness can be made to yield, about whether there are such things as phenomenal consciousness and qualia in need of explanation, about the importance of consciousness in the overall economy of mind, and about what shape the theory will take and what methods will be used to construct it. This essay is an attempt to contribute to the debate among naturalists. My aim is to show that constructive naturalism is a better view than anticonstructive naturalism, eliminative naturalism, or principled agnosticism.

Happily, I am not alone in believing that a constructive theory is possible. Recent work by P. S. Churchland (1986), P. M. Churchland (1989), and Daniel Dennett (1991a) is in the mode of constructivist naturalism. All three take conscious experience seriously as a phenomenon or set of phenomena to be explained. No one now defends the outright elimination of our commonsense ways of conceiving of mind. To be sure, the Churchlands doubt that folk psychology will fare well as inquiry proceeds, and they expect the real illumination to be provided by neuroscience rather than by cognitive psychology or philosophy. And Dennett has his eliminativist moments. For example, he favors elimination of the concept of qualia on the grounds that it names nothing (1988c). But Dennett is not as charmed as most traditional eliminativists by the promise of neuroscience. He instead favors different styles of explanation for different phenomena and proposes a "mild realism" about the patterns our commonsense psychological vocabulary picks out (1991d). The disagreements within constructive naturalism are plentiful. The important point is that these disagreements proceed in a context of agreement that mind in general and consciousness in particular will yield their secrets only by coordinating all our informational sources at once.

I would like to think that this essay might move nonnaturalists. Perhaps it will make them see that naturalism is more resourceful than they thought. But it is important to acknowledge at the start that I provide no argument against nonnaturalism. I do not think that nonnaturalism is an incoherent view, and I am familiar enough with the dialectical moves of nonnaturalists to know that from their point of view no naturalistic story will satisfy. I will be satisfied if within naturalism the constructivist position gains credibility.

3   Consciousness and Cognitivism

Behaviorism, positivism's close kin and psychology's prude, fell from power during the 1960s, and psychologists renewed the study of mind with great energy and freedom. The new regime was cognitivism. The irony is that the return of mind to psychology attending the demise of behaviorism and the rise of cognitivism did not mark the return of consciousness to the science of the mind. Mind without consciousness? How is that possible?

In the first place, the rejection of behaviorism did not take place with complete methodological abandon. A certain appropriate positivistic reserve remained. It was one thing to draw inferences about the decay rates of visual images after brief exposures and about the structure of short-term memory and its relations to long-term memory by way of sensitive tachistoscopic experiments, reaction-time tests, and retention experiments. It was a wholly other thing to try to make scientific pronouncements about consciousness. Consciousness, after all, had press of this sort:

> O, what a world of unseen visions and heard silences, this insub-stantial country of mind! What ineffable essences, these touchless rememberings and unshowable reveries! And the privacy of it all! A speechless theatre of speechless monologue and prevenient counsel, an invisible mansion of moods, musings, and mysteries, an infinite resort of disappointments and discoveries. A whole kingdom where each of us reigns reclusively alone, questioning what we will, com-manding what we can. A hidden hermitage where we may study out the troubled book of what we have done and yet may do. An introcosm that is more myself than anything I can find in the mirror. This consciousness that is myself of selves, that is everything, and yet nothing at all.   (Jaynes 1976, 1)

Now this seemed like a good thing for a psychologist interested in gaining a reputation *not* to study. Whereof one cannot speak, one should be silent. What is essentially private is something about which science should offer no opinion. "Invisible mansions" of moods, musings, and mysteries, as appealing as they might be to mushy-minded mystics, hold no interest to the scientist of the mind.

In the second place, it seemed that one could map the mind, could provide a theory of intelligent mental life without committing oneself to any general view about the nature, function, or role of consciousness. To be sure, much work assumed that a certain amount of conscious mental activity was taking place in the domain under study. For example, re-search on imagistic rotation accepted that most people in fact experience themselves rotating picturelike mental objects. But the study of imagistic rotation was designed in part to test the accuracy of these conscious experiential reports. These experiences were not considered closed off to verbalization, nor did the verbalizations stand as the last word on underly-ing processes. The alleged "ineffable essences" were not ineffable. Despite the lack of a positive theory of the nature of consciousness, the study of specific cognitive domains that typically involve conscious experiences in those domains proceeded in a spirit of skepticism about the whole idea of inner theaters, introcosms, and realms that are in principle inaccessible.

For many, the hope was that the rhapsodic received view, with its ghostly resonances, would eventually come undone. A picture of conscious mental life would eventually emerge, but it would emerge in a piecemeal fashion, associated with deepened understanding of specific cognitive domains, and alongside rejection of the idea that there exists a specific faculty of consciousness. This would take time, however, and in the meantime no respectable, or at least no respected, psychologist was trying to provide a general theory of consciousness. The general attitude during the rebirth of cognitive psychology is aptly described by Daniel Dennett: "Consciousness appears to be the last bastion of occult properties, epiphenomena, immeasurable subjective states—in short, the one area of mind best left to the philosophers who are welcome to it. Let them make fools of themselves trying to corral the 'quicksilver of phenomenology' into respectable theory" (1978, 149). A few years later, Dennett wrote, "Consciousness is making a comeback in psychology, but there is still residual skepticism, anxiety, and confusion about how to approach this perilous phenomenon scientifically" (1982, 159).

There was a third and in some ways philosophically more interesting reason of why the renewed excitement about the science of the mind was not accompanied by the reemergence of a theory of consciousness. It was widely noticed in many domains that the project of mapping out the complex information flows and networks constituting a mind, be that done at the brain level or the level of cognition, could be done without bringing consciousness into the story. Language acquisition and semantic processing, face recognition, and the like, seemed to proceed largely unconsciously. Furthermore, the dominant philosophical theory of mind, *computational functionalism*, had powerful affinities with the thesis of conscious inessentialism. *Conscious inessentialism* is the view that for any intelligent activity *i*, performed in any cognitive domain *d*, even if *we* do *i* with conscious accompaniments, *i* can in principle be done without these conscious accompaniments.

Most skeptics of strong artificial intelligence, the view that computers can in principle display any mental ability we display, press worries that machines cannot be given consciousness. Conscious inessentialism can be read as making this objection irrelevant. Mind does not require consciousness. All the input-output relations between stimuli and responses could be preserved in a system that passed the toughest conceivable Turing test, a test in which a computer must produce behavior indistinguishable from that of a person. To be sure, such a system might totally lack experience. But that simply proves the point: consciousness is not essential to intelligent mentality.

One can see how commitment to conscious inessentialism makes respectable the idea of a science of the mind that pays no significant attention to consciousness. It also explains why AI workers, be they members of aboriginal von Neumann tribes, true believers in the power of serial computation, or young connectionist upstarts devoted to massive parallelism, are not obsessed with finding the right wiring diagrams to make conscious-ness emerge. Most everyone has abandoned the old illusion that conscious-ness is definitive of the mental, that each and every mental event is a conscious one. AI workers also think that a certain kind of species chauvin-ism has made us hang onto a second illusion. We think that consciousness, even if not involved in all mental activity, is essentially involved in our intelligent and purposeful activity. But it is not, since, the argument goes, any set of input-output relations can be subserved by an endless multi-plicity of internal connections, and thus the toughest conceivable Turing test can be passed by systems totally lacking consciousness.

I reject conscious inessentialism. Consciousness *is* essentially involved in being intelligent and purposeful in the way(s) in which we are. Computa-tional functionalism, in part because it normally involves commitment to conscious inessentialism, is the wrong sort of functionalism for the philoso-pher of psychology to be committed to. It would not be the wrong sort of view if the question were, What sorts of systems can preserve the input-output relations that we take to be (partly definitive) of intelligence and purposefulness? It would not be the wrong answer to that question because the answer to that question is simply the long disjunctive list of possible mechanical and biological models that could realize the proper input-output relations. Rather, computational functionalism is the wrong sort of view for the philosopher of mind to be committed to if he or she sees the project as continuous with that of explaining how intelligent, purposeful life occurs in humans and other earthly creatures. So long as there are tastes and smells and thoughts, there are conscious events to be explained. If these conscious events are not epiphenomenal, then they need to be mentioned in our full explanations. Furthermore, it is crucial to emphasize that neither input-output equivalence nor even some richer form of compu-tational equivalence is the same as strict mental equivalence. Our behav-ioral outputs are actions; that is, they are bodily movements identified and individuated in part by the intentions and motives that constitute them. When we drive, we *signal* the intention to turn. When we laugh at a joke, we are *enjoying* the joke. Our robotic equivalent that drives just like us but lacks a motivational economy merely moves the turn signal. Our robotic equivalent that laughs at a joke but lacks a complex cognitive and conative economy does not enjoy it or think it funny.

I take the nature and function of conscious mental events and the actions they figure in as fundamental. For this reason I favor a form of functional-ism that analyzes input-output relations in terms of the processes that mediate and subserve them in the normal biological cases, not in any possible cases whatsoever (Van Gulick 1988, 1990).

There is a fourth reason, partly related to and partly independent of the previous reasons, why the reemergence of mind did not result in consciousness returning to its former pride of place. Call it the *epiphenomenalist suspicion*. In many domains in which there are in fact conscious accompaniments of the mental activity under study, it was noticed that those conscious accompaniments did not play any obvious or important causal role. First-person, phenomenological reports of the way things seem provided interesting data about experiences of imagery, short-term memory in matching tests, and so on. But the reports of conscious experience often seemed, in Dennett's wonderful analogy, to be like the press releases of the government spokesman who is out of the decision-making loop himself. A government spokesman is often one of the last persons inside the government to know what is going on. His role is quite unlike that of a truly important government functionary, the Secretary of Defense or State, for example, who exerts a firm hand in what is going on at each crucial choice point. Indeed, the press agent may, unbeknownst to himself, be engaged in massive dissembling—strategically misrepresenting the facts at the behest of those in the know. Other times he may mispeak, not so much because he is being called upon to play the role of mispeaker, but because he is too many communicative links away from the original action, like the fourth or fifth player in a game of "telephone."

The emergence of cognitive science has been accompanied by the surprising reappearance of the sort of epiphenomenalism found attractive a century before, during the birth of the science of the mind. Recall Thomas Huxley's brazen pronouncement that the "soul stands to the body as the bell of a clock to the works, and consciousness answers to the sound which the bell gives out when it is struck.... We are conscious automata" (quoted in James 1890, 131). Perhaps consciousness stands to the mind-body as the President's press agent stands to the workings of the Oval Office, the Departments of State and Defense, the National Security Council, and the Office of Management and Budget. The fact that the press agent's speech acts occur *after* the important causal activity and decision making have taken place insinuates the possibility that consciousness may play an analogous role in the governance of our individual lives.

One might resist the analogy by insisting that consciousness simply is not like the President's press agent. It is like the President himself. But this is precisely the unquestioned assumption being challenged. Furthermore, even if we accept that consciousness has a presidential role, it is important to remember that Presidents differ greatly in the amount of control they exert. Many think that Ronald Reagan had, by historical standards, relatively little control of the government. According to this view, Reagan was the entertaining and eloquent spokesperson for a cadre of smart and hardworking powers (actually layers of powers), some known to outsiders, some unknown. This is not to deny that Reagan felt as if he were in charge in his role as "The Great Communicator," first as Governor of California and eventually as President. The point is that one can feel presidential, and indeed even *be* the President, but still be less in control than it seems from either the inside or the outside.

The epiphenomenalist suspicion is healthy up to a point. This is because we tend both to think that more of mental life is conscious than it in fact is, and because we tend to overstate the causal role of consciousness. But epiphenomenalism is ultimately implausible. There are, we will see, various good reasons to ascribe consciousness a function.

4   Conscious Shyness and the New Mysterianism

So far I have isolated four reasons why the reemergence of the study of mind associated with the rise of cognitivism did not result in the simultaneous reemergence of grand theorizing about consciousness. Each reason gives rise to a distinctive form of "conscious shyness." First, there was a certain methodological scrupulousness, a vestige of behaviorism's draconian restrictions on the study of the "inner" and the "unobservable." Second, there was the view that one could analyze various aspects of mentality with a background commitment to the existence of conscious experience in the domain under study but without a commitment to any general theory of the nature and function of consciousness. Third, there was the belief, inspired by computational functionalism, that consciousness was not in fact metaphysically essential. The thesis of conscious inessentialism says that there are possible worlds in which creatures computationally identical to us do not possess consciousness. Fourth, there is the epiphenomenalist suspicion, the suspicion that the role of consciousness may be far more limited in our case than consciousness itself (not surprisingly) thinks it is, and thus the study of consciousness is of less importance in the overall project of understanding the mind than we standardly think.

An approach is conscious-shy if it sidesteps or tries to finesse the study of consciousness for any of the above reasons. Conscious shyness has, as it were, four causes. A scientist of the mind can be conscious-shy because she is methodologically modest, practicing a sort of enlightened neopositivism. Alternatively, she might believe in the reality of consciousness but think that it names such a vague or, what is different, such a heterogeneous set of phenomena that it is not the sort of thing for which a general theory can be developed (at least not yet). Different still, she might be attracted to the brand of functionalism that thinks that the aim is to explain intelligent mentality in its most abstract form, that is, in terms of the metaphysically essential properties required for the explanation of intelligence in any possible world that contains it, not in terms of the contingent properties associated with just our kind of minds, which might, not surprisingly, be especially dear to our hearts. Finally, she might simply think that we should

postpone any general theorizing about the role and function of consciousness until the evidence gives further indication of the extent to which
consciousness is involved in the causal fray, until, that is, there is evidence
that it does play a significant role in the overall economy of mind. Even if
consciousness plays a presidential role in the mind, there is still the question of whether it is presidential in the way Reagan was or the way FDR
was.

Besides the causes cited so far for conscious shyness, there are still other
causes for the even stronger reaction of eschewing altogether the scientific
study of consciousness. Nonnaturalists have their own reasons for thinking
that the problem of consciousness will not yield to science, but there are
naturalists who think this too. Anticonstructive naturalism, or the new
mysterianism, is the view that consciousness, despite being a natural phenomenon, will *never* be understood. Whether its causal role is significant or
not, it will not be understood. The "old mysterians" were dualists who
thought that consciousness cannot be understood scientifically because it
operates according to nonnatural principles and possesses nonnatural properties. Consciousness might be understood in other ways, for example, by
invoking supernatural phenomena (for some sophisticated contemporary
defenses of supernaturalism, see Swinburne 1984 and Adams 1987). Unlike
the old mysterianism or contemporary supernaturalism, the new mysterianism is a naturalistic position. Mind and consciousness exist, and they
operate in accordance with natural principles and possess natural properties. But the new mysterianism is a postmodern position designed to
drive a railroad spike through the heart of scientism, the view that science
will eventually explain whatever is natural.

Colin McGinn is a new mysterian, a proponent of anticonstructive or
noumenal naturalism. He thinks that naturalism must be true. There is no
other credible way to think about the relation of consciousness and the
brain than as a natural relation. Nonetheless, he thinks, we will never be
able to set out a credible constructive theory of that relation.

McGinn writes, "We have been trying for a long time to solve the
mind-body problem. It has stubbornly resisted our best efforts. The mystery persists. I think the time has come to admit candidly that we cannot
resolve the mystery" (1989, 349). McGinn thinks that "we know that
brains are the *de facto* causal basis of consciousness," but "we are cut off
by our very cognitive constitution from achieving a conception of that
natural property of the brain (or of consciousness) that accounts for the
psychophysical link" (1989, 350). McGinn thinks that there is some natural
property or set of properties P that accounts for consciousness. Consciousness comes with our kind of brain. It supervenes on neural activity in our
kind of brain.

McGinn simply thinks that it is in principle impossible for us to comprehend P. (McGinn is somewhat unclear whether it is P that we cannot understand or *how* it is that P accounts for consciousness or makes the existence of consciousness "intelligible.") What natural property P causes certain neural events to be consciously experienced by realizing these very conscious states is closed to us. If an omniscient God exists, then God knows all about P and how it gives rise to consciousness. But both P and the intelligible connection between P and consciousness are closed to us, the very systems in which the intelligible connections in fact obtain.

Although the doctrine is mischievous, coming from a naturalist, it is a coherent position. There are limitative results in physics and mathematics, for example, Heisenberg's Uncertainty Principle and Gödel's Incompleteness Theorem, that tell us of in-principle impossibilities faced by the physicist and mathematician. It is conceivable that just as we cannot know the position and momentum of an electron at one and the same time, or just as we can know that a certain sentence in arithmetic is true though it is in principle impossible for us to prove it within arithmetic, so we can know that consciousness is a natural phenomenon though it is in principle closed to us to know what sort of natural phenomenon it is.

It might be thought that there are limitative results within psychology itself that lend the position support. A child at each stage of cognitive development can understand certain questions or problems that are only solvable at the next stage, a stage she has not reached (Fodor 1991a). But the lesson of cognitive limits in mental development runs against the new mysterianism. For the child always eventually solves the problems she faces. None of the mysteries faced are terminal (Dennett 1991c).

It is important to see that the new mysterianism is different from principled agnosticism. The agnostic thinks that we do not understand what form a naturalistic solution to the consciousness-brain problem would take, so we ought not to confidently claim that naturalism is true. Thomas Nagel sometimes plays the agnostic. In his famous paper "What Is It Like to Be a Bat?" (1974), Nagel argues that there can be no remotely plausible naturalistic account of consciousness, that something essential will always be left out of even our very best theory. Nagel writes that "Consciousness is what makes the mind-body problem really intractable.... Without consciousness the mind-body problem would be much less interesting. With consciousness it seems hopeless" (1974, 165–166). But Nagel adds this important clarification: "It would be a mistake to conclude that physicalism is false.... It would be truer to say physicalism is a position we cannot understand because we do not at present have any conception of how it might be true" (1974, 176). In his book *The View from Nowhere*, Nagel puts it this way: "We have at present no conception of how a single event or thing could have both physical and phenomenological aspects, or how if it did they might be related" (1986, 47). Because we do not understand what form a constructive naturalistic solution to the problem of consciousness would take, we cannot assign credibility to the claim that physicalism is true or to the claim that it is false. Intellectual honesty requires that we be agnostics.

Thanks to some recent work in neuropsychology, cognitive science, and philosophy, we have, I think, the beginnings of a credible theory of consciousness. We can therefore start to sketch the outlines of a constructive-naturalistic theory. Conscious shyness can be overcome, the new mysterianism can be shown to be at least premature, and perhaps some agnostics can be converted.

5   Subjectivity, Objectivity, and the Natural Method

The question is by what method consciousness is to be studied. I propose that we try the most natural strategy, what I call the *natural method*, to see if it can be made to work. Tactically, what I have in mind is this. Start by treating three different lines of analysis with equal respect. Give phenomenology its due. Listen carefully to what individuals have to say about how things seem. Also, let the psychologists and cognitive scientists have their say. Listen carefully to their descriptions about how mental life works and what jobs consciousness has, if any, in its overall economy. Finally, listen carefully to what the neuroscientists say about how conscious mental events of different sorts are realized, and examine the fit between their stories and the phenomenological and psychological stories.

The object of the natural method is to see whether and to what extent the three stories can be rendered coherent, meshed, and brought into reflective equilibrium. The only rule is to treat all three—the phenomenology, the psychology, and the neuroscience—with respect. Any a priori decision about which line of analysis "gets things right" or "has the last word" prejudges the question of whether different analyses might be legitimate for different explanatory purposes and thus compatible with each other, or at least capable of peaceful coexistence. As theory develops, analyses at each level are subject to refinement, revision, or rejection.

One might think that the natural method must either be the preferred method or at least have been tried (it is "natural," after all) and have been shown to be deficient. This is a plausible but false thought. The natural method is certainly not the canonical method at the present time. Principled agnostics think that the concepts, categories, and methods of phenomenological, psychological, and neuroscientific analyses cannot be brought into harmonious relations. The new mysterianism or anticonstructive naturalism is the view that no method is promising. Any proposed methodology for cracking the mystery of consciousness will need to base its promises on the idle hope that the mystery of consciousness can be made to yield. Some philosophers, Richard Rorty calls them "intuitive realists" (1982), favor phenomenology over all else. On the other side, verificationists, who are ruled by the law of silence on all matters not intersubjectively available in some strong sense, have terrible allergies to phenomenology. Meanwhile, many functionalists believe that neuroscience might yield an interesting picture about how mind is implemented, but they are skeptical that it can shed any light on how the mind works. Psychological explanation, according to standard functionalism, is autonomous. Eliminativist neuroscientists, on the other hand, think that the true and complete story of mind will emerge from the story of the brain and that those who start from higher-level descriptions are in constant danger of being led astray by the silly theories embedded in our ordinary ways of thinking about the mental. So, the natural method is decidedly not the currently preferred method.

The question remains, Was it tried and discarded because in fact it did not work? The answer is no. Phenomenology alone has been tried and tested. It does not work. But all we know is that taken *alone* it does not work. Phenomenology alone never reveals anything about how "seemings" are realized, nor can it reveal anything at all about the mental events and processes involved in conscious mental life, like acoustic or visual decoding, which don't *seem* any way at all. But it is incredible to think that we could do without phenomenology altogether.

Cognitive psychology alone also does not work. Explanations at the psychological level can provide illuminating models of mental activity. But psychological explanations need to be constrained by knowledge about the brain. There are always more functional hypotheses compatible with the facts than can be true. Functional psychological analyses involve posits of all manner of processes, processors, and processing. Neuroscience constrains such positing, but the study of the brain alone will yield absolutely no knowledge about the mind unless certain phenomena described at the psychological or phenomenological level are on the table to be explained.

Imagine an utterly complete explanation of the brain framed in the languages of physics, chemistry, and biochemistry. What has one learned about mental function? The answer is nothing, unless one's neuroscientific inquiry was guided in the first place by the attempt to map certain mental functions onto the brain. This is easy to see. There is much exciting work now underway linking robust phenomenological states with distinctive types of neural activity. For example, PET scans (positron emission tomography) reveal that normal anxiety, anticipatory fear, and panic attacks involve different kinds of brain activity (M. Raichle, personal communication). Such research not only draws us closer to understanding the deep structure of these different kinds of states, it also has important implications for psychopharmacology. It is well known that tranquilizers effective in treating severe anxiety are not as effective in treating panic disorders. Sometimes antidepressants are more effective at preventing and moderating panic attacks than tranquilizers. It is natural to think that panic is simply extreme anxiety and thus simply more of whatever neural activity subserves anxiety. Despite certain strong phenomenological similarities, however, it appears that anxiety and panic involve profoundly different kinds of neural activity. The neurological difference is not one of degree but of kind.

6   The Natural Method: Three Examples

Let me give three very different examples how the natural method of seeking reflective equilibrium works.

Splitting auditory attention
There are many well-known studies of the splitting of auditory attention. In one well-known paradigm (Lackner and Garrett 1973), subjects are asked to pay attention only to the left channel in a set of earphones. In this channel they hear an ambiguous target sentence such as 'The lieutenant put out the lantern to signal the attack.' In the unattended right channel lots of irrelevant noise is produced plus the sentence 'He extinguished the flame.' Afterward the subjects are interviewed. This gives us a phenomenology. They tell us what they heard in the attended channel, and they insist that they heard nothing in the unattended channel. They were told, after all, not to listen. Subjects are good at keeping meaningful sounds received at the unattended channel from becoming conscious, or so it seems. This well-known phenomenon is known as the "Broadbent filtering effect."

It turns out, however, that when subjects are asked to choose between two interpretations of the target sentence 'The lieutenant put out the lantern to signal the attack'—(1) 'He extinguished the lantern to signal the attack' and (2) 'He put the lantern outdoors to signal the attack'—they display a decided preference for the interpretation consonant with the semantically related sentence 'He extinguished the flame', which they claim not to have heard in the unattended channel. It is known from controls that there is no preference for one meaning over the other without cuing. The best inference, therefore, is that the subjects did in fact "hear" the sentence that they are phenomenological blanks about.

There are several explanations at the psychological level compatible with these data. The favored explanation is that acoustical processing occurs in both the attended and unattended channels. The noise acoustically parsed in the unattended channel is sent on for semantic processing, and meaning is attached to the noise (how else can we explain the semantic effects of the "noise" in the unattended channel?). Meanwhile, the sentence on the attended side is an object of explicit awareness, it is remembered, and it is available for explicit report afterward. The semantically decoded sentence on the unattended side is also remembered. But because the sentence was never consciously processed, it is not consciously retrievable from memory in the form in which it was received and processed. Nonetheless, because its semantic content was fixed and received by memory, this content affects the disambiguation task in a reliable way. Subjects are unaware of having heard the sentence 'He extinguished the flame', but the content of the sentence flows smoothly through the cognitive system and causes the subject to interpret 'put out' as 'extinguished'.

This explanation *could* be true. But how can we be assured that this psychological analysis is true? There are alternative analyses. Here is one alternative. What really happens is that the noise in the unattended channel is conscious for only an instant. The brevity of the conscious episode explains why it can't be remembered as it was in fact experienced.

The first analysis takes the phenomenology as authoritative about how things were in the experimental situation. The alternative analysis disregards this authority, at least partially. It seems to the subject as if he were never consciously aware of the noise in the unattended channel. But he is wrong. His memory fails him. At the instant the sentence "He extinguished the flame" came through the right channel, he heard it. There was a seeming connected to that noise. He just didn't remember it later.

How could one make a motivated choice between these two analyses of dichotic listening? Or, to consider a more radical alternative, how could one decide that both were worthless?

Here brain science might prove useful. Neuroscience will need to tell us whether, and if so, how, the functional distinctions made by both hypotheses among acoustic, semantic, conscious, and memory processing are preserved in the brain. The brain scientist cannot begin the study of linguistic processing in general and semantic disambiguation in particular, nor can she undertake to examine the legitimacy of the distinction between acoustic processing and semantic processing without taking both the phenomenological and functional accounts seriously. But whether the distinction between acoustic and semantic processing can survive careful study of the process of linguistic comprehension by brain scientists remains to be seen.

Suppose that the psychologists' functional distinctions among acoustical and semantic processors, memory, and the like remain intact and that we are left with the choice between the original hypothesis involving no consciousness of the contents in the unattended channel and the alternative hypothesis of a lost flash of consciousness. There are philosophers who think that brain science will never be able to help us choose between hypotheses at this level of grain (Dennett 1991a). But I say, "Never say never." How conscious mental states are realized is something that neuro-science may someday yield fine-grained information about. It has recently been suggested that subjective awareness is linked to oscillation patterns in the 40 hertz range in the relevant groups of neurons; that is, neurons involved in a certain decoding task "synchronize their spikes in 40 Hz oscillations" (Crick and Koch 1990, 272). The 40 hertz patterns can be sustained for very short periods of time, in which case there is rapid memory decay, or they can resonate for several seconds, in which case they become part of working memory, give rise to more vivid phenomenology, and are more memorable. Suppose that this hypothesis turns out to be corroborated across sensory modalities and that short-term 40-hertz oscillations are observed to occur when the sentence in the unattended channel is presented. Combining present theories of short-term and working memory with such a finding would lend support to the second, initially weird, idea that the sentence in the unattended channel makes a conscious appearance (it's a 40-hertz oscillation, after all) but it is not remembered.

Neural correlates of subjective visual attention
One way to study conscious experience is to correlate particular qualitative types of experience with particular kinds of activity. One fascinating set of studies linking particular types of awareness with particular types of neural activity has recently been done on rhesus macaques and exploits the well-known phenomenon of rivalry. Gestalt images, like the necker cube or the duck-rabbit illusion, are rivalrous. The stimulus pattern stays the same, but perception flip-flops. Binocular rivalry is a particular type of rivalry that exploits the fact that the visual system tries to come up with a single percept even though the eyes often receive different visual information. In experiments involving binocular rivalry the visual input presented to the two eyes is incompatible. For example, a line moving upward is presented on the left, and a line moving downward is presented on the right. "Be-cause such stimuli cannot be fused by the cyclopean visual system, the perception alternates between the right eye alone or the left eye alone" (Logothestis and Schall 1989, 761). Humans report such alternations in perception. But how, one might ask, does one find out a monkey's pheno-menology? The answer is that one trains the monkey prior to the experi-ment to be a reliable reporter of whether it perceives a line moving up or a line moving down. This can be done by training monkeys to give bar-press reports or, more surprisingly, by training the monkeys to execute a saccade (a quick eye movement) to a spot on the left if a downward movement is perceived and to a spot on the right if an upward movement is per-ceived. A monkey's report of how things appear at any moment (its phenomenology) provides psychophysical data about the rate of percep-tual shifting and raises interesting questions about why there is shifting

perception as opposed to a winner-take-all lock on one of the rival perceptual interpretations. But the phenomenological data ("The line is now moving upward") and the psychophysical data about the time between perceptual switches yield no information about what is going on in the brain, and in particular they yield no information about what neuronal events are involved in the shifting perceptions. This is where looking at the brain helps.

It is well known that monkeys have as many as 20 to 25 visual areas in the neocortex. The bulk of retinal output projects through the lateral geniculate nucleus of the thalamus to the primary visual cortex at the back of the brain that computes edges. Other areas are interested in color and shape, position relative to the organism itself, facial features, and motion and depth. Motion detection occurs primarily in the middle temporal and medial superior temporal areas in the superior temporal sulcus (STS). So the activity of neurons in the STS were monitored as the monkeys reported upward or downward motion. The study of the effect of the rival stimuli on 66 single neurons indicated that the "activity of many neurons was dictated by the retinal stimulation. Other neurons, however, reflected the monkeys' reported perception of motion direction" (Logothetis and Schall 1989, 761). The principle of supervenience says that every difference at the level of mentality must be subserved by a difference at some lower level (but perhaps not conversely). This experiment indicates how the robust phenomenological difference between an upward or downward moving image might be subserved (although undoubtedly not exclusively) by small but detectable changes in activity in the cortical areas subserving motion detection.

The experiment is an excellent example of how subjective awareness can be studied by drawing together information gathered at different levels of analysis and by distinctive techniques. First, there is the assumption that there is something it is like for a monkey to have visual experience. Second, good old-fashioned psychological techniques of operant conditioning are used to train the monkeys to provide reports about what they see. Finally, these reports are linked with detailed observations of the activity of 66 distinct neurons to yield information about the distinct brain processes subserving perceptual experiences of upward and downward moving lines. This is knowledge by triangulation. The natural method works.

Conscious event memory
Many years ago a famous neurological patient H.M. had medial-temporal-lobe surgery to cure his epilepsy. H.M.'s ability to remember new events and facts died with the excision. Still, H.M. remembered how to perform standard motor tasks and how to use language. Indeed, to this day H.M. is something of a crossword puzzle aficionado. His intact semantic memory is

tapped by questions directly before his eyes, and his place in the puzzle is visually available to him. When H.M. is away from a puzzle he is working on, he cannot remember how far along on it he is or even that he is working on a puzzle. There are other sorts of games or puzzles that H.M. was not familiar with before surgery but that he has become good at. The Tower of Hanoi puzzle requires that one move a set of rings down a three-post line-up (one ring and one post at a time) so that in the end they are in order of size on the last post. When the game was first taught to H.M., he played as poorly as any first-timer. But gradually he caught on. Each time the puzzle is presented to him, he claims never to have seen it before. But even after long periods of not working the puzzle, H.M. shows the clear effects of prior experience. He is better than any novice and invariably starts at a level of proficiency close to where he left off. H.M. has no conscious declarative memories about the Tower of Hanoi puzzle, but quite clearly information has sunk in about how to do it.

H.M.'s good general intelligence and his semantic memory can sustain him during a short period of newspaper reading. But minutes after he has read the newspaper, he is blank about what he read. It is tempting to say that H.M. has an intact short-term memory but no long-term memory. But this is too simplistic for a variety of reasons. First, he retains information over the long term about how to do the Tower of Hanoi puzzle. The information is just not retained consciously. Second, when he does a cross-word puzzle or reads a newspaper, he depends on something longer than short-term memory, which on standard views is very short. As long as H.M. is paying attention to a task, like a crossword puzzle or a newspaper article, he can retain information about it. When his attention is removed from the overall task his memory goes blank.

H.M. can give us a phenomenology, a set of reports about what he remembers and what he doesn't. He also reveals in his behavior that he remembers certain things that he can't consciously access. Other human amnesiacs provide further phenomenological and behavioral data. Putting together the phenomenological and behavioral data with the knowledge that there is damage or excision to the medial temporal lobe leads to an initial hypothesis that this area plays some important role in fixation and retrieval of memories of conscious events.

The medial temporal lobe is a large region that includes the hippocampus and associated areas, as well as the amygdala and related areas. Magnetic resonance imaging (MRI) has allowed for very precise specification of the damaged areas in living human amnesiacs and in monkeys. This research reveals that the hippocampus is the crucial component. When there is serious damage or removal of the hippocampal formation, the entorhinal cortex, and the adjacent anatomically related structures, the perirhinal and parahippocampal cortices, the ability to consciously remember novel facts or events is lost. Removal or serious lesions of the amygdala profoundly affect emotions, but not memory. It is not as if memories were created and set down in the hippocampal formation. The hippocampal formation is necessary to lay down memories, but it is not remotely sufficient for the conscious memory of facts and events. For habit and skill learning, it is not even necessary.

The complex network involved in fixing such memories has now been mapped in some detail by using monkey models and by drawing inferences about human memory function based on comparative deficit and normal data. Larry Squire and Stuart Zola-Morgan (1991) report an elegant experiment in which monkeys were given a simple recall task. Each monkey was presented with a single object. Then after a delay (15 seconds, 60 seconds, 10 minutes), it was presented with a pair consisting of the original object and a new one. The monkeys were trained to pick the novel object to get a reward. The task is trivial for monkeys with intact hippocampal formations, but there is severe memory impairment (increasing with latency) in monkeys with destruction to the hippocampal formation. The procedure is a reliable test of perceptual memory.

A skeptic could admit this but deny that there is any evidence that monkeys *consciously* remember what they saw. To be sure, the information about the original stimulus is processed and stored. The monkeys' behavior shows that these memories are laid down. But for all we know, these memories might be completely unconscious, like H.M.'s memories for the Tower of Hanoi puzzle. They might be. However, on the basis of anatomical similarities between monkey and human brains, the similarity of memory function, and evolutionary considerations, it is credible that the monkeys' selection of the appropriate stimulus indicates what they consciously remember, and thus that it can be read as providing us with a phenomenology, with a set of reports of how things seem to them.

The next step is to put the phenomenological and behavioral data from humans and monkeys together with the data about specific types of lesions suffered and join both to our best overall theories of the neural functions subserving memory and perception. Coordination of these theories and data yield the following general hypothesis. When a stimulus is observed, the neocortical area known to be sensitive to different aspects of a visual stimulus are active. For example, in the simple matching task, the areas responsible for shape and color detection are active. In a task where the object is moving, the areas involved in motion detection become involved. Activity of the relevant cortical areas is sufficient for perception and immediate memory. "Coordinated and distributed activity in neocortex is thought to underlie perception and immediate (short-term) memory. These capacities are unaffected by medial temporal lobe damage.... As long as a percept is in view or in mind, its representation remains coherent in short-term memory by virtue of mechanisms intrinsic to neocortex" (Squire and Zola-Morgan 1991, 1384). A memory is set down only if the information at the distributed cortical sites is passed to three different areas close to the hippocampus and then into the hippocampus itself. The hippocampus then passes the message back through the medial temporal lobe out to the various originating sites in the neocortex that processed the relevant aspects of the stimulus in the first place. The memory is laid down in a distributed fashion. It is activated when the connections between the hippocampus and the various areas it projects to are strengthened by, for example, the request for recall. Once the memory is laid down and especially after it is strengthened, "Proust's principle" comes into play. The memory can be reactivated by the activation of any important node, e.g., the one subserving object shape or color, even smell or sound, without having to be turned on by the hippocampus directly. In this way the hippocampal formation passes the "burden of long-term (permanent) memory storage" to the neocortex and is freed to make new memories (Squire and Zola-Morgan 1991, 1385). This theory is credible and powerful. It explains how damage to the hippocampal formation can destroy the capacity to form new memories, and it explains why old memories are retained despite hippocampal destruction—their storage has been assumed by the neocortex.

Here again is an elegant example of the natural method. There are the phenomenological and behavioral data coming from H.M. and other human patients. There are the behavioral data coming from the monkeys, which I claim ought to be read as informing us about how things seem to the monkeys. There is the prior work linking visual processing with certain brain processes. And there is the eventual theory that explains how conscious memories are fixed, how they are recalled, what they are doing when they are not active (they are dispositions laid down in neural nets), and so on.

The three examples taken together show the power of the natural method. They also show that there is nothing about the phenomenological concept of consciousness that renders it logically incompatible with the terms and concepts of a science of the mind. The best strategy is one that promotes the search for relations among the phenomenological, information-processing, and neural levels (Wimsatt 1976; P. S. Churchland 1986; Shallice 1988; McCauley, in press). In practice, the search for relations will require give-and-take in various places, especially in our commonsense characterizations of mental events. There are a host of possible relations that might be discovered to obtain among the different levels. Presumably, each and every mental state is a neural state; that is, presumably, token physicalism is true. But there are multifarious relations of dependency, covariation, and supervenience that might obtain between mental events and neural events (see Kim 1990 for an analysis of many of these relations). The evidence suggests that there are some domains, for example, color vision, in which relatively neat mappings exist between mental-state types and neural-state types and thus for which some sort of identity theory may be true. There are other domains, for example, semantic memory, where strict type identity between the mental state that subserves my understanding of the term 'chair' and the mental state that subserves yours is less credible (of course, this may well be due to the fact that despite prima facie semantic sameness, 'chair' for me and 'chair' for you do not belong to the exact same mental kind, since they mean somewhat different things). There may well be concepts and theories designed for understanding phenomena at the macro level, concepts such as that of the self and theories of self-consciousness and narrative self-representation, for example, that are autonomous in the sense that they do not depend on showing how self-representation is achieved at the micro level in the brain (Fodor 1981; McCauley 1986, in press). The science of the mind requires an account of self-consciousness and self-representation, since these are genuine phenomena. The account must be compatible with what is deemed possible and credible by neuroscience, even if our theories of the self are not perspicuously expressible in neuroscientific terms. In the end, the best bet is that all the various relations mapped out as possibilities in the debates among identity theorists, functionalists, and eliminativists—relations of type identity, token identity, reduction, autonomy, and outright elimination (perhaps there is no id)—obtain in some domains.

The method of seeking reflective equilibrium among the phenomenological, psychological, and neuroscientific levels is deployed throughout this essay. Its merits are for others to judge. But if I am right that there are insights about the conscious mind to be gained at the level of first-person and third-person phenomenology, at the level of functional psychology, and at the level of brain science, it would be foolish to proceed in any other way.

Chapter 2
Quining Consciousness

1 What Quining Is

A book should be about something. A philosophical theory about something that does not exist is something nobody needs. It is normal to say many false things as one theorizes about some set of phenomena. But it is bad if one's theory trades in fiction at the level of core ontological commitments. Philosophers are a bold and brazen group, and the phenomenon of denying the existence of something that everyone thinks exists has been observed among them with enough frequency to have been named. 'To quine', a verb in honor of W. V. O. Quine, means to deny resolutely the existence or importance of something seemingly real or significant, for example, the soul (Dennett 1988c). Quining consciousness—resolutely denying its existence and recommending that the concept of consciousness join the concepts of the ether and demonic possession in the dung heap of intellectual history—has been seriously proposed.

Since some philosophers have said that there is no such thing as consciousness, I need to start with basics and explain why I think consciousness exists. To give my argument some force, as involving more than a simple expression of a place in my heart for the concept of consciousness, I will try to explain why even those philosophers rightly read as thinking that there is (or might be) no such thing as consciousness in fact think (or should think) that there is some such thing as consciousness. This is paradoxical, but it is true.

Two formidable arguments for quining consciousness involve attempts to secure an analogy between the concept of consciousness and some other concept in intellectual ruin. It has been suggested that the concept of consciousness is like the concept of phlogiston or the concept of karma. One shouldn't think in terms of such concepts as phlogiston or karma. And it would be a philosophical embarrassment to try to develop a positive theory of karma or phlogiston. There simply are no such phenomena for there to be theories about. Let me explain why the analogies with karma and phlogiston do not work to cast doubt on the existence of consciousness or on the usefulness of the concept.

2   *The Phlogiston Objection*

Patricia Churchland writes,

> It sometimes happens in the history of science that well-used, highly
> entrenched, revered and respected concepts come unstuck. That is,
> under the suasion of a variety of empirical-cum-theoretical forces,
> certain concepts lose their integrity and fall apart. Their niche in the
> theoretical and explanatory scheme of things is reconstructed and
> reconstrued, and new concepts with quite different dimensions and
> dynamics come to occupy the newly carved niche. The "spirits"
> and "principles" of alchemy, the "crystal spheres" of pre-Galilean as-
> tronomy, "daemonic possession" of Medieval medicine, "phlogiston,"
> "ether," and "signatures," are now nought but dry bones of an earlier
> intellectual ecology.... A similar fate may befall concepts respected
> and revered in our own prevailing conception of how humans
> work.... The concept on which I mean to focus is consciousness.
> (1983, 80)

Churchland goes on to speak of "the erosion of the concept" and of
"misgivings about the traditional conception of consciousness."

The main problem with the orthodox concept of consciousness is that it
finds its meaning within a web of theory committed to false views about
unity, transparency, and first-person incorrigibility.

> In our naivete, it seems now that conscious states are a single, unified,
> *natural* kind of brain state, but we should consider the possibility that
> the brain is fitted with a battery of monitoring systems, with varying
> ranges of activity and with varying degrees of efficiency, where
> consciousness may be but one amongst others, or where these sys-
> tems cross-classify what we now think of as conscious states. States
> we now group together as conscious states may no more constitute a
> natural kind than does say, dirt, or gems, or things-that-go-bump-in-
> the-night.   (P. S. Churchland 1983, 92)

The passage expresses a basis for suspicion about a certain view of consciousness—the view that "conscious states are a single, unified, *natural*,
kind of brain state." It is important to see that even if this suspicion proved
true, it would not prove that consciousness does not exist. One can deny
that x is a natural kind without denying that x exists. Dirt, gems, and things
that go bump in the night exist. They are even kinds of a sort. They simply
are not *natural* kinds. They don't figure in any interesting or unified way in
scientific explanation.

Second, this way of stating the objection to the concept of consciousness should make one wonder what the orthodox concept of consciousness

is. Indeed, it should make one wonder if there is any such thing as the orthodox concept. What Gilbert Ryle (1949) called the "official doctrine" was the Cartesian doctrine of the "ghost in the machine," the doctrine that placed an incorporeal mind inside the body. If Ryle's official doctrine is the orthodox concept, those who in their naiveté think that conscious states are a single, unified, natural kind of brain state hold an unorthodox concept, since this view involves a commitment to materialism about consciousness. Are ordinary folk materialists about consciousness? I doubt it.

The idea that consciousness is unified, self-luminous, incorrigible about its own contents, *and* brain-based is a view that has recently been dubbed "Cartesian materialism" (Dennett 1991a). It is a bad view, because it takes all the most questionable tenets of the Cartesian theory of consciousness, detaches them from an incorporeal soul, and reattaches them to the brain. But it is unclear how widespread the view is and, if it is widespread, among whom it is widespread.

My suspicion is this. There is no single orthodox concept of consciousness. Currently afloat in intellectual space are several different conceptions of consciousness, many of them largely inchoate. The *Oxford English Dictionary* lists 11 senses for 'conscious' and 6 for 'consciousness'. The meanings cover self-intimation, being awake, phenomenal feel, awareness of one's acts, intentions, awareness of external objects, and knowing something with others. The picture of consciousness as a unified faculty has no special linguistic privilege, and none of the meanings of either 'conscious' or 'consciousness' wear any metaphysical commitment to immaterialism on its sleeve. The concept of consciousness is neither unitary nor well regimented, at least not yet.

This makes the situation of the concept of consciousness in the late twentieth century very different from that of the concept of phlogiston in the 1770s. I don't know if ordinary folk had any views whatsoever about phlogiston at that time. But the concept was completely controlled by the community of scientists who proposed it in the late 1600s and who characterized phlogiston as a colorless, odorless, and weightless "spirit" that is released rapidly in burning and slowly in rusting. Once the spirit is fully released, we are left with the "true material," a pile of ash or rust particles.

The chemical revolution of the late 1700s transformed much more than the theory parcel involving phlogiston. But it did truly and deservedly result in the elimination of the orthodox concept of phlogiston. Phlogiston theorists were right that burning and rusting could be explained in a unified way. They were wrong, however, in two crucial respects. First, the substance involved was not phlogiston; it was oxygen. Furthermore, oxygen was not a spirit but a gas, and as such it has a certain atomic weight. Second, the substance in question, oxygen, was gained, not lost, during the processes in question.

The concept of phlogiston was introduced to name the colorless, odorless, and weightless spirit released during rusting and burning. The reason for saying that there is no such thing as phlogiston depends both on the falsehood of the claim that some substance is lost during burning and rusting (the opposite is true) and on the fact that the substance involved in the actual process, namely oxygen, is not *anything* like phlogiston. So phlogiston gets eliminated from our scientific vocabulary. There is nothing in the world that fits its description. The substance that plays its proposed role in explaining burning and rusting is oxygen.

The first point is that if I am right that the concept of consciousness is simply not owned by any authoritative meaning-determining group in the way the concept of phlogiston was owned by the phlogiston theorists, then it will be harder to isolate any single canonical concept of consciousness that has recently come undone or is in the process of coming undone, and thus that deserves the same tough treatment that the concept of phlogiston received.

There is a second reason for resisting the analogy. The case of phlogiston is one in which a concept was banished because it served no explanatory purpose. The phenomena it was designed to explain received a better explanation in terms of a new theoretical posit. McCauley (in press) points out that the replacement of phlogiston by oxygen is an *intra*level replacement: the replacement takes place among terms designed for the same level and type of analysis. Neuroscience, cognitive psychology, and first-person phenomenology do not purport to describe phenomena at the same level of analysis. They have an *inter*level relation, and "the history of science offers no precedent for theory elimination in interlevel contexts" (McCauley in press).

It is useful to think of the situation in terms of what is in need of explanation (the explananda), rusting and burning, and what is posited to do the explaining (the explanans), phlogiston. No one doubts that rusting and burning are phenomena in need of explanation. They are retained as explananda across both the phlogiston and oxygen theories. The question arises as to whether the concept(s) of consciousness functions primarily to characterize phenomena to be explained or to characterize posits that play significant roles in explanation. I don't want to get too fussy, because if I am right, there are too many different views of consciousness available to say anything definitive about the role any particular concept plays, yet it is plausible to say that the concept of consciousness is deployed both in contexts in which it is to be explained, analyzed, or thickly described and in contexts in which it (or some species of it—it is a genus term after all) is deemed explanatory. Questions like 'What is the nature of consciousness?' 'How is consciousness realized?' 'What types of conscious states are there?' put consciousness forward as a phenomena in need of more precise characterization and explanation. Statements from the high-browed 'Consciousness explains why the meaning of life arises as an issue for *Homo sapiens*' to the more mundane 'I wear this perfume because it smells great to me' deploy consciousness in explanatory roles. In the first case a temporally persistent property of mind is posited; in the second case a specific conscious state is posited. In both cases a causal role is attributed.

I want to acknowledge that an extraordinary number of truly ridiculous answers can be given to the first set of questions, questions about the nature and possibility conditions of consciousness, but I want to insist that this is not because conscious mental states are silly or misguided things about which to seek better understanding. Like rusting and burning, consciousness conceived of in a minimalist sort of way, points to a robust set of phenomena in need of explanation. Phlogiston was a bad way of explaining the phenomena of rusting and burning. Oxygen is better. Perhaps most of what has been said in answer to our pressing questions about consciousness are rubbish. I think that this is probably true. But this wouldn't show that consciousness is not a legitimate object of philosophical and scientific scrutiny, any more than the failure of phlogiston theory showed that rusting or burning were not in need of explanation.

Phlogiston couldn't explain anything, because it didn't exist. It follows that phlogiston itself required no explanation. But consciousness exists. What it is, whether it is in any interesting sense a unified kind, is something we do not yet know.

One might resist this line of analysis by claiming that concept, theory, explanandum, and explanans cannot be neatly pulled apart. If our theories about consciousness are deeply mistaken or if the concept of consciousness systematically fails to fulfill the explanatory role it is designated to play, then it simply does not make sense to hold that there is some legitimate object of inquiry that remains, despite these systematic failings, and that is worth the time of day. I have three responses. First, the phlogiston case is an example where a robust enough set of phenomena, rusting and burning, do in fact retain their right to be explained despite the utter falsehood of the first-pass explanations. Second, I have suggested the possibility that no one is an authority on the concept of consciousness (yet), and so it is something of an idle game to try to count up all the false or silly things said about consciousness, in the attempt to conclude that the canonical concept is worth abandoning. It is unclear what, if anything, the canonical concept is. Counting false or misguided statements about consciousness might allow us to mount a case for conceptual confusion. But it would be harder to show that the confusions originate from a singular orthodox concept and, even if it did, that the confusions were so weighty, numerous, and irreparable that the concept simply had to go. Third and relatedly, insofar as one can judge such matters at the present time, not all the explanatory functions attributed to conscious states are fantastic. Consider two examples of everyday consciousness discourse: "She ate so much cake because it tasted so good." "The normally reliable clerk couldn't shake the vivid memory of the nightmare. The memory kept interfering with his calculations, and his work before lunch was a total disaster." Both these explanations are probably incomplete, but they may well place specific tokens of conscious mental states in their right explanatory roles. At least it is not crazy to think that they say something true and nothing false.

I said at the start that I intended to show that even those philosophers who propose quining consciousness share (or should share) the conviction that, across the various incompatible theories in which it is embedded, the term points to some phenomenon or phenomena in need of explanation. I don't want to insist that they share my faith in any particular explanations containing the superordinate term 'consciousness' and its subordinate terms 'smell', 'sight', '(conscious) memory', and so on. The theory of consciousness I favor is a neurophilosophical one, so it will be good if I can have the eminent neurophilosopher Patricia Churchland in my camp, at least on the issue that the concept of consciousness picks out something(s) in need of explanation. This requires that I explain how her view involves a belief in consciousness, despite her well-motivated misgivings about much that is said about consciousness.

Here are two pieces of evidence indicating Churchland's commitment to consciousness as a phenomenon to be explained, and thus to a ground internal to her own thinking for resistance to the consciousness-phlogiston analogy.

Toward the end of the paper "Consciousness: The Transmutation of a Concept," in which Churchland suggests the phlogiston analogy and thus insinuates the possibility of outright elimination of the concept of consciousness, she writes, "Finally, it must be asked, how should we try to understand what consciousness is?" (1983, 92). Rather than suggesting that the question is ill formed or misguided, that there is nothing to be understood, and rather than advocating complete elimination, an idea that haunts some passages in the paper, Churchland promotes the idea of concept *transformation*, mentioned in the paper title. Indeed, in response to her question of "how should we try to understand what consciousness is," she promotes what she later describes as the coevolutionary strategy (1986). We need to study the "neurophysiological differences between conscious and nonconscious states. We need to work out views on the nature of attention, vision, and dreams by *yoking descriptions of attention, vision, dreams and so on, framed in phenomenological and functional terms, to credible brain research*" (1986, 362, my italics). What consciousness is will be understood only after such coevolutionary give-and-take among different levels of description and among adjacent sciences has been given time to wend its way toward a thick and rich description of the phenomena we now have a very incomplete sense of. This is straightforward advocacy of the natural method I recommended in the first chapter.

In *Neurophilosophy*, Churchland says this about the earlier paper, in which she suggested that consciousness *might* turn out to be like phlogiston: "In a previous publication (1983) I argued that consciousness, as it is circumscribed in folk psychology, probably is not a natural kind, in much the way that impetus is not a natural kind. Nor, for example, do the categories 'gems' and 'dirt' delimit natural kinds. That is to say, *something* is going on all right, but it is doubtful that the generalizations and categories of folk psychology either do justice to that phenomenon or carve Nature at her joints" (1986, 321). Later in the same passage she clarifies the problem with the concept of consciousness in this way: "The brain undoubtedly has a number of mechanisms for monitoring brain processes, and the folk psychological categories of 'awareness' and 'consciousness' indifferently lump together an assortment of mechanisms" (1986, 321).

Many of the worries expressed in these passages fall under the oversimplification charge, which I will take up when I discuss the karma objection below. What I want to emphasize for now is the admission that "*something* is going on all right." With phlogiston, nothing is going on at all. But with consciousness, something is going on. Rusting and burning have always been going on. When phlogiston theorists called the shots, justice was done to neither phenomenon. Now we understand rusting and burning better. The phenomena stayed on the explanatory platter despite the disappearance of what could allegedly explain them. It is not unreasonable to hold out the same hope for consciousness. With consciousness, unlike with phlogiston, we are in something like the situation lyrically described in Bob Dylan's song: "Something is happening, but you don't know what it is, do you Mr. Jones?"

The upshot so far can be expressed in this way. If the concept of consciousness required that there be a faculty of consciousness, a unified place where conscious experiences first awaken on the input side and are first generated on the side of willful action, then neuroscience spells doom for the concept. Consciousness will go the way of phlogiston. There is simply no place in the brain that plays the conceptualized role. Fortunately for the friends of consciousness, the very vagueness of the concept allows that conscious experience may yet receive a noneliminativist account within a mature science of the mind. Unlike the concept of phlogiston (and perhaps unlike the concepts of the id and the libido), the concept of consciousness was not initially designed to play an explanatory role in science. It therefore never received precise characterization, such as required the renunciation of ontological commitment to phlogiston once it was discovered that there simply is no substance being released in rusting and burning and hence that there is no phlogiston.

To be sure, some have thought that consciousness, if it is anything at all, must be a unified faculty. But the concept was never tied so firmly to that use—which, it is worth noting, is neutral between materialism and dualism—that those who think that consciousness is an emergent property of brain states rather than a faculty can be accused of violating the logic of the concept.

There are conceptions of consciousness and ways of deploying the term in explanatory contexts that deserve to be quined. But even if all the extant conceptions of consciousness deserve this tough treatment, the phenomenon of consciousness, however poorly understood, is robust enough to stand up and keep its ground against those who would quine it under.

3   The Karma Objection

In a paper entitled "A Reason for Doubting the Existence of Consciousness," Georges Rey points out that concepts can change their meaning over time as a result of empirical findings. Water was always wet, drinkable, and so on. We now know that it is also H_2O. About consciousness he writes, "If it is anything at all, it is whatever empirical scientists— psychologists, psychobiologists, but probably not merely philosophers— will in the course of their researches discover it to be" (Rey 1983, 2). This is true.

If consciousness is anything at all, empirical science, broadly construed, will tell us what it is. But perhaps consciousness isn't anything at all. Rey worries that the concept of consciousness may be like the concept of karma. According to Rey, "There is nothing that will properly serve for what the users of the term ['karma'] were 'getting at.' Consequently the term *fails to refer*. It involved a wrong, excessively simplistic way of thinking about things" (1983, 5, my italics). The concept of consciousness shows signs of similar failings.

There are actually three different objections embedded in Rey's argument. First, there is the possibility that there "is nothing that will properly serve for what the users [of the term 'consciousness'] were 'getting at.'" Second, there is the objection that the logic of the concept of consciousness may incorporate at its core a deep falsehood or set of falsehoods, for example, regarding incorrigibility or unity, and that this falsehood will render the concept unsalvageable. Third, there is the objection that the concept of consciousness may be "too simplistic" to serve the explanatory role(s) it is designated to serve.

Let me start with the last objection and work backward. The idea that the concept of consciousness in all its uses is at present too simplistic seems uncontroversially true. We don't yet understand consciousness very well or deeply. And as Patricia Churchland points out in the passages quoted above, 'consciousness' and 'awareness' simpliciter are terms hardly refined, perspicuous, or fine-grained enough to serve in illuminating ways in the generalizations of a mature science of the mind. Such superordinate terms function at this point in time as gross gestures toward significant classes of (we think) related phenomena in need of analysis, taxonomizing, and explanation. If there is a deeper, less superficial understanding to be gained, it will emerge as scientific inquiry advances.

But Rey suggests that the excessive simplicity of the concept of consciousness infiltrates ordinary explanatory discourse in such a way that it does more harm than good and sheds more darkness than light. We ought to be open to the possibility that the concept should be weeded from the conceptual landscape. Pruning won't work to get the concept back in shape. Quine it and plant anew.

The analogy with karma is supposed to help us see the potential wisdom of ridding ourselves of the concept. 'Karma' refers to the good or bad fortune that accrues to an individual on the basis of the good or bad deeds she has performed in previous lives. Good fortune results from good karma; bad fortune from bad karma. The objection of excessive simplicity is that we know that the causes of good and bad fortune are multifarious. But explanations of all the instances of good or bad fortune in terms of karma assimilate this multifarious and heterogeneous array of causal antecedents of good and bad fortune into one single kind. We lose sight of specific and useful information when we gloss all human events in terms of karma. The claim is that the same mistake is made, and the same loss of fine-grained understanding is incurred, when 'consciousness' is used in explanation.

The charge of oversimplification is misleading in two important respects. First, although hippies (when there were hippies) and others uninitiated into the Hindu life form might utter sentences of the form "x happened because of good (or bad) karma," orthodox Hindus rarely talk this way. The metaphysical commitment to a background theory in which the idea of karma functions essentially is quite compatible with causal discourse in which particular instances of good and bad fortune are individuated much as we individuate them, and in which the proximate and distal causes of these events are isolated much as we isolate them. Hindus say the car crashed because the brakes failed and that a person died of cancer, just as we do (see Shweder 1991 for an illuminating discussion of karma discourse). Second, the point that the background commitment to a possibly dubious metaphysic does not infect all Hindu discourse and prevent Hindus from providing rich, true, and largely uncontroversial accounts about the causes of events applies analogously to our own possibly misguided theories of consciousness. Dubious theories of consciousness abound. But listen to the ordinary discourse of philosophers and everyone else. We are forever explaining things in terms of tastes, smells, thoughts, and the like. Materialists and immaterialists get along surprisingly well in communicating such matters. The words 'conscious' and 'consciousness' are invoked relatively infrequently in ordinary causal discourse. But even when they are, they cause little trouble in communicative flow. Just as Hindu talk of the proximate causes of car accidents and death can be meshed with a karma or nonkarma metaphysic, so too most ordinary discourse in which conscious mental events are invoked can be meshed with any number of background views of consciousness. Both Cartesians and non-Cartesians can agree that a woman wears a particular perfume because she loves the fragrance, despite their deep metaphysical differences about how loving some fragrance is realized.

The point is that the first objection turns on the exaggerated impression that a background commitment to a karma metaphysic will engender simplistic explanations in terms of karma. But this is not so. Similarly, our everyday mental discourse shows no signs that some single, overly simplistic concept of consciousness obstructs our ability to pick out the multifarious array of types of conscious mental events that figure in the overall economy of human mental life.

The second objection actually rests on an implicit acknowledgment that far from being too simplistic, our theories of both consciousness and karma are extremely complex. The trouble is that they are also false, irreparably so. With karma the problem is that it essentially involves a belief in reincarnation. Since we do not believe in reincarnation, we cannot use the concept of karma in any meaningful way. What is the parallel false and ineliminable belief associated with consciousness? Rey suggests that it is the "Cartesian intuition," the belief in the infallibility of first-person, present-tense beliefs about the contents of consciousness (1983, 3–7; 1988, 6).

Like Rey, I think the Cartesian intuition is false. But I think that it is implausible to claim that it is an ineliminable component of the concept of consciousness. To show that it is, one would need first to point to an orthodox concept of the sort that I earlier denied exists, and then one would need to establish that the false belief could not be disengaged from the concept without draining it of its very integrity. In the case of karma there actually exist certain canonical texts that legislate criteria for coherent usage. Because of the canon, it is hard to see how the belief in reincarnation could be dropped and the concept maintained. For consciousness, however, there is no orthodoxy. Instead, there are many competing views of the nature of the phenomenon. Orthodox Cartesians may be stuck without *their* concept of consciousness if the Cartesian intuition must go. But it is unclear that *any* remotely credible philosophically and scientifically attuned concept of consciousness will need to incorporate the problematic intuition if it is to be a bona fide concept of consciousness. In his 1988 paper and in conversation, Rey has indicated that he favors an analogy between consciousness and the soul over the original consciousness-karma analogy. This suggests that he thinks that there is an orthodox concept and that it is a Cartesian concept, or at least an immaterialist one. It is this linkage that I deny exists.

I do think that there is something that binds all the various concepts of consciousness and that cannot be given up. Conscious experience names the class of mental states or events that involve awareness. A conscious experience is a state such that there is something it is like to be in it. Luckily, these ideas are vague and compatible with all manner of theoretical refinement.

The shared component is minimal enough that I see no real impossibility in an orthodox Cartesian abandoning his theory of consciousness and going back to the drawing board to explain consciousness. That is, there is no incoherence in the idea of an orthodox Cartesian abandoning the specifically Cartesian idea of consciousness without discarding the idea that there is a phenomenon or set of phenomena worthy of the name and in need of explanation. To see this, consider the following parallel. The earth was conceived of as stationary from the point of view of Ptolemaic astronomy. For Copernicans, it is in constant motion. Thus in one sense, for Copernicans there is no such thing as the earth, Ptolemaically conceived. But there is nothing incoherent about a convert from Ptolemy's system to Copernicus' system saying, "I used to think that the earth was stationary and at the center of the universe. I no longer believe either thing. But I haven't changed most of my other beliefs about the earth."

If one is absurdly fussy, one might claim that he is speaking nonsense when he refers in the first and last sentences to "the earth." His earth is gone, a figment of a bygone ontology. But an alternative is to understand the case in this way. This convert is simply indicating that the zillions of shared beliefs about what he has always called "the earth," along with his opponents, remain despite the fact that he has recently dropped two formerly cherished beliefs about its nature. Except when he was involved in earlier theoretical disputes, the shared component, "this heavenly body we call home," was the default, and it is available now, as it was before, as common conceptual ground.

This suggests that even the Cartesian can convert. There may be no such thing as consciousness, conceived in orthodox Cartesian terms. But as with the earth, there is a robust enough phenomena to maintain allegiance to, the phenomena of conscious experience, while weaning oneself from cherished but dubious dogma. The various available notions of consciousness partake, as best I can surmise, of only one ineliminable belief, the belief in conscious experience. Various theories about consciousness may need to be adjusted or abandoned as particular facts about the nature of conscious experience emerge. But the phenomena itself is too robust to think that we will ever be driven to question the minimal default assumption that conscious experiences exist. That assumption alone binds all the different views of consciousness and is ineliminable. No quining is possible.

This brings me to the final objection embedded in the claim that the concept of consciousness might turn out to be like the concept of karma. This is the idea that for 'consciousness', like 'karma', there may turn out to be "nothing that will properly serve for what the users of the term were 'getting at'" (Rey 1983, 5). Part of my response to this suggestion is contained in what I have just said about the previous objection. The types of conscious experiences are simply phenomenologically too robust to think it likely that we will someday decide that there is nothing there that we, the users of the term, were getting at—nothing real, that is, that we were trying to explain.

Here the analogy with karma plays a trick on us. Karma is a doctrine to the effect that "the natural order" is "a moral order in which events happen for an ethical purpose, namely, to promote an equitable distribution of rewards and punishments" (Shweder 1991, 157). This idea that nature is just (karma) is elaborated in the sacred scriptures—the Vedas, the Puranas, and the Epics—and it is closely tied to an elaborate ethical code (dharma) about which Hindus are knowledgeable. Karma and dharma are intertwined when it comes to explaining or justifying, in a rock-bottom way, the ways of the world and the obligations of Hindus. The concepts of karma and dharma are elaborate social constructs that frame all experience (they can frame experience without infiltrating every experiential episode). They explain, as I have said, the ways of the world and the obligations of men and women. Karma can be illuminated in terms of dharma, and vice versa. Together they function as ultimate metaphysical explanations. But they are not themselves phenomena to be explained in some deeper way.

It is easy to imagine that someone might become disenchanted with the "way of worldmaking" involved. That is, we can imagine that someone might lose faith. For a person no longer in the grip of the relevant picture of the world, it makes sense to say that she no longer sees the world in the way that the concepts of orthodox Hinduism usefully get at. She sees good fortune, bad fortune, and so on, but the concept of karma no longer provides illumination of these phenomena.

For there to be a clear parallel with consciousness, the situation would need to be one in which there was not only an orthodox concept of consciousness but also an elaborate orthodox theory that explained the nature, role, kinds, and so on, of conscious events in the overall economy of life. But I deny that either an orthodox concept or an orthodox theory exists. There are several competing theories of consciousness, some old (dualism, parallelism, epiphenomenalism), some new (for example, consciousness is a public-relations homunculus, a serial control device laid over a set of massively parallel processors, a simulation stage for contemplated action, a functional adaptation for quickly getting in touch with the sensory environment or for formulating hypotheses about other minds).

Now imagine that any one or even all these theories of consciousness fall out of favor. Would we then be tempted to say that there is nothing that these various theories were getting at? The answer is no, and the reason has to do with a fundamental disanalogy with karma. The concept(s) of consciousness occurs in (at least) two separate locations in explanatory space. There is consciousness as used to pick out what is in need of explanation, and there are the various theory specific ways of explaining these phenomena and deploying the concept in explanatory discourse. Consciousness occurs sometimes as explanandum and sometimes as explanans. Things are different with karma. It is all explanans. This is not to deny that people who believe in the world of karma and dharma "see" karma and dharma in the world. It is simply to say that once one stops believing in the metaphysical theory in which karma figures, there is no longer any karma. The weal and woe, the good fortune and misfortune, of humankind remain. But the framework within which karma explains these ubiquitous features of human life is gone. The former true believer will admit that there was after all nothing that her concept of karma was getting at. But because consciousness is a robust phenomena to be explained across the various theories of consciousness, it, unlike karma but like good and bad fortune, remains as a force to be reckoned with even as each contending theory rises and falls.

Let the true believer in any particular theory of consciousness lose faith in that theory, and she will still acknowledge, I maintain, that there are phenomena to be explained, namely conscious experiences. There is as little likelihood that those of us who point to conscious experience as a set of phenomena in need of explanation will discover that there is nothing that we were getting at as that rusting and burning, good luck and bad luck, will disappear from the set of phenomena we rightly seek to understand.

What I have said rests not one iota on the assumption that we know what is phenomenologically given in a way not influenced by all manner of abstract thought, nor on the assumption that the ways things seem will turn out, as inquiry proceeds, to be understood in the ways they are understood at the start of inquiry. I simply maintain that within the web of belief, consciousness as a phenomena to be explained has a secure place at the observational periphery. It exerts an ineliminable tug for us to develop a theory of it.

Other everyday phenomena—sound, pitch, light, color, and temperature—have had deep, surprising explanatory and predictive theories constructed about them. The explanations of light and color in terms of electromagnetic waves of various lengths, of the temperature of a gas in terms of mean molecular kinetic energy, of radiant heat as long-wavelength electromagnetic waves, of sound as compression waves, and so on, all show that "the fact that a property or state is at the prime focus of one of our native discriminatory faculties does not mean that it is exempt from possible reconception within the conceptual framework of some deeper explanatory theory" (Churchland and Churchland 1990, 250).

Conscious awareness is as ubiquitous as light, sound, heat, and color. Indeed, one might argue that it is even more ubiquitous than any of these, since there is light and sound and heat and color only insofar as these phenomena are revealed in experience. But the important point is that despite its ubiquitousness, despite its phenomenological robustness, consciousness is something we understand very superficially. There is every reason to think that it will succumb to our attempts to plumb its depths without at the same time losing the salient characteristics that press us to understand more deeply what it is.

One final point. It is by no means clear that W. V. O. Quine himself would approve of quining consciousness. Quine rejects the conception of consciousness as a hidden hermitage of ineffable essences. But Quine insists that the repudiation of Cartesian mentalism "is not to deny that we sense or even that we are conscious" (1952, 213). Quine endorses an "effortless physicalism." We discard Cartesianism, and "we just appropriate the mentalistic terms.... We even continue to speak of the states as mental. The only change is that we reckon mental states as states of the body" (Quine 1985, 5). Be a physicalist about consciousness. Quine says you can do it effortlessly. My motto is, Don't quine when Quine says not to.

Chapter 3
Consciousness and the Brain

1 Mind, Brain, and Experience

How can there be such a thing as subjectivity in the natural world? That is the question. The view that subjectivity is easy to understand if we think of it as part of an immaterial world has proved to be an illusion. The view actually explains nothing, and it fits miserably with the evolutionary requirement that we understand ourselves in naturalistic terms. The best tactic is to assume, as an inference to the best explanation, that subjectivity is realized in the brain, and to examine how what must be the case is the case.

The human nervous system is beginning to yield its secrets. Some of the air of mystery that surrounds the problem of consciousness can be dispersed by paying attention to emerging knowledge about the nervous system. The nervous system has extremely complex biochemical and organizational structure. We must not be put off by the fact that the brain looks dopey. Rest assured: it isn't.

Evolutionary theory allows us to think of subjectivity as a special kind of sensitivity. There are kinds of sensitivity that probably do not involve subjective experience, in even the lowest-level sense of the term. For example, there is the light sensitivity of unicellular organisms like paramecia. A short distance up the phylogenic scale, there are the chemical sensors of the scallop that cause it to move when an unfamiliar object intrudes into its space. Information is being received, and living creatures are responding to this information, but there is no reason at this point in time to think that paramecia or scallops can feel or experience anything at all. This gives us a first approximation of what eventually needs to be explained. What is it about some physical systems that makes them subjects of experience, creatures that feel something?

Consider the brain. It is estimated that the brain contains roughly 100 billion (10^{11}) neurons. Some think that the number may be much greater, 10^{12}, possibly as high as 10^{14} (P. S. Churchland 1986, 36). I will stick with the conservative estimate of 10^{11}, keeping in mind that it may be low by several orders of magnitude. This means that there are about the same

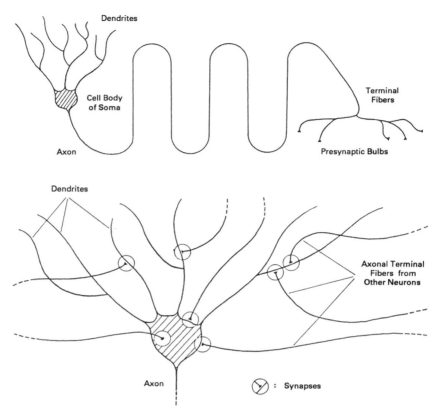

Figure 3.1
Typical neurons. (Reprinted with permission from P. M. Churchland 1988, 131, 132.)

number of neurons in each brain as there are stars in the Milky Way galaxy. There are three main types of neurons, differentiated by their involvement in various kinds of activity: sensory neurons, motor neurons, and inter-neurons (the ones involved in everything else: message transfers between the sensory and motor neurons, memory, higher-level thought, and so on). The tripartite typology of neurons is a functional one. Neurons within each type differ greatly in their specific size, shape, structure, and function.

A typical neuron is shown in figure 3.1. When a depolarization pulse (an "action potential" or "spike") runs down an axon, it causes release of its characteristic neurotransmitter, for example, acetylcholine, dopamine, serotonin, noradrenalin, at the bulbs. Depending on the neurotransmitter released and the receiving sites at the other end, this pulse will serve to excite or inhibit the synapse by creating a positive or negative charge.

Neuronal cells are almost always jittering. A spike is simply a very powerful jitter, a jolt. A second determinant of neural behavior, other than depolarization itself, is its frequency. If 3,000 inhibitory synapses are active only once per second and 300 excitatory synapses are active 30 times per second, then excitation dominates, and (all else being equal) the neuron will fire (P. M. Churchland 1988).

If one harbors doubts that a system of dopey neurons could remotely begin to account for the nature and range of thought and the plasticity of cognition, consider this. A typical neuron has synaptic connections emanating from on the order of 3,000 other neurons (this is an average: some neurons have as many as 10,000 synaptic inputs, others as many as 100,000, and some only a few). That makes for on the order of 10^{14} distinct possible synaptic connections (10^{11} neurons times 10^3 synaptic connections), that is, 100 trillion synaptic connections. If each of these 10^{14} connections is capable of 1 of only 10 possible weights, or activation levels, at any given time (this is a conservative estimate), then the total number of distinct neural states is $10^{10^{14}}$, or $10^{100,000,000,000,000}$. This number cannot be written out in nonexponential form: 10 with a 100 trillion zeros would fill all imaginable space and then some. Paul Churchland puts the number in perspective: "To get some idea of the size of this number, recall that the total number of elementary particles in the universe is generally estimated to be about 10^{87}" (1989, 132).

Even if we assume that 99 percent of these states don't add up to anything cognitively worthwhile, that still leaves $0.01 \times 10^{100,000,000,000,000} = 10^{99,999,999,999,998}$ states capable of doing worthwhile cognitive labor. And if we reduce the estimate to 99.9 percent nonfunctional states and only 0.1 percent functional (10^{-3}), that still leaves $10^{99,999,999,999,997}$ functional states. Suppose that 99.9 percent of these states subserve functional but nonconscious states. That still leaves on the order of $10^{99,999,999,999,994}$ states for *conscious* mental life!

Neurons jitter in ensembles, in populations organized on portions of horizontal sheets or in vertical threads or columns. We can picture the sheets as stacked in layers. Indeed, staining techniques have shown that the cortex consists of six distinct sheets, and the superior colliculus, the cerebellum, the thalamus, the olfactory lobe, and the hippocampus also have a layered look (P. S. Churchland 1986, 117). To form an abstract picture of the brain, imagine that each sheet contains numerous abstract designs. The recognizable boundaries between the designs on a sheet represent a functional group. These distinct patterns might, of course, run through space occupied by other patterns. Imagine further that the sheets are loosely joined by a system of threads (columns). Some threads run all the way from the top to the bottom; others connect only several intermediate layers. Imagine that sometimes air flows under a single sheet or under part of a sheet. The portion of the sheet lifted is very active, the parts far from the lifted portion are hardly active at all. Next imagine that the vertical threads are put into various wavelike motions. This will have the effect of activating portions of many sheets. Depending on the number of columnar threads activated and the strength of the waves, the global activation pattern will be massive or relatively localized. Invariably, activity will resonate horizontally and vertically. A sheet active at the start of some process may become active again and again, since the waves it sends out can resonate back to it numerous times before the process dies down.

This is only a picture. But it may help in thinking about the brain, for it captures certain salient features of neural composition, structure, and function. The activation of neuronal groups are determined not only by stimulation occurring at the sensory periphery but also, especially the more we as individuals know, from projections from next-door neighbors (horizontal projections) as well as from above (descending axonal projections). A nice example of a descending projection that exerts control occurs in visual processing. The optic nerve ends in the lateral geniculate body in the thalamus. From there visual information radiates upward to various locations in the visual cortex. Sometimes the visual cortex projects signals back to the lateral geniculate to get it to change or adjust the information it is sending, for example, to zoom in on a particular feature of a stimulus (P. M. Churchland 1988, 139).

A different sort of example where both horizontal and vertical projection are involved occurs in setting down long-term visual memories. Perception of a visual scene involves processing its various aspects (object shape, motion, color) at different locations in the neocortex. For the scene to be remembered, information must be sent to the hippocampus. But this is not enough. The memory is laid down only if the information is sent back up again to the areas of the neocortex involved in the original perception. It is as if the brain needs to trace over an experience to firm it up as memorable (Squire and Zola-Morgan 1991).

The brain is a network in which functionally segregated neuronal groups respond in parallel to various aspects of some stimulus and pass the information they compute back and forth to each other and to various other regions involved in perception and cognition. For example, the visual cortex of a monkey contains on the order of twenty or more functionally segregated areas dedicated to visual processing. Visual detection occurs as these distinct areas decode stimuli at blazing speed. Perception is the result of global coordination among the system of functionally distributed processors, each performing its distinctive computations (computing edges, motion, depth, and so on) and passing signals back and forth vertically and horizontally. Recurrent patterns of activation, synchrony among parallel processors, and signals passing between processors yield a unified perception, quite possibly without the involvement of any single perception center. To be sure, different types of sensory information project to fairly specific areas in the cortex, with each hemisphere representing the opposite side of the body. And there is some evidence that the association cortex is responsible for integrated perceptions involving more than one modality, for example, seeing and smelling a flower at once. But there are invariably gaps, sometimes quite large, among various projection points in the brain for a sensory modality. Perceiving is best thought of as an emergent product of synchronized parallel processing. Visual perception requires performances by all the players in the visual cortex. Perception is produced when all the players play their part. It is not required in addition that there is some central point where it all comes together and perception happens. Coming together just amounts to all the players doing their part.

Presumably, the same sort of story is involved in higher-level cognition. Cognition, even more than sensation and perception, involves continual updating of our knowledge of the world and the bringing to bear of previously acquired knowledge to current experience. People react to the world in similar ways not because their underlying weight configurations are closely similar on a synapse-by-synapse comparison but because their *activation spaces* are similarly partitioned. "Like trees similar in their gross physical profiles, brains can be similar in their gross functional profiles, while being highly idiosyncratic in the myriad details of their fine-grained arborization" (P. M. Churchland 1989, 234). Just as there is no single unified perception center, so there is no central faculty of thought, no "thought center." What there is instead is massively parallel processing involving coordination of disparate neural areas. The totality of active partitions constitute, or give rise to, what is being thought.

Positron emission tomography (PET) and very recently turbo-charged magnetic-resonance imaging provide amazing opportunity to watch thought in action, to map experiences onto brain processes, and thus to practice the natural method of coordinating the phenomenological, psychological, and neurological levels of analyses. Oxygen and glucose can be tagged with normally occurring radioactive substances, such as oxygen-15 or nitrogen-13, which emit positrons as they decay. PET scanners detect positron emission and produce extremely reliable images of blood flow (by imaging tagged oxygen) and glucose activity (glucose is the sole energy source for brain cells) in live human brains in real time (Raichle 1987). There is robust evidence showing vivid differences in brain activity in persons engaged in phenomenologically distinct mental activities (Phelps and Mazziotta 1985). For example, listening to music, imagining a tune, solving arithmetic problems, and remembering a conversation light up different brain parts or, in certain cases, light up the same parts to different degrees. Too many different areas light up for us to think that any one is the center of consciousness, and no one is sure which lit-up areas serve conscious mental activity and which parts serve nonconscious processing (which, of course, may well be necessary for conscious processing). Activity of lots of processors in different locations is required if certain kinds of thoughts are to occur. But no one place always lights up or lights up with such brightness that it looks like the masterworks.

One causal feature of the brain that can't be emphasized enough and that differentiates the brain from every computer has to do with the neurotransmitters and the family of other neurochemicals permeating nervous tissue. Neurotransmitters (neuromodulators and neuropeptides) don't just function to turn neurons on or off. They are also involved in how things feel qualitatively (Bradford 1987). Neurotransmitter levels are becoming increasingly implicated in diseases like Parkinsonism and schizophrenia, in anxiety disorders, and in dreaming. Some extremely effective new antidepressants, Prozac, for example, work by inhibiting the reabsorption of serotonin by the neurons releasing it. It is not that serotonin reabsorption causes depression or that serotonin levels alone are responsible for depression. But serotonin seems to be implicated in the complex causal etiology of at least certain forms of depression.

2   The Evolution of Darwin Machines

The best picture of the mind is one in which the mind is the brain and the brain is what William Calvin (1990) calls a "Darwin Machine." The brain is a biological device in which pressures to achieve adaptive coordination between the organism and the external world operate to select populations of neurons, from predisposed groups, to recognize certain patterns in the external world and within the body itself and to activate certain appropriate motor routines in response to the patterns recognized.

Higher-level thought, planning with foresight and problem solving, involve processes analogous to those involved in natural selection. We select approaches to problems that have worked in similar situations in the past. In utterly novel situations, we spin out novel problem-solving strategies by mixing previous solution strategies, creating "idea mutations" as it were. We try some of these, and if they get the job done, there is selection in their favor in the future. As George Mandler puts it, the general rule is, "When current conscious constructions do not account for the state of the world, then a new conscious state will be initiated" (1985).

Actually, the picture of the brain as a massively parallel Darwin machine suggests a particular gloss on Mandler's point that the system works by creating new ideas when old ones fail. If current conscious constructions do not account for the state of the world, new conscious constructions will be generated. But these new conscious constructions need not, indeed, they typically will not, be generated consciously themselves. In 1943 Kenneth Craik proposed the hypothesis that the nervous system is capable of modeling the external world and itself and of simulating possible worlds and possible actions based on past experience. Craik realized that such anticipatory modeling would need to operate largely unconsciously to be maximally efficient. In a very efficient cognitive system a new conscious state would be initiated only when the nervous system was finished unconsciously weighing, in parallel, various possible scenarios and action plans. William Calvin explains how the brain conceived as a massively parallel Darwin machine could do the job that Craik thought it in fact did:

> A Darwin Machine now provides a framework for thinking about thought, indeed one that may be a reasonable first approximation to the actual brain machinery underlying thought. An intracerebral Darwin Machine need not try out one sequence at a time against memory; it may be able to try out dozens, if not hundreds, simultaneously, shape up new generations in milliseconds, and thus initiate insightful actions without *overt* trial and error. This massively parallel selection among stochastic sequences is more analogous to the ways of darwinian biology than to the "von Neumann" serial computer. Which is why I call it a Darwin Machine instead; it shapes up thoughts in milliseconds rather than millennia, and uses innocuous remembered environments rather than noxious real-life ones. It may well create the uniquely human aspect of our consciousness.   (Calvin 1990, 261–262)

Dennett (1991a) puts forward a similar idea in the form of his "multiple drafts model." The brain is continuously processing information, surmising the state of the self and the world, and plotting actions. The intracerebral Darwin machine produces zillions of idea germs, topic sentences, wonderful but ultimately useless paragraphs, all competing for space in the final published draft. The conscious mind is as often a recipient of final drafts that result from the frothy competition among nonconscious draftsmen as it is a participant in the rush to publish or perish. Normally, only well-worked-over late or final drafts are published, that is, become conscious, and only then when action is called for. Of course, some causally efficacious final drafts never become conscious at all; the system doesn't need them to.

On both the Darwin-machine and multiple-drafts model, consciousness has a serial, Jamesian, Joycean, or von-Neumannesque character. The fact is that the mind of which it is an aspect is a massively parallel device that does most of its work unconsciously.

The capacities to think ahead, to recognize novel situations as harbingers of good or ill, and to speedily and imaginatively solve problems are among our most valuable. They were almost certainly key to the survival and proliferation of our species. But most of the evaluation and recognition is done unconsciously. Dennett writes that the "key to control is the ability to *track* or even *anticipate* the important features of the environment, so all brains are, in essence, *anticipation-machines*" (1988b, 6). Overall, our brain is the most powerful anticipation machine ever built. But compared to us, other systems are more sensitive to, and thus better anticipators of, certain classes of events, especially those relevant to their survival. Snakes, for example, are reliable detectors of impending earthquakes, more reliable, some say, than scientific instruments sunk far deeper in the ground.

What function might sensory or perceptual consciousness serve? Such consciousness could enable an organism to be sensitive to stimulus saliencies relevant to its survival and to coordinate its goals with these saliencies. Informational sensitivity without experiential sensitivity (of the sort an unconscious robot might have) could conceivably serve the same function. Indeed, it often does. But the special vivacity of perceptual experience might enable quicker, more reliable, and more functional responses than a less robustly phenomenological system, and these might have resulted in small selection pressures in favor of becoming a subject of experience. At least this is one possible explanation for why Mother Nature would have selected a mind with capacities for robust phenomenological feel in the sensory modalities. It is good that reptiles are sensitive detectors of earthquakes. It enables them to get above ground before disaster hits. It is good that we feel pain. It keeps us from being burned, cut, and maimed. Persons who are bad pain detectors are in a great deal of danger of these sorts of harms. Like photoreceptor cells designed for vision and wings for flight, the capacity to experience pleasure and pain is a design solution that Mother Nature has often used in different lineages of locomoting organisms.

The story of how exactly consciousness evolved is underdetermined by available information. For reasons just mentioned, direct selection for sensitivity to pleasant and painful stimuli is credible. Evidence that there are six basic emotions universal among humans—distinguished by their qualitative feel, movements of the facial musculature, and their underlying biology—suggests that there was also selection at the species level for a phenomenologically robust "emotive economy." The important work of Ekman, Levinson, and Freisen (1985) vindicates Darwin's hypothesis that the emotions of fear, anger, surprise, disgust, happiness, and sadness occur across cultures. The universality of these emotions, their early emergence in our development (very possibly in primate development), and the evolutionary rationale that can be given for them make a strong case for their natural selection.

Powerful emotional dispositions and experiential sensitivity to pleasant and painful stimuli seem like enough sensitivity to gain fairly robust biological fitness. Any system equipped with such a "conative economy" (Dennett's phrase) should do well when it comes to the activities that determine biological fitness: fleeing, fighting, food gathering, and sex. Why, then, did we evolve to possess the higher-order mental and linguistic capacities capable of creating culture, art, history, science, and schemes of self-comprehension? One possible answer is contained in what I already said about selection for anticipation machines. What capacities a particular type of organism needs to have depends essentially on what kind of organism it is, what dangers lurk in its ecological niche, what it needs to do to live long enough to reproduce, and so on. Creatures our size (we used to be smaller) would not have been given great odds for survival by some primeval bookie. Ancestral humans were not nearly as fast or as strong as predators, which, we can assume, savored the taste of their flesh. In addition, human young need constant longer-term care than any other mammal. Also, even when humans were hairier, we were still not nearly as well suited to contend with the vagaries of global weather as other animals. So how did we survive?

The short answer is that someone had the bright idea to use tools and the rest of us caught on. Hunting, gathering, and clothing became possible once tool making was invented. But food sources could quickly become scarce, so we moved a lot. Nomads need to make quick studies of new niches. They need to learn what in the new locale is useful, what is harmful. And they need to anticipate in advance when the next move is advisable. Creatures who are relatively weak and who move a lot would rationally want to have sophisticated capacities of thought, attention, anticipation, and plasticity of response. Mother Nature, of course, doesn't give creatures what they want or need unless they themselves produce a few mutations with the capacities that would enhance the reproductive fitness of these mutants relative to their normal fellows. Selection follows upon differential reproductive success.

Since we possess the relevant higher-order capacities, the inference to the best explanation is that once upon a time such mutants appeared among our ancestors. It is important to emphasize that the story does not involve direct selection for the capacities to create mathematics, art, politics, and science. It is just that creating these things were possible once sophisticated capacities of thought, attention, and plasticity of response were in place.

Mutants capable of higher-order conscious thought might seem to require that the emergence of consciousness needed to occur not once— when it arose for pleasure and pain, sensation, and the emotions—but a second time—when it arose for conscious thought, planning, self-consciousness, and so on. The simplest assumption, however, is that the mutants' higher-order conscious capacities piggybacked on the first not as free riders but as further developments of the first set of conscious capacities. Roughly, the idea is that conscious sensitivity to pleasure and pain, to the sensory environment, and to situations that require one to fight, flee, or engage the affections of a fellow already confer a certain fitness. The higher-order conscious capacities do not so much supply us with new fitness-conferring equipment as they enhance and improve upon the initial equipment. Conscious recognition of such regularities in nature as seasonal changes and the capacity to plan ahead for such regularities dramatically increase our ability to arrange the world so that we experience more pleasure than pain (see Calvin 1991 on the importance of climatic change for the evolution of mind). The sort of mutation most likely to be selected for (and probably also to have emerged in the first place) would be one in which the higher-order capacities linked up to the first-order capacities, for whose service they were, so to speak, designed. There is, of course, nothing like perfect coordination among the parts of the brain. Structurally, the human brain is triune, with an old mammalian brain on top of a reptilian brain, all covered by our large neomammalian brain. Emotional life appears to originate in the lower parts, and it displays a certain amount of impenetrability to control from above.

It seems uncontroversial that one or two mutant nervous systems with the capacities for higher-order thought would have proliferated like crazy. It is harder to explain exactly why the capacity for higher-order thought would take a conscious form. Since thought did take a conscious form in our case, however, we can engage in further thought experimentation about the relative merits of different types of design for a conscious system. Imagine that there were two populations of thoughtful mutants (the paleontological evidence indicates that there were several species of hominids existing alongside *Homo sapiens*). The first group did all its anticipating consciously and tried out all possible options for action under the full light of consciousness. The second group computed many options simultaneously in parallel networks and passed on for conscious reflection only things worth worrying about and options worth considering. Assuming that both systems were equally smart and would reach the same conclusions under the same circumstances, one might think that neither group would be favored over the other. But if speed of processing mattered, and it almost certainly did and does, then the second group would have been favored. This is because of the well-known computational bottleneck problem (P. M. Churchland 1988). A hungry sabertooth demands one's attention, but one had better not spend too much time consciously determining that it is a hungry sabertooth or reflecting on how to respond to its presence unless one doesn't mind being lunch. So the second group would have displaced the first. All else being equal, Darwin-machine mutants will win in a head to head battle with von Neumann—machine mutants.

Higher-level consciousness did not need to come into being. This is true for two reasons. First, we did not need to exist. Had it not been for our ancestral mutants, we would not have evolved, survived, and proliferated. Second, it is conceivable that there might have evolved creatures as capable as us and more or less behaviorally indistinguishable from us who can get by on pure informational sensitivity and unconscious higher-level problem solving (for example, the way a computer plays chess) without ever experiencing a thing. We, however, did not evolve that way, and so consciousness came into being. The nature of brain tissue guarantees us that there will be no fossils of consciousness. The project of recounting the causal origins of consciousness as we know it involves us in what Dennett (1986) aptly describes as "software archeology." We need to reconstruct a credible tale from present brain structure and function and from the tangible evidence of what our nonhuman and hominid ancestors lived like. The true and complete story may eternally elude us. It undoubtedly involves not only majestic feats of engineering but also all manner of quirky contingency, free riders, and emergent properties, which would not have been in the plans of an omniscient designer. Still, the more we know about what consciousness is and how it is realized, the better positioned we will be to provide more specific hypotheses about how and under what conditions it emerged in the first place.

The sketchiness of the story of the emergence of consciousness is analogous to the sketchiness of the story of the emergence of life. It was not until the mid 1950s that a remotely credible theory of how life *might* have emerged was put forward and tested. Experiments showed that adding electricity to an environment of hydrogen, ammonia, and methane started some amino-acid-building activity. Amino acids are the building blocks for proteins, which are necessary but not sufficient for DNA. But no one is sure that this is exactly how life evolved. This is because we are not certain what the primeval inorganic materials were or in what amounts they existed, whether the consummating action took place in the seas or in marshes, and what form of life was the very first to arise. Furthermore, even if someone actually got a unicellular life form to emerge in an experiment like that just described, this would not prove that life on earth in fact evolved that way. It would only show that we have come upon one of the ways in which it might have evolved. The natural history of life and mind are intimately bound together. We know that DNA is the basis for life and that the brain is the basis for mind. But we do not possess a full explanation of how DNA or our nervous system evolved. Because of the very nature of natural history, it is unlikely that any story in either domain will force a clear-cut choice among several viable alternative scenarios, at least in the near term.

3   Neural Darwinism

The theory of "neural Darwinism" or "neuronal group selection" helps bring together and extend some of the insights about brain composition, structure, function, and evolution discussed so far (Edelman 1987, 1989; also see Changeux 1985). Five ideas are especially important.

First, it is mathematically inconceivable that the human genome specifies the entire wiring diagram of the brain. The genome, powerful as it is, contains too few instructions by several orders of magnitude to build a fully functional brain. The synaptic connections that evolve in a brain over time are the complex causal outcome of genotypic instructions, endogenous biochemical processes, plus vast amounts of individually unique interactions between organism and environment (Edelman 1989, 30; Hundert 1989, 237). It follows that talk of the brain as hard-wired is misleading. To be sure, the overall structure of the brain is fixed by our genes and certain neuronal paths, and certain specific areas are designed to serve certain dedicated functions. But the "wires" in the brain are soft, even those built during fetal development and those serving specific functions. Furthermore, all the wires are capable of being drawn into novel and complex connections with indefinitely many other segments of the neural network. The key to our magnificent abilities as anticipation machines involves fixing gross architecture while leaving the development of connections at the microstructural level undedicated and adaptable.

Second and relatedly, individual brains are extraordinarily diverse in terms of structure and connectivity. Identity theory has some credibility in the domain of sensory experience. Certain characteristic neural patterns subserve similar cross-personal sensory experiences. But by and large, most mental states probably do not involve strict identities between types of mental and neural states. Thus one and the same conscious mental state, for example, believing that a speeding fire engine is coming from behind, is almost certainly subserved by compositionally distinct neural states in all the different drivers who have that thought. Once massive connectivity is added in, it is no surprise that this thought kicks off a series of other, different thoughts for each of us. One person worries about the victims and their property, and another that he will be delayed. A third is thrown into a Proustian reminiscence of summer nights in his childhood spent with grandfather, the fire chief, at the station. He feels the humid summer breeze on his face as he rides to a fire, and the smells of burning embers and pictures of lonely stone chimneys well up in him. Neural connectivity is the mother of "meaning holism" and the "drift of thought," the way the meaning of each term connects idiosyncratically with the meaning of many others. We are good at keeping attention focused, but certain events send thought reeling to unanticipated places, some welcome, others not. Neural connectivity helps explain why this happens so easily.

That said, it is worth emphasizing that the issue of whether there are or are not type correspondences between complex thoughts and brain processes is by no means settled. I said that there were probably no *strict* mind-brain type identities at the level of thought. But this is compatible with there being interesting and useful correspondences and mappings between the mental and the neural levels. A lot depends on how strict and fine-grained we demand the type-identities to be, and that depends largely on considerations relative to particular interests. Neuron for neuron and synapse for synapse matches between brain states and mental states are nowhere to be found, even within the same individual from one moment to the next. Even type correspondences between sensations and brain processes are nonexistent if we demand that the identities satisfy extremely fine-grained criteria. But at gross functional levels, interpersonal and intrapersonal identities may be abundant. Indeed, work with PET scans and other brain-imaging techniques indicates that there are certain gross typological correlations between feeling and thought types and types of brain processes. Remember, "brains can be similar in their gross functional profiles, while being highly idiosyncratic in the myriad details of their fine-grained arborization" (P. M. Churchland 1989, 234). Despite its unpopularity, some very complex version of identity theory could turn out to be credible, at least in certain domains. Personally, I hold out some hope for it. Massive parallelism is compatible with identity theory, and no philosophical song and dance about the possibility of Martians and robots with our kinds of minds should make us abandon the prospect that there might turn out to be some, perhaps many, interesting species-specific type identities (Lewis 1980).

The third, fourth, and fifth theses of neural Darwinism further clarify the prospects for a complex form of mind-brain identity theory and indicate some of the problems such a theory will face. The third thesis is that neuronal ensembles projecting through many levels are selected during experience to map and thereby to represent certain saliencies. Which ensembles represent what is jointly determined by the genetically specified receptivities of different neural locations (so visual processing takes place in areas dedicated to vision and not to audition) and by the neuronal groups available for selection and strengthening at the time a stimulus is presented. But the jobs of all ensembles are not assigned in advance, as they are, for example, on the view that the mind contains all concepts innately. On such a view, experience merely acts to trigger what is there (Fodor 1975, 1981). On the neural-selectionist view, the brain is a vast territory with contours roughed out by nature and more than enough room for all comers. Experiences come looking for squatter's rights, for room to make a life. The brain makes room in various ways. Sometimes it simply gives over unclaimed terrain; other times it sets up time-sharing and multiple-tenancy arrangements. Selection is involved in that the world plays an important part in determining which neuronal groups are activated for what roles. It does not simply trigger neuronal groups preset to work for a particular boss, should he turn up, and give the marching orders they passively await. Nonetheless, once a neuronal group is assigned to a task, that group shows up regularly for the job.

Fourth and relatedly, the neuronal network retains representations, but not in permanently coded files. It retains representations as dispositions to reactivate distributed activation patterns selected during previous experience. Once a particular distributed activation pattern has reached an equilibrial state so that it is activated by a certain type of stimulus pattern, it frames novel occurrent stimulation with that activation pattern. This leads to quick and easy identification of the stimulation and, depending on its connections to other neuronal groups, to the right motor response. The neuronal groups are selected to detect certain constellations of features. The groups are extremely sensitive but not overly fussy. This explains why we are so quick to identify degraded stimuli, for example, letters written in new and obscure handwriting. The right pattern of activation is turned on by any stimulus that possesses a sufficient number, or some adequately patterned configuration, of the relevant features. The stimuli need not be exactly the same as the stimuli that the neuronal group was initially trained to detect. Indeed, a system that could only recognize duplicates of previous stimuli would be of no use at all in our fluid ecological surround. Recognition and recall do not involve permanent storage, and thus lost space each time a particular pattern becomes recognizable. Rather, neuronal groups play multiple roles. My red detectors are activated whenever red is before me. But when red things are not before me, my red detectors are available for other recognitional labor—purple and orange detection, for example.

Fifth, a neuronal system functioning according to principles of ontogenic (lifespan) selection, as opposed to phylogenic (species-level) selection, is fluid in several respects: (1) It can gain, retain, revise, and abandon all sorts of thoughts, ideas, desires, and intentions in the course of a life. (2) The system can lose certain neurons to death, or in a labor dispute, one function can lose neurons to some other function, without any loss in functional capacity. If the capacity to recognize a banana as edible is subserved by parallel activity in numerous recurrent layers of neuronal groups, then all manner of degradation and loss of members is compatible with continuous high performance. Neuronal destruction can, of course, reach a point where the amount of neuronal degradation is great enough to lead to functional incapacitation in certain domains, as it does, for example, in Alzheimer's patients. (3) Neuronal dedication to a task is not fixed for all time once the neuronal group subserving the recognitional or motor task in question is well honed. For example, the neuronal group responsible for pressure detection on two adjacent fingers will "segregate into groups that *at any one time* are nonoverlapping and have sharp boundaries" (Edelman 1989, 52). But these dedicated groups can shift boundaries over time because of differential experience, or possibly even randomly. Imagine the boundary between the United States and Canada shifting several miles one way or another each day along its entire expanse (Calvin 1990, 175).

4   Self and Nonself

One of the most important things a well-designed system will need to be sensitive to is the distinction between self and nonself, between me and not me, between inner and outer (James 1890, Dawkins 1976, Dennett 1991a). "As soon as something gets into the business of self-preservation, boundaries become important, for if you are setting out to preserve yourself, you don't want to squander effort trying to preserve the whole world: you draw the line. You become, in a word, *selfish*" (Dennett 1991a, 174). Self, in the relevant sense, is not the self of narrative awareness, the thick self constitutive of personal and social identity (more about that self later). It is the subject of interoceptive signals that alert the organism to its own homeostatic state—to its autonomic, neuroendocrinological, and hedonic condition. There is some evidence of a neurological basis for the distinction between self and nonself. Edelman conjectures that perceptual consciousness arose in part because of selection pressures favoring coordination of "the two kinds of nervous organization"—that representing the inner and that representing the outer. In particular, there were evolutionary pressures favoring the selection of neuronal groups capable of retaining information about the relations between certain outer things and events and internal homeostasis and well-being. A phenomenologically robust discrimination system capable of keeping straight the difference between self and other, inner and outer, was selected for this purpose. Edelman writes,

> I shall use the term 'self' and 'nonself' in a strict biological sense, not in the personal or psychological sense of 'self-awareness', or in the social or philosophical sense of 'personhood'. In richly endowed nervous systems, these portions must be organized differently but also be in communication. While neural parts of the first kind (e.g., the hypothalamus, pituitary, various portions of the brain stem, amygdala, hippocampus, and limbic system) operate within developmentally given parameters, those of the second kind (e.g., cerebral cortex, thalamus, and cerebellum) operate largely through ongoing exteroceptive sensory interactions with the world, that is, through experience and behavior.   (1989, 94)

The hypothesis is that consciousness emerged as a solution to the problem of segregating and coordinating inner and outer perception. Consciousness emerged with the development of segregated neural equipment subserving, on the one hand, internal hedonic regulation and, on the other hand, information processing about the state of the external world. Enhancement occurred with the evolution of a memory system capable of retaining hypotheses about what things have or lack hedonic value and projecting them onto novel (possibly even future) states of affairs.

Neurally, things can go awry in various mechanisms that maintain the right sort of attentiveness to the inner and the outer and to the boundaries between. There is evidence that the dorsal parietal region of the cortex is essential to concern for the well-being of the self. Lesions in these areas result in a loss of self-concern. Conversely, lesions in ventral (temporal) regions of the cortex diminish attention to and awareness of the external world (Gardner 1983, 266). The frontal lobes, meanwhile, are thought to be especially important in the maintenance of the hedonic self/nonself memory system (Edelman 1989).

This story about the emergence of consciousness about self and nonself is credible. Perhaps it is true. Some sort of sensitivity to the boundaries of the self is a necessary condition for survival: "The origin of complex life forms on this planet was also the birth of the most primitive sort of self, whatever sort of self is implied by the self-regard that prevents the lobster, when hungry, from eating itself" (Dennett 1989, 9). Lobsters, I suspect, are dim experiencers. The important point is that designing systems that make the self/nonself distinction is one of the very first design problems Mother Nature faces. Either Mother Nature makes us experientially sensitive to the self/nonself distinction, or she makes us informationally sensitive to it. She has no choice but to make us sensitive to the distinction. Otherwise, predation will start with the nearest tasty morsel, possibly oneself! One really need not picture Mother Nature as faced with a choice between informational sensitivity and experiential sensitivity. Experiential sensitivity is really just a kind of informational sensitivity. It is one type of design that endows a system with informational sensitivity.

The good thing for this sort of story about the evolution of conscious sensitivity to the self/nonself distinction is that, like the story of the evolution of photoreceptor cells for vision or wings for flight, it offers a design solution that we know is not unique to humans. Something like the requisite conscious sensitivity is common among many organic systems that have made it this far. If one is a mere photosynthesizer and ground-nutrient absorber, the self/nonself distinction is not one that the system needs to be sensitive to. But if one depends on eating for survival, one will need the requisite sensitivity. For reasons we do not completely understand, such sensitivity appears to have been conferred on many species in its phenomenologically robust form (Griffin 1981).

5   Sensory Qualia and Neural Vectors

My initial question was, How can there be such a thing as subjectivity in material world? The barebone sketch provided so far of the structure, function, and evolution of our partly conscious, massively parallel brain shows that we can make progress on this question by reformulating it into two more manageable questions: (1) Under what conditions and under what selection pressures might the conscious mind have evolved? (2) How does conscious experience arise from a system of 100 billion well-connected neurons set in a soupy mixture of neurochemicals in which the only things that happen are activations of sets of neurons at different rates and changes in the composition of the soup? These questions, like the original question, might be asking us to dispel *all* mystery, or they might be asking merely for some relief from mystery. Minimally, we want a plausible picture of the evolution of the conscious mind and a plausible picture of how a rambunctious bundle of nervous activity, set in its complex biochemical environment, can ever add up to experiences that are clearly individuated by the subjects who experience them as, for example, the taste of lemonade, the smell of a rose, the feeling of sadness or elation, and so on. Explaining how something is actualized is a way of diminishing the sense of overwhelming awe at its very possibility.

For us, the lowest level of conscious experience involves sensory qualia: experiences of taste, touch, sight, and the like. If we can beat back the mystery surrounding sensory qualia even a little, we will have gained some ground, for it is here that many think the intractability problem begins. Here is one hypothesis for sensory qualia sketched by Paul Churchland (1988, 1989). The basic idea is that different sensory qualia are produced by distinct but characteristic spiking patterns of the sensory pathways that project through the brain. This hypothesis is simply the inference to the best explanation for sensory qualia. The evidence in favor of this analysis comes mainly from two different directions.

First, there is the phenomenological and behavioral data indicating that there are sensory experiences and that they have some cross-personal regularity. Persons across cultures pick out the same chip as typical red; persons across cultures claim to see images in which horizontal or vertical lines come to the fore or recede to the ground in predictable patterns, depending on the stimuli presented.

Second, there is information about the nervous system. The story about spiking frequency has the virtue of fitting the two sets of data together in a coherent matter. It predicts, for example, that sighted, non-color-blind people will report seeing red only if there is neural activity of a certain sort going on. To be more precise, the story for color, taste, and olfaction run as follows.

For color there are three distinct kinds of color-sensitive cells (cones) in our retinas, which are sensitive respectively to short, medium, and long wavelengths of light. There are over 120 million light receptors in the eye, of which 7 million are foveal cones. Whatever information is gathered must be passed up the optic nerve, with a mere 1.2 million fibers (Hardin 1988, 33). Color perception originates in different levels of activity in the three kinds of cones. Each experience of a particular color or shade is subserved by a unique ratio of activity in the three cone types and by the complex pattern of neural activity it gives rise to. This suggests the "hypothesis that a visual *sensation* of any specific color is literally identical with a specific triplet of spiking frequencies in some triune brain system" (P. M. Churchland 1989, 104). This hypothesis was put forward by Hermann von Helmholtz in 1860, and twentieth-century brain science shows some version of it to be almost certainly true (Calvin 1990, 144–145; see Hardin 1988 for a discussion of some of the main points of controversy).

For taste there are four distinct kinds of receptor cells on the tongue. For olfaction there are six or seven distinct sensory receptors. In general, for each domain there is a small set of sensory receptor cells that classify inputs subserving the relevant types of sensory experience—experiences of taste, color, and smell.

The story so far may look hopelessly thin and inept: Three or four receptor cells to explain the seemingly endless multiplicity of tastes and colors? So much for the naturalists' story! But here we have to be careful. As we have seen in the case of color, the receptor cells are not each responsible for one and only one taste or color. If that were so, your capacity to see any particular color would evaporate upon the death of the neuron or neuron type responsible for it.

The essential feature of the receptor cells is that they can vary across a fine-grained continuum in their degree of activation. It is the ratio across receptor cells of their activity along their idiosyncratic continua that determines what is experienced. The involvement of ensembles of cells explains how death or inactivity of individual neurons have no significant effect on experience or information pickup.

It is best to think of each sensory cell in each domain as a variable that can take on different numerical values, each representing a different level of stimulation. So for taste, we have the set of variables $\{S_{t_1}, S_{t_2}, S_{t_3}, S_{t_4}\}$. We then define a sensory coding vector as any determinate list of numerical values representing the level of stimulation assigned to the four variables. The proposal, then, is simply this: for each and every human taste there is a unique sensory coding vector. The extraordinary range of sensory experience in the taste modality is explained by the extraordinary but not infinite set of values that can be taken by each receptor cell and the vast combinatorial possibilities available among the four cells. The same story goes for olfaction, color, and so on. If we suppose that there are 10 distinct discriminable states that each receptor cell can give rise to, we can distinguish 10^3 colors, 10^4 tastes, 10^6 or 10^7 odors, and so on.

The choice of 10 as the number of discriminable states for each kind of receptor cell is just a matter of convenience. It is almost certainly a serious underestimation for each sensory modality. Hardin suggests that there are between 7 million and 10 million distinguishable colors (1988, 127). If this is true, we would need to posit on the order of 200 discriminable states for each of the three kinds of color receptor cells.

The natural method requires that we sometimes use information from the psychological or phenomenological levels to generate neural hypotheses. Estimating the discriminative sensitivity of each type of color receptor on the basis of estimates of our psychological color sensitivities is one example of this method in practice. Here is another example. If it is true that bloodhounds are capable of distinguishing every person on the planet by smell, they could do so with the same number of odor receptors as we have so long as these were about three times as sensitive as ours. If each receptor cell can give rise to 30 discriminable states along its axis, 30^7 (22 billion) unique odor discriminations are possible. Alternatively, a system with 10 odor receptors capable of 10 distinct states would also do the job, since it would be capable of 10 billion unique discriminations (it is estimated that there will be 6.3 billion humans on earth by the turn of the century).

The vector-coding story of sensory qualia is credible. Its credibility undermines the claim that qualia are inherently mysterious and that nothing, at least nothing scientific, can be said about them. The nonnaturalist may not be moved, claiming only to see that certain neural correlations have been cited between two different metaphysical kinds. But those naturalists who claim that consciousness is forever mysterious, that no constructive theory can be offered, and those agnostics who say we do not yet know how naturalism could be true ought to see that this story about qualia lends support to the idea of a coherent and constructive naturalism. As Paul Churchland rightly points out,

> This approach to understanding sensory qualia is both theoretically and empirically motivated.... It suggests an effective means of expressing the allegedly inexpressible. The "ineffable" pink of one's current visual sensation may be richly and precisely expressed as a 95Hz/80Hz/80Hz "chord" in the relevant triune cortical system. The "unconveyable" taste sensation produced by the fabled Australian health tonic Vegamite might be poignantly conveyed as a 85/80/90/15 "chord" in one's four-channeled gustatory system.... And the "indescribable" olfactory sensation produced by a newly opened rose

might be quite accurately described as a 95/35/10/80/60/55 "chord" in some six-dimensional space within one's olfactory bulb.   (1989, 106)

Sensory qualia, according to the proposal being offered, are just the characteristic spiking frequencies or activation patterns in the relevant neural pathways. (These activation patterns include, I emphasize, changes in the biochemical environment produced in the creation of the activation pattern.) Functional locations or spaces in the continua of values that each set of pathways can take correspond to what psychologists call "just-noticeable differences." If for me Pepsi and Coke taste different, this is because the activation ranges in the relevant pathways are distinct *and* I am sensitive to their distinctness.

The story with sensory coding vectors may generalize beyond qualia associated with the five familiar sensory modalities. Take facial recognition. Persons with prosopagnosia cannot recognize faces, but normal persons take for granted their abilities to *re-*cognize faces. I emphasize the '*re-*' because the crucial thing is that once we see a face, we experience it as seen before, and this is true even if we can't associate a name to the face. It is possible that facial recognition works according to the vector-coding strategy (P. M. Churchland 1988, 150). There are several good reasons for thinking that the neural network contains a sector built for facial coding. First, there is decisive evidence that certain sorts of right-hemisphere damage to the parietal lobe causes prosopagnosia. Second, thanks to the work of David Hubel, and Torsten Weisel, and others, we know that receptor cells in the eye are very sensitive to the different orientations of lines, and we know from work on coordination between the visual and motor systems that we are good at judging distances (from our body to a cup we want to grasp, for example). Third, there are good evolutionary reasons to think that there would have been selection pressures to build networks capable of quickly and effortlessly recognizing the faces of members of the same species. A system that quickly recognizes its mate, fellow travelers, and its enemies will do better that a system that does not.

We consciously recognize faces, but we are not conscious of how we recognize faces. The most plausible hypothesis is that the facial-coding sector operates as an unconscious geometrician. It detects some of the main facial aspects: eye shape, distance between eyes, mouth width, nose length and width, distances between eyes and nose, nose and jaw, ear to ear, jaw and hairline, and so on (this proposal helps us understand how facial recognition can survive long time gaps: the relevant geometrical relations are fairly well preserved as faces age). There are, let us suppose, 10 or 12 saliencies such as these to which we are sensitive and as few as 10 values that can be encoded for each (this is probably a underestimation, although

Paul Churchland works with 5 and he may know something I don't know). This would allow for unique vector assignments for between 10 billion (10^{10}) and 1 trillion (10^{12}) faces. More than enough!

6   Experiential Sensitivity versus Informational Sensitivity

Our informational sensitivities far exceed our conscious sensitivities. If the sensory-vector story is true for sensory qualia, it is true in the following sort of way. For any qualitative experience q, q has the qualitative character it has because q is both a token of a type of neural activation in the relevant sensory pathway and at the same time a token of the relevant experiential state type. The thesis is not that for each different vector there is a distinct sensory quale. The Pepsi and Coke case shows why. Coke and Pepsi almost definitely differ in the activation vector they cause. Not all persons are *experientially sensitive* to all significant differences in the sensory vectors. To some people, Pepsi and Coke taste the same. Now a person might be experientially *in*sensitive to the difference between two stimuli while at the same time he or she is *informationally sensitive* to the difference. If the person who honestly claims to experience no taste difference between Pepsi and Coke reliably chooses Pepsi in blind forced-choice situations, we must infer that some complex calculation of information differences, in interaction with a complex economy of desire, is taking place. For the vector-activation story to be credible, there will have to be some underlying difference in the Pepsi and Coke vectors subserving the eventual behavioral difference. All distinct sensory experiences are subserved by distinct vectors. But not all distinct vectors subserve distinct experiences. This is why the hypothesis is that a sensory experience occurs *only if* there is the relevant sort of nervous activity in the sensory pathways. The hypothesis says "only if" rather than "if and only if" for two reasons. First, the relevant sensory vector is necessary, but possibly not sufficient, for the relevant sensory experience. Neural activity quickly spreads from the sensory periphery up and outward throughout the brain. More neural activity than the right sensory coding vector may be needed to experience red, for example. Certain attentional mechanisms may need to be in play. Second, the sensory vector that unambiguously differentiates Pepsi from Coke might be active without the whole system experiencing the difference. The activated vector may nonetheless play an important role in our overall psychological economy.

The distinction between experiential sensitivity and informational sensitivity is useful across a wide array of domains. But it is hardly pure. First, there is a grey area of what Freudians call preconscious experience, where some stimulation to which we display clear informational sensitivity is not in awareness but can be brought into awareness. The capacity of some individuals to become sensitive to what it is about the taste of Pepsi that makes them prefer it, even when they are initially unaware of any experience that could subserve such a preference, suggests that there are attentional mechanisms that can be brought into play to bring to experience what is initially only a neural difference, that is, an informational difference. Second, in the Coke and Pepsi case, both tastes are experienced. It is the difference in taste that is not experienced. There are other kinds of cases in which there is informational sensitivity but no experiential sensitivity at all. Indeed, the literature on subliminal perception indicates that for each sensory modality, there is a level of stimulation at which experience fails to occur but information about stimuli is received and processed. For example, emotionally threatening words presented below the visual experiential threshold cause changes in auditory sensitivity and vice versa (Dixon 1987). On my view, we are informationally sensitive to such stimuli, but we are not consciously sensitive to them. Third and correlatively, dreams are consciously experienced. We are notoriously bad at remembering our dreams when awake, but they involve phenomenologically robust experience (Hobson 1988; Crick and Koch 1990, 265).

All things considered, the distinction between experiential sensitivity and informational sensitivity has a credible basis. Subjective consciousness, as I am using the concept, refers to experiential sensitivity. But it is important to emphasize that all subjective consciousness also involves informational sensitivity, even if it is only the sensitivity involved in the awareness of what it is like to be in whatever state one is in. But the reverse is not true. Pure informational sensitivity is nonconscious. That is, there is such a thing as informational pickup and processing without phenomenal awareness.

7   Identity Theory to a First Approximation?

To a first and rough approximation, identity theory seems true for the type identity of sensory qualia within persons and, if we allow for differences in individual brains, within the species. One advantage of this story is its compatibility with evolutionary theory. A certain uniformity in receptor-cell sensitivity and in mappings from the sensory periphery to the cortex could easily have been selected for because of the overwhelming survival importance to ancestral humans of getting the basic features of the external world right. For example, the discovery that distinct receptor cells in the hand subserve the detection of pain, temperature, vibration, and pressure comes as no great surprise in view of the great importance of the hands in the evolution of *Homo sapiens*. Patricia Churchland writes,

> Neurons carrying information from the sensory periphery terminate at selected areas of the thalamus, where they are arranged in a

somatotopic representation of the body. These thalamic areas in turn project to selected areas of the cortex, all in very orderly fashion and with substantial reciprocal projection from the cortex. In the cortex neurons are again mapped in such a way as to preserve neighborhood relations of body parts, though there are some interesting discontinuities. Accordingly, neurons responsive to stimuli on the index finger are between neurons responsive to stimuli on the thumb and those for the middle finger, but distant from those for the big toe or the scalp. (1986, 128–129)

The evidence suggests that the lemniscal system (the system subserving sensory perception of touch, deep pressure, limb position, vibration, and conscious proprioception in general) projects fairly precisely through the spinal system, to the thalamus, and onto the cortex. The spinothalamic system (which detects pain, temperature, and some kinds of touch) projects onto the cortex via spinal and thalamic routes in a somewhat coarser manner than the lemniscal system does. Specialized detector cells working in parallel, along with the iteration of their findings through many layers of neuron ensembles, explains how a complex experience of hot, painful pressure on one's finger can happen with such rapidity.

I have said that identity theory is only approximately true for sensory qualia. I say "approximately" for two reasons. First, though the maps for certain sensory qualia project relatively neatly through the network hierarchy, not all the mappings are so tidy. There are precise mappings for certain sensation types (for example, color sensation, taste, touch and vibration), but the mappings are coarser and less consistent for other sensational types (for example, pain and temperature). Second, there is the evidence mentioned above of changing boundaries and *intra*individual variation of neural maps. The mappings from the sensory receptors to the cortex are remarkably fluid within a certain range. William Calvin writes,

> In the 1980's, we were all shocked to hear (from Michael Merzenich, Jon Kaas, Randy Nelson, and their colleagues) that somatosensory cortical maps were a day-to-day affair, changing size if the hand was exercised more; if a particular fingertip was regularly rubbed on something,... more cells in the somatosensory cortex would come to specialize in that finger. And conversely, the size of the receptor-field center for a cell specializing in that finger would become stronger.... Usually when this happened, the new forefinger cells would come from cells that formerly specialized in adjacent fingers—but sometimes from cells that formerly specialized in the face! The face's connections to such versatile cells were turned down to nothing, while the forefinger's connections were enhanced—and so a "retrained worker"!...But they also noticed that some changes in cortical

boundaries seemed to occur spontaneously from week to week, even though the monkey wasn't being trained and was just moving about his cage. For example, the boundary between face and hand cells in the cortex moved from week to week, back and forth—some weeks the cells near the boundary were face specialists, other weeks the very same cells were thumb specialists. To neurophysiologists, this was approximately as if you had told us that the state line between California and Oregon was moving a few miles back and forth from week to week for no apparent reason.   (1990, 175)

Even if we accept this story of iterated distributed mappings through neuronal layers with somewhat fluid boundaries for sensory perception, we still need an explanation for the fact that we are experientially sensitive to certain saliencies but informationally sensitive to these plus some. The explanation, according to neural-network models, will once again simply have to do with characteristic patterns of activation and connection within the nervous system, perhaps even within the system as a whole. This explanation does not simply posit the divide between experiential sensitivity and informational sensitivity as an inexplicable surd. As I have insisted, consciousness did not need to evolve at all. But since it did, there are resulting design constraints. An optimally designed system with finite powers better not be conscious of everything. Any efficiently designed finite cognitive system will be sensitive to far more than it is conscious of.

One mistake to stay away from is positing a center of consciousness, a specific faculty devoted to consciousness, that receives some but not all messages causally relevant in human activity. Some patterns of neural activity result in phenomenological experience; other patterns do not. The story bottoms out there. It bottoms out just as the explanation of complex life bottoms out in the microstructure of the double helix.

The analogy to the genetic code indicates that the story's bottoming out does not mean that dead silence ensues or that we can say nothing more about the way in which some kinds of somatosensory activity subserve certain kinds of experience, and other types of nervous activity do not give rise to experiences. We know, for example, that informational sensitivity to fine hair movement in the ears is very important to the maintenance of balance, and we can say something about the patterns of neuronal activation involved. But no one experiences the position of the hairs in his or her ears. In fact, most people don't even know that there are fine hairs in their ears. And it is not clear that all the effort in the world could overcome the phenomenological impenetrability of the existence and movement of our ear hairs! Furthermore, the account implies—and there is already considerable confirmation for the hypothesis—that phenomenological distinctions in conscious experience (differences in color, speech, shape, musical perception, and so on) are subserved by different types of neural activity.

To blunt the force of a likely criticism, it might be better to say the story will eventually bottom out in the fine-grained *details* of the story. The criticism I have in mind originates with John Locke's *Essay Concerning Human Understanding* (also see Levine 1983, Adams 1987). Locke claimed that the qualitative experiences of colors or sounds bear no intelligible relation to the corpuscular properties of matter that give rise to these very experiences. The connection between a rose and *seeing* red or between hitting the middle key on a piano and *hearing* middle C seems utterly arbitrary. God could just as well have made hitting middle C cause the smell of honeysuckle or the experience of yellow or the sound of B sharp. He could have done this, but he didn't. Since he didn't, we can look for features of the connections between physical stimuli and consciousness of them that diminish the sense of arbitrariness. When Locke wrote, the connections between the physical and the phenomenal were very poorly understood. Given the state of seventeenth-century science, one could have credibly wondered why playing middle C causes people to hear something, as opposed to see or smell or taste something. We now know more. We can add significant and convincing detail to certain parts of the story. The reason that some objects gives rise to a red experience has to do with the fact that they emit light waves of certain frequencies. These waves are picked up by cells that specialize in light (they can't do sound). They give rise to a sensation of red rather than green because of the length of the wave and the complex structure of the various channels involved in color discernment. Similarly, sounds of different sorts are heard when compression waves are picked up by a system designed for audition (it can't do color, although it is involved in olfaction). Robert Van Gulick rightly says, "The more we can articulate structure within the phenomenal realm, the greater the chances for physical explanation; without structure we have no place to attach our explanatory 'hooks.' There is indeed a residue that continues to escape explanation, but the more we can explain relationally about the phenomenal realm, the more the leftover residue shrinks toward zero" (in press a). The best hypothesis is that a heterogeneous array of neural activity subserves the heterogeneous types of subjective consciousness, and that the science of the mind will increasingly provide more and more detailed stories that diminish the sense that inexplicable or arbitrary links obtain.

If this much is right, the question remains of whether there is or is not some deep commonality among all the different neural arrays that subserve the different types of conscious experience. Francis Crick, one of the discoverers of the double helix, has recently turned his attention to consciousness. Crick suggests that there is tantalizing evidence that neuronal oscillations in the 40-hertz range subserve different kinds of consciousness and thus that despite the fact that consciousness comes in many forms, there exists "one basic mechanism (or a few such) underlying them all" (Crick and Koch 1990, 267).

This could be true. It is early in the game. But it is not too early to know that immaterialism is a nonstarter, and that the brain is up to the job that it in fact most certainly does of generating subjective consciousness. It is also not too early to abandon the idea that there is one central place where all experiences happen, where all thoughts come together. Sensation, perception, cognition are subserved by neural events taking place in multifarious neural locations. Massive parallelism, massive connectivity, and unimaginably great computational power make it clearer how the brain could produce experience without there being any one way in which it does so or any one place in which it does so. That said, it is still entirely possible that some brain location or some pattern of neural activity could turn out to be a necessary condition of conscious experience (see Baars 1988, Crick and Koch 1990, and Edelman 1989 for some contrasting suggestions about essential areas and patterns). Not sufficient but necessary. We'll see. It is an empirical question.

This chapter began with the question, How can there be such a thing as subjectivity in the material world? I have not answered that question directly. Instead, I have tried to make the question seem less perplexing by providing some sense of how consciousness might have evolved, as well as some sense of the awesome power of the brain. The brain is a supremely well connected system of processors capable of more distinct states, by several orders of magnitude, than any system ever known. This, I hope, provides some reassurance that the brain is complex enough to be our *res cogitans*—our thinking thing.

Chapter 4
Qualia

As mentioned above, "to quine" means to deny resolutely the existence of some seemingly undeniable phenomena, one's immortal soul, for example. In his paper "Quining Qualia" (1988c), Dennett recommends the tough action suggested by the title. There are no such things as qualia. Quine qualia!

This is a bad idea. Qualia are for real. Dennett himself says what they are before he starts quining. Sanely, he writes, "'Qualia' is an unfamiliar term for something that could not be more familiar to each of us: the *ways things seem to us*" (Dennett 1988c, 43). A superordinate term for the ways things seem to us is innocent enough. Surely, things do seem in certain ways to us. Furthermore, characterizing the multifarious ways in which things seem is an important component of the natural method. It pins down the phenomenological features of mind so that we can check for relations among the phenomenological, psychological, and neurological levels.

Dennett's exasperation with the concept of qualia comes not so much from doubts that things seem in certain ways, that is, that we go into multifarious kinds of "internal discriminative states" (1991a, 373). His belief that it is time to discard the concept of qualia comes from the idea that qualia have further alleged features: they are atomic, nonrelational, ineffable, incomparable, and incorrigibly accessible from the first-person point of view. It is this extended list that makes the concept of qualia problematic, for its effect is to put qualia in the class of things about which nothing can be said from the third-person point of view. On this analysis, qualia are things about which the science of the mind can offer no illumination. But it is a contentious list. It pins on the friend of qualia the implausible view that qualia are essentially and exclusively qualitative, that is, that they have no other properties than those implicated in their subjectively available aspects. Quining qualia is an overreaction. The qualitative "ways things seem to us" aspect of certain mental states can be the most salient feature of these states, and the only feature available in the first person, without being the only features of these states. This is the view I want to defend.

The first-pass, noncommittal characterization of qualia as the ways things seem to us is well suited to do genuine taxonomic and explanatory work in the science of the mind. This characterization is useful so long as we do not join it to some contentious theory of qualia according to which first-person seemings exhaust the nature of states with a seeming aspect. Dennett says that when "your kite string gets snarled up, in principle it can be unsnarled, especially if you're patient and analytic. But there's a point beyond which principle lapses and practicality triumphs. Some snarls should just be abandoned" (1991a, 369). So it is, Dennett thinks, with the qualia snarl. Ditch the snarled kite!

I'm more hopeful. There isn't one snarled string. The problem is that two distinct strings have gotten ensnarled. One string is attached to an ordinary box kite that announces that there are certain ways things seem. The other string is attached to a gaudy kite that ostentatiously flies banners announcing that the ways things seem consists of a set of atomic, non-relational states that possess ineffable properties known deeply, incorrigibly, and exclusively from the first-person point of view.

We can immediately improve matters by freeing the box kite from the extraneous one tangled up with it, the one that immodestly depicts qualia as possessing special problematic features: being atomic, ineffable, and incorrigibly accessible from the first-person point of view. Ditch the second kite, but get the first kite flying again once it is freed. The box kite announces on one face that qualia are the ways things seem. The fact that it is a box kite helps to capture the idea that qualia have depth and hidden structure. Furthermore, the box kite flies no extraneous banners committing it to the problematic properties. Qualia, as they are depicted on the box kite, can have other properties than those available in the first person. This is ruled out by the banners the second kite flies (see figure 4.1).

2   What Qualia Are

Subjective consciousness is what I seek to explain. Qualia help specify the types of subjectivity. Specifying the types of conscious experience is something we cannot do without if we are to generate and test hypotheses about the links between the phenomenological, the psychological, the physiological, and the neural. Furthermore, qualitative states figure in explanations. Seeing a red light rather than a yellow or green light figures in the explanation of why people stop their cars at some times and not at others. Part of the work of the preceding chapter was devoted to showing how certain qualitative experiences—experiences of color, smell, taste, and even pressure, temperature, and pain—can be understood in neuroscientific terms. Qualia exist, and qualia can be naturalized.

Qualia pick out types of subjective experience. Qualia pick out the different ways things seem to us. Charles Sanders Peirce used the concept

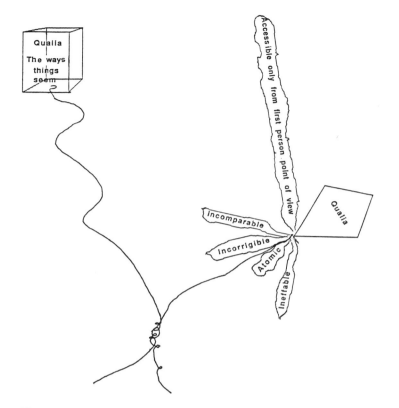

Figure 4.1
Dennett thinks we should ditch qualia because the kite string that flies their colors is too
snarled to be worth untangling. My diagnosis is that there are two kites that have become
ensnarled. The box kite on the left simply announces on one face that qualia are the ways
things seem. The fact that it is a box kite captures the idea that qualia have depth and hidden
structure. Qualia as are depicted on the kite on the right can have no other aspects than
those that are available subjectively. So Dennett is right that one kite should be ditched. But
it should be ditched only after it is disentangled from the kite on the left, which, once free,
can fly again. (Drawing courtesy of Joseph L. Dropkin.)

of qualia very broadly to specify the multifarious ways in which things seem:

> The *quale*-consciousness is not confined to simple sensations. There is a peculiar *quale to purple*, though it be only a mixture of red and blue. There is a distinctive *quale* to every combination of sensations— There is a distinctive *quale* to every work of art—a distinctive *quale* to this moment as it is to me—a peculiar *quale* to every day and every week—a peculiar *quale* to my whole personal consciousness. I appeal to your introspection to bear me out.   (Peirce 1898, par. 223)

A quale is a mental event or state that has, among its properties, the property that there is something it is like to be in it. The superordinate category of distinctive feels is dubbed "qualia." So there is the quale my experience of red, here and now, which belongs to the species of red experiences, which belong to the genus of color experiences, which fall under the superordinate category of experiences with feel.

Qualitative experience has a holistic quality. This does not preclude, however, that the work of analysis might require decomposition into different aspects for certain purposes. We sometimes mark off the qualitative component of an experience from its content component, for example, "I'm pleased [that Mary got the job]." But even in such cases it is important to recognize that the content [that Mary got the job] is constitutive, from the first-person perspective, of the quality of the experience. The experience is one of being pleased that Mary got the job. Despite the fact that experience is holistic, there may be philosophical reasons to separate the narrow qualitative aspect from the content in the example given, since logically and in fact, they do come apart. I might, after all, have been disappointed that Mary got the job.

Qualitative experience might also yield to neural decomposition. Seeing colored shapes is qualitatively holistic. I see a red triangle or a green octagon. I do not see red and then a triangle, or green and then an octagon. Nonetheless, we know that the visual system detects color and shape in different processors and somehow binds them together (Treisman and Schmidt 1982). The phenomenology of even simple visual experiences does not remotely reveal their deep structure.

Like Peirce, I see no principled reason for restricting the concept of qualia to the feels of sensations. 'Qualia' picks out the types of qualitative experience. Not all qualia are sensational. Conscious moods, emotions, beliefs, desires, possibly even what it is like to be me have distinct qualitative character.

My recommended use of the term 'qualia' is more useful and principled than the sense that picks out the feels of sensations only and that characterizes such feels in terms of a problematic cluster of properties: being atomic, nonrelational, ineffable, incomparable, and incorrigibly accessible from the first-person point of view. There are no qualia with these properties. Quine the properties, but don't quine qualia. Leave the real qualia alone.

Quality is contrasted with quantity. Do subjective experiences have nonqualitative aspects? The answer is yes. Subjective experiences occur at particular spatial locations in the form of distributed neural activity. The neural properties of qualitative experiences are not revealed in the first-person point of view. They are, however, part of the structure of such experiences.

There are four reasons why we need the concept of qualia. First, the concept is needed to distinguish mental states with feel from those without, though we must allow, of course, that feels differ greatly in degree and kind. One might wonder what a mental state is without feel. Subliminal perception, knowledge without awareness informational sensitivity without phenomenal awareness, might be credibly thought of as involving or consisting of mental states without feel. These are cases where a content component occurs without any qualitative accompaniment whatsoever. Are all conscious states qualitative? I think so. Some philosophers think that there are conscious states whose contents are "transparent, unclouded by a subjective feel or aspect" (this is Ken Winkler's formulation). I think that conscious beliefs have a distinctive qualitative character, as do desires. Cases where conscious states might seem nonqualitative are ones where the way the thought seems is exhausted by saying what propositional attitude is taken toward what content. But the fact is that such thoughts seem in a certain way.

Corralling all conscious propositional-attitude states into the stable of qualitative states is controversial. But I think that it is plausible and that skeptics might be skeptics because they think that experiences with qualitative character must have the sort of robust qualitative feel that sensations have (Jackendoff [1987], Baars [1988], and Goldman [1991] defend the idea that conscious thought has qualitative character).

In any case, the second reason why we need the concept of qualia is that subjective experience is illuminatingly taxonomized in terms of mental state types with distinctive feels. It is extremely doubtful that the taxonomy picks things out in the most illuminating or optimal way, even from the phenomenological point of view. But the vocabulary in whose terms we have learned to distinguish sensations, moods, emotions, and different kinds of thoughts serves useful everyday functions. Interpersonal communication is facilitated by the acquisition of a mentalistic vocabulary that abounds with terms for qualitative types.

Third and relatedly, whatever imperfections the vocabulary of qualitative distinctions suffers from, it sets the agenda for hypothesis generation and theory construction at the lower levels. There is evidence that heightened activity in the left frontal lobes is linked to cheerfulness and low activity to depression (Henriques and Davidson 1990). The PET-scan techniques and brain-wave research that have led to this finding link temperament and mood on the one hand and brain states on the other. Nothing would have been illuminated had not the phenomenological evidence concerning cheerfulness and depression, and personality measures of these states, been in place prior to the examination of the brain. Similarly, it is inconceivable that we could sketch any credible story about the neurobiology of color, taste, and odor perception without having phenomenological descriptions to hook the exploration onto. Likewise, the important work showing that there are characteristic cross-personal muscular and physiological correlates of certain basic emotions—sadness, disgust, happiness, surprise, anger, and fear—involved testing the hypothesis that such links exist and could not have proceeded without giving our subjective emotional types their due (Ekman, Levinson, and Freisen 1985).

Not all qualitative types pick out coherent sets of experiences. Consider Peirce's catalog. We say such things as "It's been a great week" or "I've felt great this week," but it is wrong to think, as Peirce does, that there is a "distinctive *quale* to every day and every week." We make summary judgments about what a day or a week has been like and how it has gone for us, but it is doubtful that there is some distinctive quale each day or week has for us. I think that things are somehow different with "my whole personal consciousness." Peirce is right that there really is something distinctive that it is like to be an individual self. Not all of personality is experienced. But for most persons there is an aspect of identity that is experienced as their *personal* identity and that is bound by memory connections, dispositional characteristics, intentions and plans of certain sorts. The self is a complex construct. But the complex it depicts is presumably realized in some unique way in the life history of the brain and behavior of each individual. The burden falls to neuroscience to explain how the feelings of personal identity and continuity maintain such a strong foothold in our phenomenology.

The fourth reason for embracing the concept of qualia is embedded in what I have already said, but it is worthy of being marked off on its own. There is no stronger evidence for the thesis of the heterogeneity of kinds of subjective consciousness than the heterogeneity of qualitative types available in ordinary talk. Some have complained that the concept of consciousness is too simplistic (Rey 1983, 1988), that it "indifferently lumps together" a heterogeneous assortment of state types (P. S. Churchland 1986, 321; Wilkes 1988a, 1988b). To be sure, it is a big mistake to think that the states that make up consciousness are a single, undifferentiated class. But it seems to me that the manifold of qualitative types, as unrefined and superficial as it might be in certain respects, already displays a clear commitment to the heterogeneity of the types of consciousness.

Those who would quine qualia are bothered by the fact that they seem mysterious—essentially private, ineffable, and not subject to third-person evaluation. Qualia are none of these things. In addition to having none of these defects, qualia have the unnoticed virtue of providing powerful evidence for the heterogeneity of subjective experience. Some qualia, such as color experiences, are associated with a single sensory modality; others, such as shape experiences, are open to more than one modality. I can see a square, feel a square, maybe even echolocate a square. Red and green are as different as can be colorwise, and the evidence shows that this phenomenal incompatibility is explained by the underlying neurobiology. But unalike as they are, red and green are phenomenologically more alike than red is to any taste or any shape. The feel of a square, as perceived through a single modality or multimodally, is phenomenologically more similar to the feel of any other shape than it is to the feel of any odor, color, or taste. And the sense of self is as qualitatively different as can be from all these qualitatively distinct sensory experiences, as are sensory experiences from beliefs, hopes, desires, and expectations. Heterogeneity reigns among qualia.

3 Sensational and Nonsensational Qualia

Qualia provide a typology of experiences with qualitative aspects. The concept of qualia has both a wide sense and a narrow sense. Much of the trouble caused by the concept comes from focusing exclusively on the narrow sense, which associates qualia with sensations, especially sensations involving only one sensory modality. Color experiences are everyone's favorite qualia. This is due in part to the fact that colors, unlike shapes, can be perceived by only one sense and can therefore seem private and capable of going undetectably awry in ways not possible with multimodal experiences, like experiences of shapes. Together, the wide and narrow senses of 'qualia' cover the same gamut that 'conscious experience' in the broad sense covers.

The wide sense of 'qualia' comes straightforwardly out of the analysis of 'qualia' as the name for the superordinate category under which fall all types of experience with subjective, first-person, phenomenological feel. Beliefs, thoughts, hopes, expectations, and propositional-attitude states generally, as well as large narrative structures, are qualitative (or have qualitative components) in this sense. The wide sense is rarely noted, but it is well grounded. In our phenomenology, beliefs (when they are experienced) are experienced differently from desires, and desires differently from expectations. When a person says, "I believe that snow is white," there is almost never any doubt that she is in a state of belief rather than a state of desire. How should we explain this? The best answer is that there really is a certain way it feels to be believing something and that way of feeling is different from the way it feels to be desiring something (see Goldman 1991 for an argument in defense of the "phenomenal 'parity'" of the attitudes). The qualitative feel of propositional-attitude states is underestimated. It is an interesting question whether going into a certain brain state with a beliefy feel (or desirey feel) *causes* us to confidently assert a belief (or a desire) or whether going into some such state is actually *constitutive* of believing and desiring. Nothing in our current science enables us to answer this question of whether the relation is causal or constitutive, but the question can be explored as we learn more about the connections among the brain, certain kinds of thoughts, and certain kinds of speech acts.

Qualia in the wide sense lurk in the philosophical literature concerning absent qualia. The species of zombielike beings allegedly just like us except that they lack inner lives altogether do not simply lack smells and tastes and sounds. They don't simply lack qualia in the narrow sense, by which I mean the subjective experience of non-propositional-attitude states, primarily of sensations. They lack all conscious propositional thought as well. In his thought experiment of a Chinese-speaking room (1984), John Searle attacks the sufficiency of the Turing-test for establishing real equivalence between human and machine by describing a system that is absent qualia in that it does things that are normally mediated by conscious intentional states—it answers questions in Chinese—but that are not so mediated in the thought experiment. Searle originally framed the problem as one of absent intentionality, the Chinese-speaking room had no contentful representations, but the problem can also be seen as a problem of absent consciousness. Even if the room is Turing-identical to a Chinese speaker and even if it represents Chinese speech production somewhere along the way, there is nothing it is like to be the Chinese-speaking room.

4   Inverted Qualia

The development of a theory of subjective consciousness requires that the phenomenological, psychological, and neuroscientific analyses be brought into reflective equilibrium. The possibility of an integrative theory of the sort discussed in chapter 1 hinges on the possibility of getting at qualia. Thought experiments involving allegedly undetectable qualia inversions present problems. Indeed, Dennett's program to quine qualia (1988c), to disqualify them (1991a), is motivated largely by the fact that inverted qualia are thought to establish that there are discriminative states *independent* of all other dispositions, reactive attitudes, and even radical adjustments in our neural wiring. Dennett thinks that the properties that engender thoughts about principled undetectability are knots in the string of the kite we must now ditch. I think that experiences are qualitative, but I also think that they have other properties than those available in their subjectively available aspects. Indeed, I deny that qualia are closed off to objective scrutiny. The idea that qualia are in principle undetectable is proclaimed on the kite we should have no wish to launch again. But there is still the other kite, the true qualia kite. Unsnarl it from the troublesome kite, and let it fly again. It makes no claims to the effect that the properties of qualia are objectively undetectable because the properties of qualia are exhausted by their subjectively available aspects. Let's see if we can make sense of this more credible conception of qualia.

Inverted qualia are normally brought on the scene to challenge functionalism. The sort of functionalism that is the target of inverted-qualia thought experiments is one that tries to "'tack down' mental states only at the periphery—i.e., through physical, or at least nonmental, specification of input and outputs" (Block 1980b, 269). Absent and inverted qualia exploit the behavioristic character of functionalism. If functional equivalence is equivalence at the level of nonmentally specified inputs and outputs, then zombies and folk with qualia inversion will be equivalent to us so long as they are equivalent to us in terms of inputs and outputs.

I reject this sort of computational functionalism. It is too behavioristic. We want to capture the actual dynamics of human psychology and behavior. This will require that we intentionally describe inputs. What stimulus is presented depends on how it is construed by the organism. One person's beautiful snake in the grass is a terrifying sight to another individual and the cause of his heart attack. Furthermore, many of our behavioral outputs are actions, where actions are behaviors characterized in terms of the motives and intentions that constitute them. One person's left turn signal is another's resting arm. Not all the mental ascriptions that enter into the intentional characterization of human perception, thought, and action will involve ascriptions of occurrently or vividly conscious mental states. But many will. At least in these cases, qualitative states are required for the identification of certain perceptions, thoughts, and actions as the perceptions, thoughts, and actions that they are.

Inverted qualia are a problem primarily because they are alleged to be undetectable. They do not directly challenge the opponent of computational functionalism, since equivalence for the opponent requires equivalence of subjective mental life. Two people with red-green inversion have different inner lives. Such persons may be input-output equivalent, but they are not mentally equivalent. But inverted qualia present an indirect problem, for if they really are undetectable, we will have no good reason to withhold ascriptions of subjective sameness in cases where in fact there is no subjective sameness. And there will be a potentially large and important class of mental causes that don't open themselves up to the usual inter-subjective tests science demands. Inverted qualia are an epistemic problem, even if they are not metaphysically problematic. The good news is that inverted qualia are in principle detectable, despite the hoopla.

Consider first a puzzle about inverted qualia in the wide sense. Imagine two individuals who have inverted beliefs relative to each other: *a* believes that *p*, while *b* believes that not *p*. Can we imagine cases in which there is such an inversion but it is in principle impossible to detect the inversion? The answer is no (Block 1980b, 288). When two people have different beliefs, those differences show up in behavior or can be made to do so. When people have different beliefs about important everyday matters, they typically say so and get into disagreements. "I am Napoleon." "You're not Napoleon." "Taxes should be raised." "Taxes should not be raised."

Sometimes, of course, differences in beliefs are not expressed straightfor-wardly. Whenever we are leaving the house in daylight, my son always picks up a basketball and shoots a couple of shots. Long after I noticed this little ritual, Ben asked me one day if I had any superstitions. I said that I was sure that I did, but couldn't think of any offhand. I asked him if he had any. Indeed, he did. Ben explained that he thinks it is good luck to make a hoop before departure. Now I don't think that. Before this admission, there was a behavioral difference between Ben and myself, but no evidence of any relevant difference in belief related to this particular set of behaviors (I in fact assumed that our behavioral difference was rooted solely in different desires). But now there is evidence of actual belief inversion. Ben believes that it is important for how one's day goes that one make a hoop before departure, and I don't think that. This belief explains Ben's ritualistic shoot-ing. But it probably would not have been revealed to me had he not reported it.

Nonetheless, Ben's belief was always in principle detectable. To believe that *p* is, among other things, to have a disposition to assent to '*p*' if queried. The point can be generalized to very abstract metaphysical beliefs that might never in fact make a perceptible impact on behavior. The person who believes that life is holy may never show signs to others of this belief. Yet it remains in principle detectable because it will show up in her verbal behavior if we make the right probes. The upshot is that we need not give in to excessive worries about the possibility of inverted qualia in the wide sense. Such inversions will, or can be made to, reveal themselves in behav-ior or speech.

But what about inverted qualia in the narrow sense? The case of the inverted spectrum is supposed to show the possibility of genuine inversion in, say, red and green sensations with no way in principle to detect the inversion. Unlike the case of qualia inversion in the wide sense, no verbal probe will detect the difference. "What color is that?" I ask pointing to a lawn, and you say, "Green," all the while seeing red. You use the language of color perfectly; you just see red when I see green, and vice versa.

I want to indicate some grounds for thinking that we underestimate the ways in which such inversion might be revealed in behavior or in the brain. In the first place, there is underestimation of the behavioral consequences of a color inversion. "The way the visual experience of color is mapped onto or used to express concepts of emotion (happiness, worry, sadness, fright, anger) may not be all that variable either historically or cross-culturally.... The association, for example, of red with anger and black (and white) with bereavement is no historical accident; very different kinds of people know how to translate the color-affect code, and they translate it in a similar way" (Shweder 1991, 246).

If there is some biological disposition to link certain colors with certain emotions, then in fact there may be detectable differences between people with normal perception and those with inverted spectra. Perhaps there is a statistically significant difference in the frequency with which those suffering color inversion say such things as "That makes me see red" when angry. They don't say this, because being angry and seeing green simply don't suitably link up in the way in which our quirky minds link anger and seeing red.

Hardin discusses possible ecological and biological foundations for the surprising analogical maps between colors and other concepts. Red and yellow are seen as "warm" hues, and green and blue as "cool." "Some are inclined to use kinetic rather than thermal terms, so red and yellow are 'advancing' and blue and green are 'receding.' Still others assimilate the distinction to a variation in brightness, with red and yellow as 'light' and green and blue as 'dark'" (1988, 129). Hardin offers the following proposal to explain these common conceptual links:

> One can readily find particular and extrinsic reasons for each of these connections. *Warm-cool*: Red and yellow are hues of fires, green and blue colors of lakes. *Advancing-receding*: If the lens of the eye accommodates so that an image formed by middlewave light is focused on the retina, a shortwave image will focus in front of the retina, and a longwave image will focus behind it. Shortwave light thus focuses like light from a more distant object, and longwave light focuses like light from a closer object. To focus on a blue patch we must therefore accommodate our lenses as we would when we focus on a distant object, while focusing on a red patch requires that we accommodate as we do for nearby objects.... *Light-dark*: The eye's sensitivity is much less at the spectral locus for blue and blue-violet than it is at the locus for yellow and yellow-orange. So, although a thing that looks blue may reflect as much light energy to the eye as a thing that looks

yellow, the blue looking thing will typically have most of its reflected energy in the neighborhood of 475 nm, where the eye is not so sensitive, and the yellow looking thing will commonly reflect more of its energy at around 575 nm, where the eye is very sensitive. So the first thing will look darker than the second one.   (1988, 129)

The idea that certain analogies are rooted in the way in which the mind is embedded in the brain and the body in the world is worth taking seriously (Lakoff 1987; Johnson 1987). Whereas inverted-spectrum cases try to have us imagine no differences in speech acts (everything we call "red," our inverted friend calls "green"), the fact is that not all speech acts involving color are likely to be so well preserved in a person suffering inversion.

If a person showed up who made all the wrong analogical speech acts, calling red things "cool," green things "warm," blue things "light," yellow things "dark," and so on, we might then start examining for color inversion. If the earlier sketched story of sensory coding vectors is on the right track, we should be able to look at receptor cells in the eye responsible for detecting short, medium, and long wavelengths of light, and at the neural networks responsible for normal color perception, to check for wiring or transmission problems. The idea that a neuroscientist armed with a good understanding of the neurophysiology of color vision and PET or MRI scanners could detect such malfunctions is perfectly plausible. Good auto mechanics can detect car problems that automotive know-nothings cannot.

We will never be in a position to prove that two individuals see red in exactly the same way. But that shouldn't worry us because things get proved only in mathematics. It is nonetheless possible that as science progresses, we might be able to make extremely well grounded judgments about experiential similarities and their neural underpinnings (Logothetis and Schall 1989; Crick and Koch 1990, 265; Henriques and Davidson 1990).

5   Intractable Qualia

Dennett's argument in "Quining Qualia" begins, as I said earlier, with the sentence " 'Qualia' is an unfamiliar term for something that could not be more familiar to each of us: the *ways things seem to us*" (1988c, 43). Dennett does not deny that there are "*ways things seem to us*." His target is a certain conception of qualia. It is a conception according to which qualia are intrinsic, atomic, unanalyzable, nonrelational, ineffable, essentially private, and immediately and incorrigibly apprehensible. My reaction to Dennett's quining qualia is similar to my reaction to the attempts to quine the whole of consciousness (see chapter 2). This is predictable, since for me all and only conscious states are qualitative. Qualia is the name for the super-

ordinate class comprising multifarious types of states with qualitative properties, that is, conscious states. What Dennett is really after is a particular
conception of qualia. It is by no means clear whether it is the orthodox or
canonical conception. To be sure, all the properties he lists have been
ascribed by someone or other to qualia. But I can't think of one credible
recent philosophical source that uses the term in a way that ascribes all or
even most of the features he lists. Dennett's heart is in the right place, since
he rightly resists the idea of atomic, ineffable, incorrigible qualia. But his
characterization of qualia is contentious; it is partly responsible for ensnar-
ing the two kite strings. On the problematic conception, qualia are essentially and exclusively qualitative, that is, they have no other properties than
those implicated in their having subjectively available aspects. This is a bad
view. Qualitative states are always realized in the brain, and they typically
have behavioral effects. So the conception of qualia he quines deserves such
treatment. But it doesn't follow that there are no qualia. There are. 'Qualia'
names what he initially says it names: "*the ways things seem to us.*" This is
the orthodox concept of qualia if anything is, and it entails *none* of the
problematic properties. The ways things seem to us provide the types of
subjective experience as discerned from the first-person point of view. This
typology is the sine qua non for theory construction and hypothesis
generation about subjective experience. Without our qualitative typologies
to start with, there are no remotely manageable connections between types
of subjective experience, other psychological states and processes, and
neural processes to seek to understand. Without qualia, there is just the
buzzing confusion of subjective mental life. With qualia, many types and
subtypes of subjective experiences are taxonomized. Qualia, as it were,
give theory a chance.

Dennett thinks that inverted qualia are no cause for worry. Like me, he
thinks that it is doubtful that the "qualophile" can tell a convincing story in
which the way things look turns out to be independent of *all* our verbal
and nonverbal reactive attitudes. So long as there are changes in blood
pressure and galvanic skin responses exhibited when experiencing red but
not green, detectable differences exist, and no opaque, nonrelational, atomic qualia haunt mental space. Dennett's inference strategy, at least sometimes, seems to be this: there are no undetectable qualia; therefore, there
are no qualia, period. My view is that there are no undetectable qualia;
therefore, there are no undetectable qualia.

Because of his general attitude toward thought experiments involving
qualia inversion, Dennett presents some thought experiments of his own,
which have the curious feature of being, as it were, undecidable or intractable. This is a bad result, so I want to help Dennett around it by using the
tactics I have availed myself of so far. Dennett rejects the global mysteria-

nism of Colin McGinn (1989, 1991), according to which the problem of consciousness is unsolvable, period. But he has a curious streak of local mysterianism in that he thinks certain specific problems of consciousness are unsolvable. There are two causes of Dennett's skepticism about the possibility of resolving certain disagreements over alternative phenomenological hypotheses. Often the hypotheses, or the problems to which they are addressed, are ill advised or badly formulated. For example, the word 'qualia' appears in the questions or the answers. Just as one cannot really resolve questions about phlogiston except by changing the subject (to oxygen), so too one cannot really resolve questions about qualia. At other times Dennett's main concern seems to be that even if we can seem to formulate credible alternative hypotheses about the ways things seem, we overestimate the resolving power of neuroscience if we think that a choice can be forced in all such cases. Since no choice can be forced by neuroscience in certain cases, the alternative hypotheses do not depict differences that we can truly understand as making a difference. Consider the following two cases.

Chase and Sanborn

> Once upon a time there were two coffee-tasters, Mr Chase and Mr Sanborn.... One day ... Chase ... confessed to Sanborn: "I hate to admit it.... When I came to Maxwell House six years ago, I thought Maxwell House was the best-tasting coffee in the world.... I no longer like it! My tastes have changed. I've become a more sophisticated coffee drinker. I no longer like *that taste* at all. Sanborn greeted this revelation with considerable interest. "It's funny you should mention it," he replied, "for something rather similar has happened to me.... But *my* tastes haven't changed; my ... *tasters* have changed. (Dennett 1988c, 52)

Dennett describes the possibilities as follows: For Chase, (a) his "coffee-taste qualia have stayed constant, while his reactive attitudes to those qualia, devolving on his canons of aesthetic judgment, etc., have shifted"; (b) he "is simply wrong about the constancy of his qualia; they have shifted gradually and imperceptibly over the years, while his standards of taste have not budged"; (c) his "qualia have shifted some *and* his standards of judgment have also slipped." For Sanborn, (a) "his qualia have shifted, due to some sort of derangement in his perceptual machinery," while his aesthetic standards have stayed the same; (b) his standards have shifted, Sanborn simply misremembers his past experiences; (c) as with Chase, there is some qualia shifting and some change in aesthetic standards. So far so good. Dennett then writes,

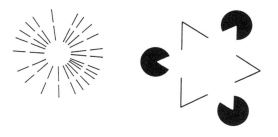

Figure 4.2
Induced illusory contours. Von der Heydt, Peterhaus, and Baumgartner, (1984) provide evidence that such subjective illusions are produced by edge detecors relatively early in visual processing and are not due to higher-level cognitive judgments. (Reprinted with permission from Dennett 1991a, 351.)

It seems easy enough ... to dream up empirical tests that would tend to confirm Chase and Sanborn's different tales.... It is obvious that there might be telling objective support for one extreme version or another of their stories. Thus if Chase is unable to re-identify coffees, teas, and wines in blind tastings in which only minutes intervene between the first and second sip, his claim to *know* that Maxwell House tastes just the same to him now as it did six years ago will be seriously undercut.   (1988c, 55)

Dennett goes on to acknowledge that neurophysiology "suitably interpreted in some larger theoretical framework could also weigh the scales in favour of one extreme or the other." He adds,

For instance, the well-studied phenomenon of induced illusory boundaries [see figure 4.2] has often been claimed to be a particularly "cognitive" illusion, dependent on "top-down" processes and hence, presumably, near the reactive judgment end of the spectrum, but recent experimental work (Von der Heydt et al. 1984) has revealed that "edge detector" neurons relatively low in the visual pathways—in area 18 of the visual cortex—are as responsive to illusory edges as to real light-dark boundaries on the retina, suggesting (but not quite proving, since these might somehow still be "descending effects") that illusory contours are not imposed from on high, but generated quite early in visual processing. One can imagine discovering a similarly "early" anomaly in the pathways leading from taste buds to judgment in Sanborn, for instance, tending to confirm his claim that he has suffered some change in his basic perceptual—as opposed to judgmental—machinery.... But let us not overestimate the resolving power of such empirical testing. The space in each case between the two poles represented by possibility (a) and possibility (b) would be occupied by phenomena that were the product, somehow, of two factors in varying proportion: roughly, dispositions to generate or produce qualia and dispositions to react to the qualia once they are produced.... In extreme cases we can have indirect evidence to suggest that one factor has varied a great deal, the other factor hardly at all, and we can test the hypothesis further by checking the relative sensitivity of the subject to variations in the conditions that presumably alter the two component factors. But such indirect testing cannot be expected to resolve the issue when the effects are relatively small —when, for instance, our rival hypotheses are Chase's preferred hypothesis (a) and the minor variant to the effect that his qualia have shifted a little and his standards less than he thinks.   (1988c, 56–57)

There is no doubt that it will be hard to decide between hypotheses such as these. But it is difficult to see why one would have confidence that rival hypotheses could be sorted out by indirect behavioral and neurophysiological evidence up to a point, but doubt that such evidence could ever provide us with evidence for favoring one of two subtly different rivals. Suppose that the evidence for the sensory-vector story turns out to be overwhelming. Now suppose that we have charted the history of Chase's taste buds and have discovered that over time there have been small differences at the taste receptors on the tongue (destruction caused by coffee), causing a shift in the vectors as viewed on PET scanners. The vectors once looked like those of others who reported that "Maxwell House tastes great." Now they look like those of people who say that they don't like the taste of Maxwell House. This still doesn't rule out some effects emanating from aesthetic standards. These, let us suppose, we understand less well. But imagine that we have discovered that certain experts in meditative technique can keep the normal sensory vectors associated with painful stimuli from occurring and that we know from these cases something about the sorts of resonating brain activity that causes sensory-vector modification from on high. In Chase's case we see none of the relevant wave patterns that would indicate the consequences of any aesthetic standards whatsoever. In his case there still is the surprising straight ballistic shot from the taste buds to his speech center. The inference to the best explanation is that his taste buds have undergone small changes that cause Maxwell House coffee to taste bad, whereas it used to taste good. His higher-level aesthetic standards may have changed some, but as far as the evidence goes, nothing from other parts of the system is interfering much with his tastings. His memory is mistaken. Maxwell House coffee tastes different now than it used to. Chase's taste buds have changed.

Dennett goes on to produce a modification of the thought experiment that is supposed to convince us of "the limited evidential power of neurophysiology." Here we are to imagine that Chase's taste buds are surgically inverted so that right after the operation sugar tastes salty, salt tastes sour, and so on. After a while Chase compensates. "He now *says* that the sugary substance we place on his tongue is sweet, and no longer favours gravy on his ice-cream." Dennett goes on to describe two rival hypotheses about Chase's current state and claims,

> There will always be at least two possible ways of interpreting the neurophysiological theory, however it comes out. Suppose our physiological theory tells us (in as much detail as you like) that the compensatory effect in him has been achieved by an adjustment in the memory-accessing process that is required to compare today's hues with those of yore. There are *still* two stories that might be told:
>
> (I) Chase's current qualia are still abnormal, but thanks to the revision in his memory-accessing process, he has in effect adjusted his memories of how things used to taste, so he no longer notices any anomaly.
>
> (II) The memory-comparison step occurs just prior to the qualia phase in taste perception; thanks to the revision, it now *yields* the same old qualia for the same stimulation.   (1988c, 58)

Dennett concludes, "These seem to be two substantially different hypotheses, but the physiological evidence, no matter how well developed, will not tell us on which side of memory to put the qualia" (1988c, 58).

But then Dennett says that although Chase will not be able to decide between the two hypotheses, physiologists "may have their own reasons for preferring (I) to (II) or vice-versa, for they may have *appropriated* the term 'qualia' to their own theoretical ends, to note some family of detectable properties that strike them as playing some important role in their neurophysiological theory of perceptual recognition and memory" (1988c, 58).

Now all this is pretty confusing. What exactly is Dennett trying to claim? He might be read as claiming that there are no qualia and therefore there are no truths whatsoever to be told about qualia. The reason that no one, neither Chase nor the neuroscientist, can help us decide between (I) and (II) is that both (I) and (II) are terminally misguided ways of formulating alternative hypotheses. By analogy, imagine that someone says to you, "I always forget, is the phlogiston slowly released in burning or rusting?" and you say "Well, the 'phlogiston'—it turns out to be oxygen—is slowly *gained* in rusting." We might reasonably accuse you of being excessively polite and allowing a certain amount of nonsense to be uttered. After all, the calm corrective "it turns out to be oxygen" really says that neither the hypothesis that phlogiston is slowly released in burning nor the hypothesis that it is slowly released in rusting can be vindicated by science, because there is no phlogiston at all.

Now Dennett is a qualophobe if ever there was one, so this way of reading him has some plausibility. In fact, I favor this interpretation, since it allows a compromise. Even though I think that there is no canonical concept of qualia, if there were, it would be the initial *"ways things seem to us"* formulation, not the easy target Dennett sets, which has the "special properties" of being intrinsic, unanalysable, atomic, ineffable, and an object of immediate, privileged, and incorrigible access. The concept of qualia that Dennett rails against names an empty set. There are no truths to be uttered about qualia in that sense.

If we view the problem in this way, as revolving around problems with the occurrence of the word 'qualia', in Dennett's sense, in (I) and (II), then we can imagine ways in which neuroscience could lead us to reasonably favor one hypothesis over the other, so long as we don't interpret the word 'qualia' in terms of its problematic meaning.

Imagine that the story continues on in this way. Chase says to his neurosurgeon, "Doc, I just saw a video tape of myself in the post-op. I was asking for gravy on my ice cream, and I was complaining about the sour flavor of the salted peanuts. That was the way I always thought it would be. Remember, I went in for voluntary sensory-tampering surgery. I wanted to find out what it is like to be a being with an entirely different taste space. But here I am six months after the operation, and everything seems back to normal. What happened?"

The doctor replies, "Yes, Chase, we've noticed this return to normalcy, and we've been following things closely. The first thing we discovered was that the apparent return to normalcy is the result of an adjustment by your memory system. We then went to work trying to figure out how your memory was doing the compensating. One possibility we explored was that memory was blasting the sensory vectors at an early point and changing what would normally produce the sort of neural vector that is associated with sincere reports of 'salty' into 'sweet' reports [this is a credible reconstruction of hypothesis II, minus the troublesome term 'qualia']. We checked out this hypothesis in your case, and that didn't seem to be what was happening. We then explored a second hypothesis [hypothesis I reconstituted]. We have had a few cases in which we have found that patients who have had your kind of surgery shift their concepts in a way that coordinates past taste experiences with new ones by misremembering what the old experiences were like. (We think this might be a compensation for the trauma of messing with all the experiential and behavioral regularities associated with a normally functioning taste space.) The reason I put it this way is that we find in such patients that the distributed brain patterns we used to see associated with specific taste terms have shifted, so that the patterns we would see preoperatively when the word 'sweet' was used, we now see when 'salty' is used, and vice versa. This is highly abnormal, but we think that what has happened is that you now call the sensory vectors you used to call sweet 'salty' and that you misremember sweet experiences as salty."

The resolution of the rival hypotheses that I have imagined is certainly no more incredible than the thought experiment that got us wondering about rival interpretations in the first place. It is the sort of resolution one might expect if one seeks coordination, some sort of reflective equilibrium, among evidence coming from first-person phenomenology and our best psychological and neuroscientific theories. The case at hand is one in which Chase knows that something is happening—he can describe it up to a point—but he doesn't understand what is happening in any depth, so he rightly cedes authority to the experts. It violates the logic of the concept of qualia as Dennett construes it for first-person authority to be ceded in this way. To think this, Dennett must think that the identification of qualia with the "way things seem to us" must be interpreted as meaning that a quale is a state such that, necessarily, being in it seems a certain way and, necessarily, there is nothing else to it. But again I claim that the concept simply doesn't need to be understood in that way. The alternative interpretation is that a quale is a state such that being in it seems a certain way. This interpretation is better because it allows us the concept of the way things seem without making seemings atomic, intrinsic, exhaustive, ineffable, and so on.

Conscious experiences have heterogeneous qualitative feels associated with them. Other psychological events lack qualitative feel. That seems innocent enough, and it avoids embracing the nonsense that Dennett tries to pin on the concept of qualia.

Metacontrast

If a stimulus is flashed briefly on a screen and then followed, after a very short interval, by a second masking stimulus, subjects report seeing only the second stimulus. In the standard disc-ring procedure, subjects swear to have only seen the ring and not to have seen the first disc flash (see figure 4.3, p. 80). Dennett and Kinsbourne claim that two rival hypotheses allegedly explain the metacontrast results and that in spite of initial appearances to the contrary, they are empirically indistinguishable.

> The standard description of such phenomena is that the second stimulus somehow prevents conscious experience of the first stimulus (in other words, it somehow waylays the first stimulus on its way to

First Stimulus

Second Stimulus

Figure 4.3
Disc and ring. (Reprinted with permission from Dennett 1991a, 141.)

consciousness). But people can nevertheless do much better than chance if required to guess whether there were two stimuli. This only shows once again that stimuli can have their effects on us without our being conscious of them. This standard line is, in effect, the Stalinesque model of metacontrast: the first stimulus never gets to play on the stage of consciousness; it has whatever effects it has entirely unconsciously. But [there is] a second, Orwellian model of metacontrast: subjects are indeed conscious of the first stimulus (which "explains" their capacity to guess correctly) but their memory of this conscious experience is almost entirely obliterated by the second stimulus (which is why they deny having seen it, in spite of their tell-tale better-than-chance guesses).... Both models can deftly account for *all* the data—not just the data we already have, but the data we can imagine getting in the future. They both account for the verbal reports: one theory says they are innocently mistaken while the other says they are accurate reports of experienced "mistakes." They *agree* about just where in the brain the mistaken content enters the causal pathways; they just disagree about whether that location is pre-experiential or post-experiential. They both account for the non-verbal effects: one says they are the result of unconsciously discriminated contents while the other says they are the result of consciously discriminated but forgotten contents. They *agree* about just where and how in the brain these discriminations occur; they just disagree about whether to interpret those processes as happening inside or outside the charmed circle of consciousness. Finally, they both account for the subjective data—whatever is obtainable "from the first-person-perspective"—because they *agree* about how it ought to "feel" to subjects: subjects should be unable to tell the difference between misbegotten experiences and immediately misremembered experiences. So, in spite of first appearances, there is really only a verbal difference between the two theories.... They tell exactly the same story except for where they place a mythical Great Divide, a point in time (and hence a place in space) whose *fine-grained* location is nothing that subjects can help them locate, and whose location is also neutral with regard to all other features of their theories. This is a difference that makes no difference.   (1992, 25–26; also see Dennett 1991a, 124–125)

Dennett and Kinsbourne go on to conclude,

One can arbitrarily, but only arbitrarily, settle on some moment of processing in the brain as the moment of consciousness, declaring all prior stages and revisions unconscious or preconscious adjustments, and all subsequent emendations to the content (as revealed by recollection) to be post-experiential memory-contamination. One could insist on some such distinction, but could not expect to get subjective support from subjects. From their point of view this would be an unmotivated revisionist proposal about how to use the word 'conscious.'   (1992, 26)

There are several things I want to say about the example. First, the example really does two entirely different things: it describes the phenomenon of metacontrast and two competing explanations for it; then—and here is where the trick occurs—it pins on proponents of either the Orwellian model (a conscious flash dashed by memory obliteration) or the Stalinesque model (informational sensitivity to the stimulus but no phenomenal awareness of it) a commitment to the existence of "the charmed circle of consciousness," "a mythical Great Divide." But this is uncharitable in the extreme. No credible researcher believes in a charmed circle or Great Divide that all conscious experiences must cross into or over on their way to becoming conscious, or in a Cartesian theater where all conscious mental events make their appearances. The principle of charity in interpretation suggests that we remove all references to these mythic places in order not to make the rivals sound silly. Second, the tale is told in a way that makes first-person phenomenology and ordinary language troublemakers pure and simple. This too is uncharitable. We start inquiry with the phenomena of consciousness as roughed out in ordinary language. But, of course, neither ordinary first-person usage nor first-person intuitions about what is happening have any special status in settling theoretical disputes about the nature of consciousness. Only a person in the grip of the illusion that she has final first-person authority on how the word 'conscious' and its cognates are to be used will claim that any theory telling her that she was conscious briefly of the first stimulus is "an unmotivated revisionist proposal about how to use the word 'conscious'." Most savvy subjects won't insist on such special authority and therefore won't need to claim that any

(Orwellian) model saying that they were briefly conscious but don't remember is "an unmotivated revisionist proposal." Whether such a proposal is well motivated will depend on the theoretical support that can be mustered on its behalf. This might be done without buying into the myth of the Great Divide.

There might be well-motivated differences between earlier and later stages of processing that, even if they can't gain us a pure pre- versus postexperiential distinction, might gain us something close to it. If we set up less vulnerable targets, then the possibility of gaining information relevant to choosing between something like the Stalinesque and Orwellian hypotheses is hardly ruled out of court. Strategies like those discussed in the case of Chase and Sanborn give reason for thinking that the rival metacontrast hypotheses depict differences that do make a difference within the science of the mind and that are potentially tractable. Could we ever be motivated to deem the class of first stimulus exposures conscious in the metacontrast experiments, despite subjects' sincere denials of any phenomenology? Of course we could. If our theory of consciousness develops so that we come to think that there is some especially salient set of neural properties that paradigm conscious events have, if we notice that these properties are involved in exposures to the first stimulus, if we have at the same time a good theory of how memory works, and if we see that the loading of the second stimulus into memory causes the first stimulus— with its content happily fixed and ever ready to be probed—to get bumped, then we would have good grounds for favoring the Orwellian scenario (see Block 1992 for some other ways to distinguish the two hypotheses).

Francis Crick and Christof Koch have proposed that subjective consciousness, despite its heterogeneous form and despite its involving disparate brain locations, involves a basic common mechanism. On the basis of preliminary studies of visual perception and some tantalizing evidence from other modalities, they write, "Our basic hypothesis at the neural level is that it is useful to think of consciousness as being correlated with a special type of activity of perhaps a subset of neurons in the cortical system. Consciousness can undoubtedly take different forms, depending on which parts of the cortex are involved, but we hypothesize that there is one basic mechanism (or a few) underlying them all" (1990, 266). The common mechanism proposed is one in which neurons in many cortical areas (relevant to vision, for example) "cooperate to form some sort of global activity and . . . this global activity corresponds to visual awareness" (1990, 267). The feature hypothesized to form the underlying mechanism is oscillation in the 40-hertz range. Groups of neurons involved in visual detection give rise to awareness when the ensemble lock into short-term oscillation patterns in this range. The hypothesis is that cross-modal aware-

ness, like seeing and smelling something, involves similarly locked oscillations in the neural groups subserving the relevant modalities.

Suppose that this hypothesis is highly corroborated. If the right sort of
oscillations are detected in both the single-stimulus case and in the two-
stimulus metacontrast case, there might be good reason to say that there
was awareness in both cases and that awareness got bumped in the second
case (the Orwellian hypothesis). If the oscillations associated with awareness are nowhere to be found in the second case, we can explain this by
saying that the neural groups involved do not achieve the required oscillatory frequency (the Stalinesque hypothesis). Since it has been estimated to
take 50 to 250 milliseconds for us to become conscious of an object, any
masking within that time frame could easily keep the right oscillatory
patterns from settling in (Crick and Koch 1990, 265). Indeed, in the original
metacontrast studies, maximal phenomenal masking of the first stimulus is
achieved when the second stimulus is presented 70 to 90 milliseconds after
the first (Fehrer and Raab 1962). This makes credible the hypothesis that
the first stimulus might in fact be bumped before we have a chance to
become conscious of it.

The point is that there might be principled hypotheses about conscious
experiences that need not appear unmotivated from the first-person point
of view—at least not if that person is not in the grip of the illusion that
she knows how consciousness works, remembers all her conscious episodes, and so on—and that could lead to a principled choice between the
Orwellian and Stalinesque interpretations.

Dennett suggests a third hypothesis, which he thinks can avoid altogether the alleged Orwellian versus Stalinesque morass.

> Here is how the Multiple Drafts model deals with metacontrast.
> When a lot happens in a short time, the brain must make simplifying
> assumptions. The outer contour of a disc rapidly turns into the inner
> contour of a ring. The brain, initially informed just that something
> happened (something with a circular contour in a particular place),
> swiftly receives confirmation that there was indeed a ring with an
> inner and outer contour. Without further supporting evidence that
> there was a disc, the brain arrives at the conservative conclusion that
> there was only a ring.... The Multiple Drafts model agrees that the
> information about the disc was briefly in a functional position to
> contribute to a later report, but this state lapsed; there is no reason to
> insist that this state was inside the charmed circle of consciousness
> until it got overwritten, or contrarily, to insist that it never quite
> achieved this privileged state.   (1991a, 142)

It is not obvious how different this hypothesis is from the one I have just
imagined being corroborated. Talk of the "charmed circle of consciousness"

aside, it is not obvious how saying that "the disc was briefly in a functional position to contribute to a later report, but this state lapsed" is intended to be different from saying that it was bumped from that position by the second stimulus. If the "lapsing hypotheses" is intended by Dennett as an empirical hypothesis, rather than as a noncommittal *façon de parler* designed to stop us from wondering about what really happens in the metacontrast case, then the "bumping hypothesis" is a legitimate empirical rival. I insist that evidence from psychophysics and neuroscience might help us choose the most credible way of conceiving of the case. Such evidence might help us to decide, for example, that it is a matter of something being bumped rather than lapsing.

Dennett is happy with his way of putting things. Metacontrast is best understood in terms of the lapsing of information that was briefly in a position to contribute to a later report. But why should we favor this way of putting things over the alternatives? It is not a bad hypothesis, but I don't see any compelling logical connection between the lapsing hypothesis and the Multiple Drafts model. An opponent of that model could favor the lapsing hypothesis. Still, it is hard to see why anyone should favor it over the alternative until more is known neuroscientifically.

But here I think we come to the real crux of the matter. Dennett is genuinely skeptical about the helpfulness of neuroscience in such cases. This is why it is legitimate to wonder whether the lapsing hypothesis is intended as an empirical hypothesis or is simply a restful metaphor designed to provide us with a comfortable picture of a matter that cannot be settled empirically. Dennett's skepticism about help forthcoming from neuroscience is rooted in two beliefs. First, there is the credible point that it will be fiendishly difficult to resolve all disagreements about the timing of events taking place over the space of milliseconds (Dennett 1991a, 101–111). Second, there is his belief that "human consciousness (1) is too recent an innovation to be hard-wired into the innate machinery, (2) is largely a product of cultural evolution that gets imparted to brains in early training, and (3) its successful installation is determined by myriad micro-settings in the plasticity of the brain, which means that its functionally important features are very likely to be invisible to neuroanatomical scrutiny in spite of the extreme saliency of the effects" (1991a, 219).

With regard to the first point, fiendish difficulties should not put us off so early in the game. Better theory about the structure and function of the brain and advances in technology might make certain hypotheses more plausible than others, even when we are talking about events occurring over milliseconds. The second point (or set of points) is *very* contentious. We don't know how recent human consciousness is. Furthermore, it is by no means clear that human consciousness "is largely a product of cultural evolution." Many features of consciousness—its streamlike character, the core emotions, perceptual sensitivities in the five modalities—are most credibly thought of as having a genotypic specification. To be sure, even features of consciousness that do have a genotypic specification will require "myriad microsettings" to achieve phenotypic realization. But the fact is that all sorts of differences in microsettings are compatible with visibility to "neuroanatomical scrutiny." The perceptual mechanisms involved in a task like metacontrast might require brain maturation, but they are not plausibly thought of as involving mechanisms that are the "product of cultural evolution ... imparted to brains in early training." There is no good reason offered to doubt the illumination that might be offered by neuroscience in the metacontrast case (or even in the Chase and Sanborn case of taste). If one accepts Dennett's contentious theory that "human consciousness ... is largely a product of cultural evolution" loaded into highly plastic brains like software, then a certain skepticism about the resolving power of neuroscience might be warranted for those aspects of consciousness that truly are the product of cultural evolution. But even so, we will have to see. We will have to look into brains and see whether and to what extent such cultural creations as the way(s) in which we think about the self, justice, and beauty, for example, have any interesting shared neural underpinnings. Despite the fact that these things are products of social learning, we don't have a clue at this point in time of how self-consciousness, ethical consciousness, and aesthetic consciousness operate in the brain. But we must not give up on brain science as a partner in the inquiry to learn more even about the many aspects of consciousness that are clearly results of cultural evolution. It is too early in the game to think that the "functionally important features [of consciousness] are very likely to be invisible to neuroanatomical scrutiny."

To conclude, there are no qualia in Dennett's contentious sense, but there are qualia. The work of this chapter has been devoted to defending that claim by unsnarling two tangled kite strings and getting the kite of qualia, real qualia, up and flying again. A theory of subjective consciousness gains its motivation from the need to explain the heterogeneous qualitative character of our mental life. The initial explanandum need not foster the illusion that all conscious experiences are diaphanous, that their beginnings and endings and their deep structure involve conscious awareness, or that we are first-person authorities about their nature. How we individuate conscious states and what we come to say about the nature of consciousness remain to be seen. But I don't see that the thought experiments of qualophiles or qualophobes isolate any deep principled intractability. Phenomenology, psychology, and brain science are credible partners in the effort to penetrate qualia and reveal the nature, structure, and causal roles of the various ways things seem.

Chapter 5
The Missing Shade of You

1   The Subject Is Experience

There is something it is like to be a subject of experience. This is uncontroversial. There is something distinctive that it is like to be each and everyone one of us. This is more controversial than the first claim. But it is true (Flanagan 1991a, chap. 3). What it is like to be you or any other subject of experience is closed off to me. This is controversial. The alleged fact that subjectivity is impenetrable spells doom for naturalism. Either naturalism is a view we do not understand, or we understand it but it is not up to the task of constructively accounting for subjectivity. This too is controversial. The aim of this chapter is to show that the controversial claims are false. What it is like to be you is not closed off to me, subjectivity is not impenetrable, and naturalism explains better than any alternative why subjectivity attaches uniquely to particular individuals.

2   The Missing Shade of Blue

In section 2 of his *Enquiry Concerning Human Understanding* (1777), Hume presents his argument that all "perceptions of the mind can be divided into two classes or species, which are distinguished by their different degrees of force and vivacity. The less forcible and lively are commonly denoted *Thoughts* or *Ideas*." The "more lively perceptions" are "impressions." Hume's copy theory is then expressed this way: "All our ideas or more feeble perceptions are copies of our impressions or more lively ones." No impression, no idea. One important piece of evidence for the copy theory, according to Hume is this: "If it happen, from a defect of the organ that a man is not susceptible of any species of sensation, we always find that he is as little susceptible of the correspondent ideas. A blind man can form no notion of colours; a deaf man of sounds" (1777, sec. 2, pars. 12–15).

Hume then produces a counterexample to his copy theory in the case of the missing shade of blue:

> Suppose . . . a person to have enjoyed his sight for thirty years, and to have become perfectly acquainted with colours of all kinds except one

particular shade of blue..., which it has never been his fortune to meet with. Let all the different shades of that colour, except that single one, be placed before him, descending gradually from the deepest to the lightest; it is plain that he will perceive a blank, where the shade is wanting, and will be sensible that there is a greater distance in that place between the contiguous colours than in any other. Now I ask, whether it be possible for him, from his own imagination, to supply this deficiency, and to raise up to himself the idea of that particular shade, though it had never been conveyed to him by his senses? I believe there are few but will be of opinion that he can; and this may serve as a proof that the simple ideas are not always, in every instance, derived from correspondent impressions; though this instance is so singular, that it is scarcely worth our observing, and does not merit that for it alone we should alter our general maxim.   (1777, sec. 2, par. 16)

It is important for Hume's theory that this counterexample turn out to be only apparent and not genuine, since, despite what he says, it is not so singular that it is scarcely worth our observing. Innumerable analogous examples can be generated across the sensory modalities.

The thought experiment raises questions about whether two different mental acts can be performed. First, can the person with no experience of $blue_5$, call him Hugh, *notice* that $blue_5$ is missing in a chart containing $blue_{1-4}$ and $blue_{6-10}$? Second, can Hugh *conjure up* an idea of $blue_5$ (remember, ideas can be dim and feeble)? A positive answer to the first question by no means requires a positive answer to the second. Hume, however, thinks that both questions are to be answered affirmatively. Hugh, the man who has missed out on the experience of $blue_5$, will notice its absence when faced with the gappy color chart, and he will also be able to conjure up the idea of $blue_5$. How is this possible? Both the noticing and the conjuring need explaining.

The laws of association might enable us to explain the noticing in this way. The law of resemblance, part of the innate structure of mind, disposes the mind to calculate the degree of resemblance or difference between the shades of blue on the color chart. The degree of resemblance is consistent except where $blue_6$ follows $blue_4$. The larger difference at this point produces the mental cramp that constitutes perceiving "a blank, where the shade is wanting," and noticing "that there is a greater distance in that place between the contiguous colours than in any other."

Noticing that a shade is missing is one thing. How is the more difficult task of conjuring up the idea of $blue_5$ accomplished? The best explanation is that Hugh does in imagination what could easily be done in the external world to produce $blue_5$. Once the gap is noticed, he mixes $blue_4$ and $blue_6$

in his imagination in the same way we would mix paints in the world. In this way blue$_5$ is conjured up and, as is the case with many ideas, is "faintly perceived," so to speak.

3   The Missing Shade of You

The missing shade of blue then presents no insurmountable problem. There are ways to get at it even if we lack direct experience of it. There is something it is like to experience blue$_5$. One who is not directly acquainted with blue$_5$ can grasp what blue$_5$ is like, even if more dimly than someone who has actually experienced blue$_5$.

Things are different with other minds than with colors. If I am not you, I cannot grasp what it is like to be you. I can perhaps conjure up the missing shade of blue, but I cannot conjure up the missing shade of you. Or so some philosophers have argued. If we imagine that there is something there is like to be each particular person and that what it is like to be each individual person constitutes a particular shade in the colorful array of possible experiencers, then for each and everyone of us, lacking direct experience of any other experiential system as we do, we know that there is some unique shade coloring the inner life of each and every person. But we cannot grasp, capture, or directly experience any shade other than the one that colors our own inner lives. Hence the missing shade of you.

4   Capturing You: The Very Idea

In his famous essay "What It Is Like to Be a Bat?" (1974), Thomas Nagel vividly forces the question that concerns us: to what extent can subjectivity be captured from the outside? Nagel thinks that subjectivity is impenetrable. His argument focuses on attempts to capture experience from the objective perspective of science, but his argument easily generalizes to the situation each of us faces in trying to understand the inner lives of other persons in ordinary, everyday circumstances. By showing how Nagel goes wrong, I can provide reasons for thinking that consciousness in general is tractable from a naturalistic perspective, and for thinking that particular subjects of experience can be known as such by other subjects of experience. Many of the same resources available to Hugh that allow him to conjure up the missing shade of blue are available to me as I try to conjure up the missing shade of you. When I conjure up the missing shade of you, do I capture or grasp you? Of course not. That would be overstepping my bounds.

Nagel's argument for the intractability of consciousness proceeds in several steps. First, he claims that "no matter how the form may vary, the fact that an organism has conscious experience *at all* means, basically, that there is something it is like to be that organism" (1974, 166). An "organism has conscious mental states if and only if there is something it is like to *be* that organism—something it is like *for* that organism. . . . We may call this the subjective character of experience" (1974, 166). Second, he claims that if the naturalist's program is to succeed, the phenomenological features of mental life, the "something it is like to be" features, must be given a naturalistic account. "If physicalism is to be defended, the phenomenological features must themselves be given a physical account" (1974, 167). Third, he denies this possibility. "But when we examine their subjective character it seems that such a result is impossible. The reason is that every subjective phenomena is essentially connected with a single point of view, and it seems inevitable that an objective, physical theory will abandon that point of view" (1974, 167). The subjective character of experience "is fully comprehensible from only one point of view." Therefore, "any shift to greater objectivity—that is, less attachment to a specific viewpoint—does not take us nearer to the real nature of the phenomenon: it takes us farther away from it" (1974, 174). Finally, he informs us that "this bears directly on the mind-body problem. For if the facts of experience—facts about what it is like *for* the experiencing organism are accessible only from one point of view, then it is a mystery how the true character of experiences could be revealed in the physical operation of that organism" (1974, 172). The argument has disturbing consequences for physicalism: "Physicalism is a position we cannot understand because we do not at present have any conception of how it might be true" (1974, 176). This view I call "principled agnosticism."

Nagel is led astray because of two implicit, misguided, and interconnected assumptions. The first source of trouble is Nagel's claim that moving away from the phenomenological surface inevitably takes us "farther away" from "the real nature of the phenomenon." Why think that how consciousness seems gets at its real nature? To be sure, the phenomenological aspects of experience are real and require an account. But unless one thinks that the conscious mind is diaphanous, one should not think that its real nature is revealed fully by its first-person appearances. The second source of trouble originates in a certain positivistic picture of science and of philosophical analyses that take science seriously. This attitude comes out in Nagel's claim that no naturalistic analysis will be able to make room for the facts of first-person phenomenology, for "the true character of experiences" (1974, 172).

As I have been framing the naturalistic project, there are a series of questions that will need to be answered and then brought into equilibrium with one another. One important part of the inquiry has to do with getting clear on whether there are any shared phenomenological features of conscious mental life, whether, that is, there is anything it is like to be a member of our species. In trying to frame an answer to this question, I will be somewhat less interested in how exactly things seem for any particular individual than in the overlap among individuals. But this greater interest in the species than in the unique features of the individuals in no way implies that the naturalist doubts that there is something it is like to be each particular one of us. The issue here is simply interest-relative. For obvious reasons, you, your loved ones, and your therapist will be much more interested in the fine-grained details of exactly how your inner life seems than will the framer of a general theory of mind.

In any case, once we get a fairly good picture of how conscious mental life seems, we will want to see if the seeming features can be interpreted realistically. That is, we will want to see how the way things seem from the first-person point of view fit with data from other, impersonal sources: from third-person phenomenology, evolutionary theory, cognitive psychology, and neuroscience. Nagel repeatedly insists that this move will involve abandoning the subjective point of view. And he claims that "any shift to greater objectivity—that is, less attachment to a specific viewpoint—does not take us nearer to the real nature of the phenomenon: it takes us farther away" (1974, 174).

But this claim is much overstated. First, there is nothing in the naturalist's approach that requires abandoning the subjective point of view as the source of human phenomenology or as a rich source of data for hypothesis generation about what is in fact going on. Indeed, part of the overall strategy I have been recommending involves a fine-grained attention to phenomenological detail, partly on the supposition that there are many different kinds of awareness with many different causal roles, some but not all of which causal roles we have reliable access to.

Second and relatedly, the claim that moving to the objective point of view "does not take us nearer to the real nature of the phenomenon; it takes us farther away" is deceptively ambiguous between two senses of 'real nature'. If 'real nature' is meant, as it appears, to refer to the way things seem to some particular person, then it is true in certain respects that becoming more objective will take us farther away from the phenomenon. But the reason for this—for why objective analysis is not as well suited as subjective analysis for gaining insight into how things seem to us in the first person—is something the naturalist can explain. It is because persons are uniquely causally well connected to their own experiences. They, after all, are the ones who have them. Furthermore, there is no deep mystery as to why this special causal relation obtains. The organic integrity of individuals and the structure and function of individual nervous systems grounds each individual's special relation to how things seem for him (Quine 1952, 213). John Dewey put it best: "Given that consciousness exists at all, there is no mystery in its being connected with what it is connected with" (1922, 62).

If, on the other hand, by 'real nature' Nagel means what is really going on in the cognitive system as a whole, including whether conscious mental events are actually playing the causal role they seem to the agent to be playing and whether they are physically realized or not, then the claim that looking at things from a more objective point of view will necessarily lead us astray is quite incredible. Its only conceivable warrant is allegiance to the bankrupt version of the doctrine of privileged access.

The important point is this: there is absolutely no reason why a naturalist cannot both acknowledge the existence of subjectivity and view getting an accurate description of it as part of the overall project of understanding human nature. It is crucial to see that description at the phenomenological level is something that can be provided from the first-person point of view and the third-person point of view. I can say how I think things seem for you, sometimes before you see that this is how they seem to you. Sometimes you will even treat my account of how things seem for you as authoritative. "You're right, I just don't feel the same way about him anymore." Saying how things seem is a project involving intersubjective give-and-take. You have special authority (but not infallibility) about how things seem for you here and now. You have very little authority if you have views about how your mental processes actually work or how mental events are realized. Getting clear on the phenomenology is not an essentially private enterprise. Good phenomenology is group phenomenology.

In his brief against naturalism, Nagel concedes that analyses of conscious mental states in terms of their neural substrate or in terms of their functional or causal roles may explain certain aspects of these states. He writes, "I deny only that this kind of thing exhausts their analysis" (1974, 167). But here he mischaracterizes naturalism. The wise naturalist is not a reductionist. He is not committed to the idea that a theory spelling out how conscious mental states are realized in the brain, even when combined with a theory of the causal role of conscious mental states, "exhausts their analysis." The analysis must also include a description of the phenomenology, perhaps a revision of the phenomenology that we started with, but a robust phenomenology nonetheless. The analysis is designed not to eliminate the phenomenal facts but to deepen our understanding of them.

A nonreductive naturalistic theory will provide a rich phenomenology, a theory of how the phenomenology connects up with behavior, a theory about how conscious mental events taxonomized into many different classes of awareness figure in the overall economy of mental life, a theory of how mental life evolved, and thereby a theory of which features of mind are the result of direct selection and which features are free riders, and finally, it will provide a neuroscientific realization theory, that is, a theory about how all the different kinds of mental events, conscious and unconscious, are realized in the nervous system. An analysis that includes a phenomenology in addition to a theory of neurophysiological realization and a theory of causal role will be as exhaustive as an analysis can be.

Here one might expect a slightly different gloss on the denial that this sort of analysis can be exhaustive in the requisite sense. No matter how well analyzed the phenomenon of consciousness is by such a (yet-to-be-developed) theory, the theory will fail fully to *capture* consciousness. Now there are several ways in which a theory that provides an exhaustive analysis of consciousness might nonetheless be said to fail to capture something important about consciousness. First, it might be charged that such a theory fails to capture what exactly conscious mental life is like for each individual person. Nagel's continual mention of the way consciousness attaches essentially to a "single point of view" indicates that this bothers him. But here there is an easy response. Theorizing of the sort I have been recommending is intended not to capture what it is like to be each individual person but only to capture, in the sense of providing an analysis for, the type (or types) conscious mind and, what is different, conscious person. Although the general analysis is not intended to do so, you, of course, are entitled to capture what it is like to be you. Indeed, it is unavoidable.

There is a second and more perplexing sort of the "failure to capture consciousness" charge. Recall that part of a general naturalistic theory will be a theory of how the human nervous system works, a theory of how mental life is realized in us. The core assumption is that although mental states are relational states involving complex causal connections with the natural and social environment as well as with other mental states, they are, in the final analysis, tokened in the brain. But Nagel, and he is not alone, finds it unimaginable that a theory of neurophysiological realization could reveal "the true character of experiences" (1974, 172), where by the latter phrase Nagel means how these experiences feel. Indeed, this worry in particular leads Nagel to the view that we at present have no conception of how physicalism *could* be true.

Yet we do understand how physicalism can be true. It can be true if every mental event is realized in the brain. Those of us who believe that all mental events, conscious and unconscious, are tokened in the brain do not believe that the theory that eventually explains *how* they are tokened will capture "the true character of the experiences" as experiences. The whole idea that the qualitative feel of some experience should reveal itself in a theoretical description of how that experience is realized fails to acknowledge the abstract relation between any theory and the phenomena it accounts for. Even the phenomenological part of the project I have recommended, which, unlike the realization theory, is directly concerned with how things seem to the subject, is itself at one remove (namely, a linguistic remove) from the experiences themselves. But the naturalist is the first to accept that a particular realization will be an experience only for the agent who is causally connected to the realization in the right sort of way. Once again, the biological integrity of the human body can account straightforwardly for the happy fact that we each have our *own*, and only our own, experiences. But this can hardly be much comfort to Nagel insofar as it shows the coherence and explanatory power of a naturalistic account of the unique way in which experiences are "captured" by their owners.

Naturalism can explain why only you can capture what it is like to be you. Only your sensory receptors and brain are properly hooked up to each other and to the rest of you so that what is received at those receptors accrues to you as your experiences. That consciousness exists at all is amazing. But given that it does, Dewey is right that "there is no mystery with its being connected with what it is connected with" (1922, 62).

In the final analysis, your experiences are yours alone; only you are in the right causal position to know what they seem like. Nothing could be more important with respect to how your life seems and to how things go for you overall, but nothing could be less consequential with respect to the overall fate of the naturalistic picture of things.

5   Grasping Experiences

Colin McGinn (1991) offers a more recent argument that makes the same mistaken presumption that if physicalism is true, a theory that explains how some set of experiences is realized or what their causal role is should enable us to *grasp* those very experiences as they are experienced by their subjects.

> Suppose ... that we had the solution to the problem of how specific forms of consciousness depend upon different kinds of physiological structure. Then, of course, we would understand how the brain of a bat subserves the subjective experience of bats. Call this type of experience B, and call the explanatory property that links B to the bat's brain P_1. By grasping P_1 it would be perfectly intelligible to us how the bat's brain generates B-experiences; we would have an explanatory theory of the causal nexus in question. We would be in possession of the same kind of understanding we would have of our own experiences if we had the correct psychophysical theory of them. But then it seems to follow that grasp of the theory that explains B-experiences would *confer* a grasp of the nature of those experiences: for how could we understand that theory without understanding the concept B that occurs in it? How could we grasp the *nature* of B-experiences without grasping the *character* of those experiences? The true psychophysical theory would seem to provide a route to a

grasp of the subjective form of the bat's experiences. But now we face a dilemma, a dilemma which threatens to become a reductio: either we *can* grasp this theory, in which case the property B becomes open to us; or we *cannot* grasp the theory, simply because B is *not* open to us.   (McGinn 1991, 9)

The reductio ad absurdum that McGinn thinks is lurking destroys two ideas at once: the idea that we could ever possess a theory that renders "perfectly intelligible" the link between subjective mental life and brain processes, and the idea that we could ever "grasp the subjective form" of the experiences of another type of creature. McGinn thinks that the problem of other minds can be solved, but only in cases where the concepts we need in understanding another's mind are concepts that refer to properties we ourselves instantiate. This condition may be satisfied for other humans; it is not satisfied in the case of us and bats. I'll come back to this issue in the final section. Right now I simply want to deal with the central argument contained in the quoted passage:

> 1. If we had an explanatory theory of the causal nexus in question, that is, a theory of how the bat's brain generates bat experiences, we should grasp the nature of the subjective life of bats.
> 2. This is because a grasp of a theory that explains a certain set of experiences should "*confer* a grasp" of the nature and character of those experiences.
> 3. If it failed to confer this grasp, we would be in the absurd position of possessing a theory that makes "perfectly intelligible" the relation between a set of phenomena we do not understand.

When the argument is laid out in this way, it becomes clearer that the notion of grasping is deployed in two different senses: there is grasping some causal theory and grasping experiences, where grasping experiences means knowing what these experiences are like. Yet there is no necessary connection between understanding a theory that explains some set of experiences ($grasp_1$) and "grasping the *character*" of those experiences ($grasp_2$). Experiences function as explananda. Good theories explain their explananda. In this way they reveal the nature of the explananda. In the case of experiences, our best neuroscientific theory will explain that there is an aspect of experiences, the phenomenological aspect, that is only grasped by the system having the experiences. McGinn wonders rhetorically, "How could we grasp the *nature* of B-experiences without grasping the *character* of those experiences?" The nonrhetorical answer is this. In understanding the theory ($grasp_1$), we understand ($grasp_1$) the nature of the experiences the theory explains in that we understand ($grasp_1$) what neural states the experiences supervene on, and we understand ($grasp_1$)

that only the systems that are suitably designed, hooked up, and so on, to have (grasp$_2$) those experiences have (grasp$_2$) them. The theory explains (grasp$_1$) why bats have (grasp$_2$) bat experiences and why we don't have (grasp$_2$) bat experiences. (For other persons, we are in something like a position of grasping$_{1.5}$ their experiences. I'll return to this issue at the end.)

The first problem thus involves equivocation of the senses of 'grasp'. Neither premise 1 nor premise 2 are credible when the relevant senses of 'grasp' are substituted. The equivocation is the source of the illusion that an understanding of some set of experiences necessarily involves grasping the character of these experiences. This takes care of the first horn of the dilemma that McGinn thinks "threatens to become a reductio." There is no incoherence in comprehending some theory that explains bat experiences without grasping exactly what bat experiences are like for bats. Indeed, the theory itself will explain why only bats grasp$_2$ their experiences.

There is still an opening. Perhaps we can be impaled on the second horn of the dilemma: "we *cannot* grasp the theory, simply because B [bat experience] is *not* open to us." McGinn has one of his rhetorical questions at the ready to suggest that this is truly an absurd view: "how could we understand that theory without understanding the concept B that occurs in it?" The horn is easily avoided by seeing that its source lies in the unreasonable expectation that grasping a theory (grasp$_1$) should "open" the experiences to us (grasp$_2$). If we don't grasp$_2$ bat experiences once we grasp$_1$ the theory that explains bat experiences, then we don't really understand (grasp$_1$) the theory. The problematic equivocation does its mischievous work again.

Furthermore, it is a perfectly common occurrence in the course of theory development in science that the phenomena to be explained are poorly or superficially understood at the beginning of inquiry. That is why one needs the theory. There is no incoherence in the idea of understanding some theory T that explains, as best we can, some phenomenon P, where P is imperfectly understood. We understand P as best we can, given the state of our theory. But we expect our understanding of P to be enriched as theory matures. For example, it used to be thought that bats were blind. It turns out that they have good vision. Bats live well and successfully by using their fine night vision and powers of echolocation. We know that much about what it is like to be a bat. Someday we may know much more. After all, it was *in the course* of the development of a theory about bats that certain facts about bat experience revealed themselves.

McGinn has one small opening. He tries to have us imagine that we are at the end of inquiry. Surely it would be incoherent for us to possess a theory that makes the causal nexus "perfectly intelligible" without our understanding fully all the terms of the theory related. A lot depends here on what perfect intelligibility consists in and what full understanding of all the terms of the theory entails. If we require that understanding the concept of bat experience (grasp$_1$) involves grasping bat experiences (grasp$_2$) we are back to the old problem. A theory of experience should not be expected to provide us with some sort of direct acquaintance with what the experiences it accounts for are like for their owners. Indeed, there is no incoherence in the idea of an extremely robust explanatory and predictive theory of bat brain and behavior that explains exactly how bat vision and echolocation work but leaves unanswered the question of whether bats experience the sights and sounds they undoubtedly compute. If we are truly at the end of inquiry, we will, I assume, have a very firm opinion about whether, how, and when bats have experiences. But being fallible, we will always have reason for doubt. We could have the full explanatory theory in place without being certain whether there is something it is like to be a bat.

6   Missing Shades Again

The same sort of response applies to Frank Jackson's (1982, 1986) well-known argument about Mary, the world's greatest color scientist. Mary lives in a black and white and gray world. She knows everything physical that there is to know about what goes on in any normal brain when the person who houses that brain experiences red. But Mary does not know what it is like to experience red. This she knows only when she escapes to the colorful world and sees ripe tomatoes and strawberries, red apples and roses, and so on. Since the facts Mary comes to know, facts about what it is like to experience red, are not captured by the most complete neuroscientific theory of color, physicalism is false. Because phenomenal properties are not captured by the most complete set of objective descriptions of the brain activity subserving these very experiences, phenomenal properties are not explained by, nor can they be identified with, physical properties.

In a recent reply to critics, Jackson (1986) provides a "convenient and accurate way of displaying the argument":

1. Mary (before her release) knows everything physical there is to know about other people.
2. Mary (before her release) does not know everything there is to know about other people (because she *learns* something about them on her release).
3. Therefore, there are truths about other people (and herself) that escape the physicalist story.

Jackson clarifies the main point this way: "The trouble for physicalism is that, after Mary sees her first ripe tomato, she will realize how impoverished her conception of the mental life of *others* has been *all along*. . . . But she knew all the physical facts about them all along; hence what she did not know until her release is not a physical fact about their experiences. But it is a fact about them. That is the trouble with physicalism. . . . There are truths about other people (and herself) that escape the physicalist story" (1986, 393). Jackson tells us that Mary "knows all the physical facts about us and our environment, in a wide sense of 'physical' which includes everything in *completed* physics, chemistry, and neurophysiology, and all there is to know about the causal and relational facts consequent upon all this, including of course functional roles. If physicalism is true she knows all there is to know. . . . Physicalists must hold that complete physical knowledge is complete knowledge simpliciter" (1986, 392).

The argument is seductive, but it is easy to defeat. The problem is with premise 1. This is a thought experiment that can be kept from starting. Mary knows everything about color vision that can be expressed in the vocabularies of a complete physics, chemistry, and neuroscience. She also knows everything there is to know about the functional role of color vision (this assumption requires charity on my part, since I think she actually lacks knowledge about the first-person functional role of color vision). She knows that when the eye is exposed to wavelengths of light in the red range, the persons whose eyes are so exposed have red channel activation, they claim to see red, they are disposed to use the word 'red' in sentences, and so on. Does Mary know what red experiences are like? No. She has never had one. Red experiences are physical events: they are complex relational states of individuals undergoing red-channel activation (in truth, there is a red-green channel that is activated differently for red and green; see Hardin 1988). Mary knows that. Her theory tells her so. But she doesn't know what red experiences are like, nor does she possess the concept of red as it is possessed by someone who has experienced red. She has never been in the appropriate complex relational state. She knows that too.

One way to avoid the seduction here is to distinguish between metaphysical and linguistic physicalism. Metaphysical physicalism simply asserts that what there is, and all there is, is physical stuff and its relations. Linguistic physicalism is the thesis that everything physical can be expressed or captured in the languages of the basic sciences: "*completed* physics, chemistry, and neurophysiology." Linguistic physicalism is stronger than metaphysical physicalism and less plausible (Fodor 1981). Jackson gives Mary all knowledge expressible in the basic sciences, and he stresses that for physicalism to be true all facts must be expressed or expressible in "explicitly physical language." This is linguistic physicalism. It can be false without metaphysical physicalism being false. This is easy to see.

One piece of knowledge Mary possesses is that red-channel activation causes red perception. Red perception is a physical event and will be understood by Mary as such. It is metaphysically unproblematic. But there is no reason to think that there will be some expression in the basic sciences that will capture or express what it is like to experience red, or that will provide Mary with the phenomenal concept of red or the phenomenal component of the concept of red. Knowledge of the phenomenological component of red requires first-person relations of a certain sort between a stimulus of a certain type and a suitably hooked-up organism. It requires seeing something red.

Jackson insists that we should interpret premise 1 to mean that Mary possesses all the knowledge that the basic sciences can provide, and he suggests that this entails that she knows everything: "Physicalists must hold that complete physical knowledge is complete knowledge simpliciter" (1986, 392). Yes and no. Physicalists must hold that complete physical knowledge is complete knowledge simpliciter in the sense that they must hold that when Mary finds out what red is like, she has learned something about the physical world. But this hardly implies that complete knowledge in the basic sciences can express or capture this item of knowledge without the relevant causal interchange between perceiver and perceived. Mary might know everything that can be expressed in the languages of completed physics, chemistry, and neuroscience, but this hardly entails that she knows "all there is to know." What else there is to know is nothing mysterious. It is physical. And it can be expressed in certain ways. It is simply that it cannot be perspicuously expressed in the vocabulary of the basic sciences.

So premise 1 is false. Mary does not know "everything physical there is to know about other people." The metaphysical physicalist will not think that what she does know—everything completed physics, chemistry, and neuroscience have to offer—is sufficient to convey everything there is to know about other people, since it is not sufficient to convey phenomenal feel! But premise 2 is true. Mary does learn something new upon her release. In light of the falsehood of premise 1, the truth of premise 2 does not support the intended reductio of physicalism. Mary really does learn something new. It isn't quite right to say that she knows *exactly* what she knew before but simply knows it in a different way, say in some non-linguistic way (P. M. Churchland 1989). The reason that this isn't quite right is because Mary will credibly claim to know something new: "So *that* is what it is like to have one's red channels turned on!" She learns what it is like to experience red. The perceptual concept of red is triggered in Mary's mind by the basic biological mechanisms that subserve normal color perception (Loar 1990; Van Gulick, in press a). Mary's red channel has been turned on for the first time. She knew all about the red channel before, but her own red channel had never been turned on. 'Experiencing red' always referred to tokens of the event type, red channel on. Mary never knew what it was like to be in a state of this type. She had never had an experience of red. She now has had direct, first-person experience of what happens to an organism undergoing red-channel activation. Perceptual capture is done in the first person. I repeat: unless her theory was radically incomplete, she knew that before she saw her first red tomato.

Mary, remember, is very knowledgeable. This is why it is implausible for Jackson to write, "The trouble for physicalism is that, after Mary sees her first ripe tomato, she will realize how impoverished her conception of *others* has been *all along*." Mary knows that she has never experienced red; she knows from her rich sensory life in the four active modalities just how heterogeneous and rich sensory experiences are. She doesn't know what it is like for others to experience red, other than that their red channels are on. But Mary is smart. She knows what she doesn't know, and she would never dare try to develop a view so firm about what it is like to experience red that her view could turn out to be false or impoverished. Mary is no dope. Yet Jackson has made her extremely smart. He can't have Mary both so smart she knows all that he says she knows, and so stupid that she will be so surprised upon seeing that first tomato. Mary will have an utterly novel experience. But it will neither throw her into a state of shock nor cause her to jump the ship of her theory. She expected the novelty. Her theory told her to.

An experience of red is how we describe the state she has never been in up to departure from the black and white room. 'An experience of red' is not in the language of physics. But an experience of red is a physical event in a suitably hooked-up system. Therefore, the experience is not a problem for metaphysical physicalism. It is a physical event after all. Completed physics, chemistry, and neuroscience, along with a functional-role description, will explain what an experience of red is, in the sense that they will explain how red experiences are realized, what their functional role is, and so on. But no linguistic description will completely *capture* what a first-person experience of red is like. That is only captured in the first person. You have to be there.

This explains why I want to deny premise 1. Mary does not have complete physical knowledge. She does not have complete physical knowledge even if she possesses complete knowledge in all the basic physical sciences. Despite her complete theoretical knowledge about everything that does happen or can happen in a human mind, there are indeterminately many neural states (all those subserving color experiences) that she has never been in. That is, there are indeterminately many bits of knowledge, those in the class of color experiences, that Mary has never possessed. These experiences, were she to have them, would be physical occurrences. She knows that, and she knows how such occurrences are realized in others. But the realization theory does not express or entail all there is to know about color experiences. The phenomenal features are conveyed only in the first person. Mary knows all the third-person, theoretical sentences that describe color sensations. But she herself has never (yet) instantiated the states that the sentences describe.

We didn't require Mary to get to this point. All "omniscient" mind theorists, if they have not had all the experiences they possess analyses for, will lack certain knowledge, and the knowledge they will lack is knowledge of physical phenomena. It is knowledge of experiences as realized in human nervous systems. The theory tells us that such knowledge requires first-person connections of a certain sort. It even tells us why it is good design to have experiences captured only by the systems that have them. It would be extremely idle labor if our theories enabled us to have experiences or engendered grasping experiences in the strong sense. But that, sad to say, is what some philosophers seem to yearn for. The plea seems to be, Don't distance me from my experiences. The right response is one of reassurance. Unless your friends are radical reductionists or epiphenomenalists, no one is trying to distance you or to disconnect you from your experiences. Don't worry. Be happy. Have your experiences. Enjoy them.

In the end, we need to beware of the temptation to think that for physicalism to be true, the basic physical sciences must be able to *capture* all truths. This is stronger than requiring that physicalism be true; that is, it is stronger than requiring that everything that happens is physical. Physicalism can be true in this sense without being able to explain everything, let alone capture everything in the languages of the basic physical sciences. There are places where physical explanation has come upon it own limits, for example, with Heisenberg's Uncertainty Principle. The principled impossibility of predicting the simultaneous position and momentum of an electron is a limit on physical explanation. But it does not undermine physicalism, the view that what there is, and all there is, is physical stuff and its relations. Indeed, the uncertainty principle is a finding that concerns two utterly physical phenomena: electron position and electron momentum.

Rather than harming naturalism, the arguments I have discussed show its power and resiliency. This is easy to see. A standard criterion of theoretical superiority is this. T_2 is better than T_1 if T_2 explains everything T_1 explains plus some of what T_1 does not explain. Now T_1 asserts that subjective consciousness cannot possibly be captured from the objective point of view. T_1 asserts this but doesn't explain it. But the naturalist's theory, T_2, explains why subjective consciousness cannot be captured from an objective point of view, insofar as it *cannot* be captured from an objective point of view. The organic integrity of bodies explains why each organism has its own, and only its own, experiences. It would have been a bad evolutionary design to have experiences sitting around disembodied. It is best that experiences are captured by and attached to the organisms to whose ongoing life they are most relevant. The project for theory is to characterize and explain our experiences, not to have them or enable third parties to have them. We ourselves will have them, thank you.

7   Refrain: The Missing Shade of You

When last seen, your colorful inner life was a missing shade as viewed from the perspective of every other subject of experience. No one else has had the experiences that constitute the unique coloration of your inner life. You, and you alone, are the subject of your experiences. Does that sound scary? Does that make you feel lonely? If it does make you feel scared and lonely, it can only be because you been seduced by two illusions. The first illusion is that somehow things would be better if others really did penetrate your being, and you theirs. Think about it.

The second illusion is that by virtue of being the sole subject of your experiences, no one else can imaginatively come to see the missing shade that is you. Though theory cannot engender such penetration, there is a powerful impulse to think that it is important in ordinary life that we penetrate each other's inner lives and capture each other's subjectivity. But what is important is not the interpenetration of being. What is important is that we understand each other. Between grasping an abstract theory of some phenomena ($grasp_1$) and having an experience ($grasp_2$), there is $grasping_{1.5}$. This is when I take your experience, as I understand it, into my mind for the sake of trying to understand what things are like for you.

There is no great mystery about how such understanding is accomplished. It involves sensitive detection of what others say, do, and intend. This is accomplished by deploying a complex psychological vocabulary to describe and explain what is detected. The rudiments of this vocabulary are acquired during the second year of life. It is then enriched throughout life as it comes to contain complex meanings that explicitly and implicitly convey the multifarious commitments of a whole form of life that has historical roots and is expressed in culture.

Once on a trip to Vermont, my daughter Kate was seated directly behind me while I was at the wheel, and I made some comment about something Kate was doing. Surprised by my perceptual powers while looking straight ahead, Kate commented that I, like my own mother (as I had reported), had eyes in the back of my head. Ben, seated next to Kate, informed us that in fact no one, not even a parent, had eyes in the back of his head. Humans are simply "mental detectors." Both ideas—eyes in the back of one's head and mental detectors—are meant to explain how humans, especially grown-up humans, can "see" what others are up to, how we can both surmise that certain behaviors are occurring and put the behaviors under the right intentional description. This metaphor of us as mental detectors is a powerful one. Just as a metal detector detects metal objects beneath the sand or between blades of grass, so too mental detectors detect invisible mental states. Good mental detectors understand a great deal about the form of life in which they live and about behavioral regularities. That is why grown-ups are much better mental detectors than children.

When the form of life is not shared, understanding is more difficult. Nagel puts the point in terms of us humans and bats: "We must consider whether any method will permit us to extrapolate to the inner life of the bat from our own case.... Our own experience provides the basic material for our imagination, whose range is therefore limited" (1974, 169). Learning about echolocation and suiting up in equipment that simulates what the best scientists think echolocation is like "will not help." "Insofar as I can imagine this (which is not very far) it tells me only what it would be like for *me* to behave as a bat behaves. But that is not the question. I want to know what it is like for a *bat* to be a bat" (Nagel 1974, 169). He concludes that we "cannot form more than a schematic conception of what it *is* like.... We may ascribe general *types* of experience on the basis of the animal's structure and behavior.... But we believe that these experiences also have in each case a specific subjective character, which it is beyond our ability to conceive" (1974, 169–170).

There are two important claims here. The first claim is that, although we might understand that bats undergo echolocating experiences, it is "beyond our ability to conceive" the "specific subjective character" of these experiences. If what is beyond our ability here is to have a sonar experience in just the way a bat does, then the point seems true but trivial. Only bats have bat experiences. But if I can form a schematic conception of the type echolocating-experience and can put myself into a position where I have an echolocating experience, then it seems plausible to say that I have gained some understanding of what it is like to echolocate, and thus that I have gained some understanding of what it is like to be a bat. The problem is understanding what failing to conceive of the "specific subjective character" of the experience of another is to be contrasted with. When do we succeed at grasping this specific subjective character of another's experience? If conceiving of the specific subjective character of the experiences of another means having the experiences exactly as the experiencer has them, then this never happens. This problem is not one that separates sighted people from bats and blind persons, it separates each subject of experience from every other. But if conceiving of the specific subjective character of another's experience means something less than that, for example, if it means understanding another or conceiving of what things are like from another's point of view, then it often happens.

The second claim, that working on echolocation "will not help," is ambiguous. It might mean that I can't have echolocating experiences. But that is patently false. All humans make some use of echolocation in getting about. If anything will help to form "a schematic conception" of what it is like to be a bat, practicing echolocation will. To be sure, this will only tell me what it is like for me to take on certain batlike properties. This seems to be why Nagel thinks that becoming a master echolocater "will not help." It will be me having echolocating experiences, not me having bat echolocating experiences. But if this is the right interpretation, then one wonders again what the contrastive case is. What other possibilities are there? When I imagine what it is like to be you, am I doing something different than imagining what it is like to be you from my point of view? How could I do anything else? All my experiences are my experiences. The most empathic act the world has ever known occurred from the point of view of the empathizer. There is no other way it could have happened. If the problem is that every attempt to understand the mental life of another must be from a particular point of view, this is a problem every subject of experience has in understanding every other subject of experience. Bats play no essential role in the argument whatsoever.

Nagel goes on to claim that persons blind or deaf from birth are other examples of cases that are "beyond our ability to conceive." And McGinn chimes in to say, "You cannot form concepts of conscious properties unless you yourself instantiate these properties. The man born blind cannot grasp the concept of a visual experience of red, and human beings cannot conceive of the echolocating experiences of bats. These are cases of cognitive closure within the class of conscious properties" (1991, 8−9).

But here we need to be reminded of our capacities to create and conjure up novel experiences. Again consider Mary, the omniscient color-vision expert. One might wonder why Mary can't conjure up color experiences in the way in which the Humean character Hugh can. The simplest answer is that Hugh has had lots of color experience. Mary has had none. Hugh can make blue$_5$ from other shades he knows about. Mary is a complete know-nothing about all colors. She, unlike Hugh, has no shades to mix. But consider this possibility. Remember that Mary knows that the sensation of red supervenes on activation of the red channel. Suppose that she discovers a novel way to tweak the red channel. She discovers that staring at a black dot for a minute and then quickly downing a shot of brandy produces red hallucinations. (Hardin [1988, 91−92] lists ten different ways to see colors without being exposed to "colorful" objects!) Mary does as well with red as Hugh does with blue$_5$, maybe even better. After all, she has the impression of red, whereas Hugh only has a faint idea of blue$_5$.

Hugh and Mary have resources at their disposal to have experiences that neither has had in the usual way. From these two thought experiments, there seem to be two ways to grasp a shade one has not seen. Either one mixes in imagination shades one already knows to form a conception of a new shade, or one figures out a nonstandard way—staring at dots and drinking strong liquor, pressing on one's eyeball, eating wild mushrooms— that activates the desired color channels. It is possible that in similar ways I can conjure up or creatively construct the missing shade of you, even if you are a very alien type of creature. I can spend time with you, read anthropological accounts about your kind, and in this way gain imaginative entry into your life form and eventually into what it is like for you to be you.

If Mary can figure out a way to turn on her red channels without retinal stimulation, perhaps the blind person with retinal destruction but intact red channels can too. If Hugh can conjure up the missing shade of blue from other color experiences he has had, I can surely conjure up what it is like to echolocate from my own limited experience.

Phenomenological opacity is a matter of degree. We never have exactly the same experiences as any other subject of experience. But this does not preclude understanding all manner of unusual subjective life forms. Nagel concedes this when he writes,

> It is often possible to take up a point of view other than one's own, so the comprehension of such facts is not limited to one's own case. There is a sense in which phenomenological facts are *perfectly objective*: one person can know or say of another what the quality of the other's experience is. They are subjective, however, in the sense that even this objective ascription of experience is possible only for someone sufficiently similar to the object of ascription to adopt his point of view—to understand the ascription in the first person as well as in the third, so to speak. The more different from oneself the other experiencer is, the less success one can expect with this enterprise. (Nagel 1974, 172)

A telling footnote attaches to this passage:

> It may be easier that I suppose to transcend inter-species barriers with the aid of imagination.... Blind people are able to detect objects near them by a form of sonar, using vocal clicks or taps of a cane. Perhaps if one knew what that was like, one could by extension imagine roughly what it was like to possess the much more refined sonar of a bat. The distance between oneself and other persons and other species can fall anywhere on a continuum. Even for other persons the under-standing what it is like to be them is only partial, and when one moves to species very different from oneself, a lesser degree of partial understanding may still be available. The imagination is remarkably flexible. My point, however, is not that we cannot *know* what it is like to be a bat. I am not raising that epistemological problem. My point is rather that even to form a *conception* of what it is like to be a bat

(and *a fortiori* to know what it is like to be a bat) one must take up the
bat's point of view. If one can take it up roughly, or partially, then
one's conception will also be rough or partial.   (Nagel 1974, 172).

Imagination is remarkably flexible. Even among persons, understanding is
only partial. For species farther away, understanding is harder. But since
these things are a matter of degree, there is no incoherence in thinking that
we can (work to) form a conception of a bat, a person blind or deaf from
birth, a person with a multiple personality disorder, and so on.

I have insisted throughout that it is possible to do phenomenology from
both the third-person and first-person points of view. A. R. Luria's *The Man
with the Shattered World* (1972), Oliver Sacks's *Awakenings* (1983), and the
essays contained in Sacks's *The Man Who Mistook His Wife for a Hat* (1985)
are masterpieces of third-person phenomenology. Helen Keller's memoirs
are a masterpiece of first-person phenomenology. These works play with
imagination, perhaps in the way in which Mary plays with black dots and
brandy, to help produce some comprehension of lives radically different
from our own. Once we gain imaginative entry into these lives, do we
instantiate the properties so described? When we read about a prosopagnosiac who moves through life without recognizing faces, do we now
instantiate the property of not seeing faces as faces? Of course not. Do we
comprehend, though, what it would be like to do so? Yes, to some extent.

We have gotten this far: Persons understand each other, but not by
penetrating each other's being, not by having each other's experiences.
Understanding another involves conceiving of the other's experiences. We
do this in a variety of ways. What we speak of as taking on the point of
view of another involves imaginatively taking on what we think things are
like for the other, and this typically requires bracketing out to some extent
what things are like for ourselves. Strictly speaking, we never take on the
other's point of view. The structure of the nervous system prevents it.

The best candidates for interpersonal experiential commonality, for mutual grasping, involve sensory experiences. There is reasonable evidence
that I can have experiences that are (almost) the same as your experiences,
when the experiences in question are sensations or low-level perceptions.
The sensory vectors for color, taste, smell, and so on, are similar across
persons. Evolution has made them so. It is not unreasonable, therefore, to
think that we know what it is like for others to experience red and blue, to
smell smoke, and to feel the sharp pain of a bee sting. Yet sensational
sameness is not something we simply need to assume is the case. When in
doubt, we can test for it.

Even when there is very deep understanding between persons, as between lovers or excellent friends, it is easy to fall into the illusion that each
has, so to speak, direct acquaintance with the inner life of the other. But
that is never the case. Often, in fact, people who understand each other

deeply are simply very sensitive to the characteristic response patterns of each other. One might know that one's best friend is prone to feelings of low self-esteem, and one might be savvy at keeping her from going into such states and good at getting her out of such states. But one is in the grip of an illusion if one thinks that a person needs to have experienced low self-esteem to know what it is like to feel low self esteem, to express appropriate concern and sympathy when a friend experiences it, and to possess the expertise to help a friend avoid experiencing it.

What are the prospects for my coming to know what it is like to be you? What are the prospects of my coming to understand not merely what it is like for you to experience colors but also what it is like for you to feel happy and sad, to be confused, to be excited over a new idea, to be in love, and in general to be you? The prospects are not good, unless I am willing to take the time and expend the energy that gaining human understanding requires. I will need to get to know you. I will need to formulate sensitive views about what makes you tick—and this is compatible with treating you as a black box up to a point. Often I will need to work at factoring out certain ways in which I am prone to conceive of things, and I will need to be careful not to project onto you what things are like for me or how I would respond to a certain situation. Time together, screening off certain aspects of my character and agenda, and avoiding projection—these are the ways in which good relationships and deep understanding are built.

Beware of the idea that it is important for one person to enter the mental life of another in the way usually intended when there is talk about really getting inside someone's head or grasping, capturing, what it is like to be another. There are other minds, and we have knowledge of them. But such knowledge never involves grasping exactly what it is like to have another's experiences or inner life. The structure of the nervous system accounts for the happy fact that we each have our own, and only our own, experiences. But we are very smart, and we possess powerful imaginations. Intelligence and imagination open doors to other minds. Intelligence, imagination, and shared life forms make for especially profitable, connected visits. Chances for visits abound. Chances for direct communion do not. If that seems like a loss, a tragic feature of the human condition, think about what a life spent in communion would be like.

Chapter 6
The Mystery of Consciousness

1   The Mystery of Qualia

Conscious mental life includes much more than sensory qualia. It also includes moods, emotions, dreams, many kinds of intentional states, various kinds of self-consciousness, conscious attention, and conscious self-control. We will eventually need a complete neurophilosophical theory of these kinds of consciousness. Noumenal or anticonstructive naturalism is the view that although naturalism is true, we will never be able to provide a naturalistic account of consciousness. It is not simply that it will be very hard to provide an intelligible analysis of these more exotic kinds of consciousness. The connection of consciousness and brain will remain eternally inexplicable. Noumenal naturalism is the claim that no convincing naturalistic account of sensory consciousness can be given. The inexplicability begins at the beginning, as it were, at the very lowest levels of conscious mental life. Forget about self-reflection, self-control, conscious life planning, and moral self-scrutiny, we cannot even provide a theory about consciousness at the level shared by us with most other animals. For this reason it makes sense to join the battle at the level of sensation, since my side says that the sensory-vector story provides a credible naturalistic account of sensory consciousness, while noumenal naturalism is the view that in-principle intractability and unknowability begin with sensory qualia. Colin McGinn is a capable and clever defender of this view. His arguments for noumenal naturalism are the focus of this chapter. The claim that naturalism is not up to the problem of consciousness is familiar, but it comes from various kinds of nonnaturalists. McGinn's argument for mystery, however, comes from inside naturalism. The position might be called "new mysterianism" to distinguish it from the more familiar kinds of mysterianism that are antinaturalistic.

The first question is whether the sensory-vector story about sensory qualia, with suitable caveats in place, is true. I think that something like it is true. It is the best explanation available. Is the story certain? Of course not. One could remain skeptical in a variety of ways. One could simply deny that anything physical could cause anything mental, or one could claim that it is very hard to be convinced that the relevant sensory vectors confer sensory consciousness. After all, one doesn't see consciousness in the brain or in the theoretically derived vectors.

> A point whose significance it would be hard to overstress ... is this: the property of consciousness itself (or specific conscious states) is not an observable or perceptible property of the brain. You can stare into a living conscious brain, your own or someone else's, and see there a wide variety of instantiated properties—its shape, colour, texture, etc.—but you will not thereby *see* what the subject is experiencing, the conscious state itself.... You cannot see a conscious state *as* a brain state. In other words, consciousness is noumenal with respect to perception of the brain.   (McGinn 1989, 356–357)

If consciousness is a property of the brain, this shows that "there *are* properties of the brain that are necessarily closed to perception of the brain" (McGinn 1989, 357).

The smart move for those of us who favor my proposed analysis of sensory qualia is to claim that consciousness is not based on direct observation. Rather it is an inference to the best explanation. Inference to the best explanation, also called abduction, proceeds as follows. One has a set of observations and a set of background assumptions (observational and theoretical). The inference drawn best explains this total set of reasonable commitments.

McGinn thinks that "no form of *inference* from what is perceived can lead us to *P*," where *P* is the property or set of properties that naturalistically explains consciousness. McGinn's position is puzzling because he is, as I have said, a naturalist. He is also a metaphysical realist. He believes in a mind-independent reality and thinks that whether or not we know what *P* is and whether or not we come to understand how *P* renders consciousness intelligible, *P* does exist, and it does render consciousness intelligible. This is why McGinn says that there "is no *metaphysical* problem" (1989, 363). He writes, "The approach I favour is naturalistic but not constructive. I do not believe we can ever specify what it is about the brain that is responsible for consciousness, but I am sure that whatever it is it is not inherently miraculous" (1989, 349).

It will be useful to set out McGinn's general argument as perspicuously as possible. Actually, McGinn offers two somewhat different arguments for his conclusion that the problem of consciousness is unsolvable. The first argument (1989) characterizes *P* as the property of brain states that would naturalistically explain consciousness, were we only smart enough to see the "intelligible connections" between *P* and consciousness. The second argument (1991) heightens the air of mystery by characterizing *P* not as a property of brain states but as some third sort of property that is neither physical nor nonphysical. In the first argument, what cannot be made fully intelligible is the *relation* between P and consciousness, where P is understood as a set of neural properties. In the second argument, P itself eludes us. P is a property of the hidden structure of consciousness, itself neither physical nor phenomenological. P would make the relation of brain and consciousness intelligible if only it were knowable. But it is not knowable. Alas, there is terminal mystery.

2   The First Argument: Why We Can't Solve the Problem of Consciousness

Here is how the first argument goes:

1. Introspection will not reveal what P is, where P is the brain property that subserves or renders consciousness intelligible.

2. Examination of the brain won't reveal what P is either. This is because for any candidate P we won't be able to *see* how P could explain or render consciousness intelligible.

3. Since perceptual closure does not entail cognitive closure (we can think about things that we have never perceived, e.g., transcendental numbers, electrons), one might think that there is some form of inference to the best explanation that will work to make the link between consciousness and brain states intelligible.

4. But there is no form of inference to the best explanation that could draw an intelligible link between any set of brain properties and consciousness. This is due to the *homogeneity constraint* on concept introduction: psychological concepts should not be introduced to explain physical phenomena, nor physical concepts to explain the psychological, unless we are forced to do so. "Inference to the best explanation of purely physical data will never take us outside the realm of the physical, *forcing* us to introduce concepts of consciousness. Everything physical has a purely physical explanation. So the property of consciousness is cognitively closed with respect to the introduction of concepts by means of inference to the best explanation of perceptual data about the brain" (McGinn 1989, 358, my italics).

Explanation of (4). The basic idea behind (4) is that perception of brain facts will never ground an inference to the best explanation of the form "P is what renders consciousness intelligible," because to explain brain facts, we only need to appeal to other brain facts. Since consciousness is not perceived by looking at the brain, and therefore is not (according to this contrived exercise) a phenomenon to be explained, to explain consciousness we do not need to introduce any theoretical concept P (referring, I assume, to some complex set of neural facts). McGinn writes, "To explain the observed physical data we need only such theoretical properties as bear upon these data, not the property that explains consciousness, which does not occur in the data. Since we do not need consciousness to explain these data, we do not need the property that explains consciousness" (1989, 359). Conversely, if we set our sights on explaining consciousness as it appears to conscious subjects, nothing will force us to introduce physical concepts to explain its existence.

5. The epistemological diagnosis fails that sees the cause of the problem in differences in how we come to understand or be acquainted with consciousness, as opposed to brain facts (including facts about our own brains), in "the peculiarity of the epistemological situation" (McGinn 1989, 359–360). That is, the impossibility of uncovering an intelligible link between brain processes and consciousness is not rooted in the fact that we have direct, first-person access to certain features of consciousness and only objective access to facts about the brain.

6. The best diagnosis is that even though there is some natural property P that explains consciousness from "the God's-eye point of view," this property is cognitively closed to us.

3   Critique of the First Argument

The upshot of the first argument is this: We cannot render the link between consciousness and the brain intelligible from the point of view of consciousness, and we cannot render the link intelligible by observing the brain. So we cannot render the link intelligible at all. The argument to this conclusion is inductive rather than deductive. Like any argument, this one depends on the plausibility of its premises, so let us take the argument one step at a time. Premise 1 seems to me uncontroversially right. Consciousness reveals nothing about my brain, not even that I have one!

Premise 2 is uncontroversially true on one interpretation and patently problematic on another interpretation. The uncontroversially true interpretation is the one according to which we will not literally see how P explains or renders consciousness intelligible by looking at the brain alone. But it is hard to understand why this should worry us. In complex scientific contexts we invariably need to bring a theory to some set of observational data in order to draw that data into a web of intelligibility. The patently problematic interpretation of premise 2 is that the "unobservability" of the link between P and consciousness prevents us from inferring that P is in fact where the link resides. This interpretation comes from reading back into premise 2 what McGinn goes on to say at steps 3 and 4.

Evidence that McGinn holds excessively high standards of intelligibility and at the same time abides overly restrictive methodological principles emerges in steps 3 and 4. Strictly speaking, step 3 is unproblematic, but it sets a trap that step 4 is designed to catch us in. The trap set in step 3 involves thinking that there might be some acceptable form of inference from some set of brain facts P to the conclusions that P subserves consciousness, that P causes consciousness, or that consciousness supervenes on P.

But in step 4 McGinn sets out some rules on concept introduction and inference that are designed to stop us from thinking that there is any such acceptable inference pattern. One reason is that "a certain *homogeneity* operates in our introduction of theoretical concepts on the basis of observation" (1989, 357–358). He clarifies what he has in mind by the homogeneity constraint on concept introduction when he quotes Nagel to the effect that "it will never be legitimate to infer, as a theoretical explanation of physical phenomena alone, a property that includes or implies the consciousness of its subject" (Nagel 1974, 183). Consciousness is a different kind of property (it is heterogeneous) from the perceptible properties of the brain, so the homogeneity constraint prohibits its introduction.

McGinn's misstep comes from forgetting that consciousness has already been introduced. We are not looking for an explanation of "physical phenomena alone," at least not physical phenomena narrowly understood. There is a prior commitment to the existence of consciousness. Thus both brain facts and facts about consciousness are on the table to be explained. We then infer that the constellation of a certain set of phenomenological reports of restricted range ("tastes sweet") correlate with certain sorts of brain activity (activation in the relevant pathways), and we infer, given an overall commitment to naturalism, that the latter explain the former.

McGinn's argument works by restricting inferential space to only the simplest, most straightforward sorts of connections. When looking at the brain, you are only allowed to draw links among brain states, and when introspecting, you are only permitted commentary on how things seem, on what reveals itself in the conscious stream. Since neither way of looking at things will by itself get you to the other, the link between the two is closed, a mystery.

To see that something has gone awry here, that the "homogeneity constraint" is overly restrictive, consider the case of the ubiquitous electron. Given a commitment to standard contemporary physics, it is the inference to the best explanation that certain observable processes in a cloud chamber are the traces of unobservable electrons. We never see the electrons directly while observing the processes in the cloud chamber, nor for that matter do we see them anywhere else. Electrons are a theoretical construct whose postulation best explains certain observable data and whose postulation is in turn supported by certain (predicted) observations.

Similar inferential moves are required to draw links between consciousness and the brain. We do not *see* consciousness when we look into the brain. Our access to the surface features of consciousness is not mediated by our senses. Consciousness is experienced in an intimate first-person way. But given a prior commitment to the existence of consciousness and a naturalistic view of the world, certain observations of brain properties, especially those reliably linked to certain kinds of first-person reports and behavior, can easily warrant the claim that such and such processes subserve sensory awareness in domain d.

The relevant sort of inference pattern occurs in the cases of blindsight. What are the data in such cases? The data includes such facts as these: there are patients who say they do not see anything on, say, their right side but who, if asked to reach in that direction or guess what is there, move their fingers and hands with the right preparatory movements to pick up the object that is there and who guess with considerable accuracy. The data also include facts such as these: such individuals typically have some sort of lesion in area V1 of the visual cortex but possess unimpaired function in the other distinct areas that the retinal image projects to. Contrary to what McGinn says, this data set is precisely the kind that warrants, as an inference to the best explanation, the invocation "of consciousness [or the lack thereof] to explain [the] data." Conversely, we need to invoke certain neural properties to explain why visual consciousness is present in normal cases and lacking in the blindsight cases. There are lesions in the striate region of the visual cortex in the latter cases but not in the former. McGinn writes that to "explain the observed physical data we need only such theoretical properties as bear upon those data, not the property that explains consciousness, which does not occur in the data. Since we do not need consciousness to explain those data, we do not need the property that explains consciousness" (1989, 359).

But my point is that to explain the observable data about the differences between sighted and blindsighted people—the former say they see something, the latter don't; the former make reliable judgments about what is in the visual field, the latter are significantly less reliable—we need to invoke the property of visual consciousness (or the lack thereof). The same reasons that warrant invoking the concept of consciousness also warrant the invocation of concepts referring to certain brain properties—an intact versus a lesioned area V1—to explain the two different kinds of consciousness.

For reasons such as these, premise 4, which espouses the "homogeneity constraint," is untenable if it is meant to render it impermissible to draw explanatory links between some set of events or processes unless all these events or processes are simultaneously observable in the domain under study. Such a restriction is totally unwarranted. It would lead us back into the dark ages scientifically.

McGinn demands that we be shown an "intelligible connection" between P and consciousness, and he claims at every turn that this cannot be done. But if one is in the proper Humean mood, one will wonder why any naturalist would set the impossibly high standard on intelligibility that McGinn sets. To be sure, we think that water *is* H_2O, and we think that this is a necessary, a posteriori truth. But we also think that it is an utterly contingent fact about the course of the universe that there turned out to be any water at all, or that it turned out to possess the molecular structure it in fact possesses. Furthermore, the necessity ascribed is provisional. 'Water is H_2O' is necessary *if* true. The truth is vulnerable to displacement, or so we think, in a way in which the truths of arithmetic or logic are not. But if there is room for skeptical doubt about well-established and allegedly necessary, a posteriori truths, then it is hard to see how any scientific theory could render any connections "intelligible," except in some standard fallibilistic sense. If the standards of necessity or intelligibility are those operative in logic or arithmetic, then *no* scientific statements will satisfy the standard, and we can be said to know nothing about the world. So this hardly seems like the right set of standards for explanation.

In one place McGinn compares the emergence of consciousness with the emergence of life on earth: "We cannot take the arrival of life as a primitive brute fact, nor can we accept that life arose by some form of miraculous emergence.... We rightly insist that it must be in virtue of some natural property of (organized) matter that parcels of it get to be alive" (1989, 353). He goes on to insist that the necessary connections that led to the emergence of life may eternally elude us. I think he is right in this. But I pointed out earlier that we possess some plausible sketches for how life emerged, and we have deep knowledge of certain connections between life as it did emerge in the form of the double helix and the phenotypic features of many different kinds of living things. Unless we hold impossibly high standards of intelligibility, the story of the emergence and subsequent natural history of life is becoming increasingly intelligible to us. The genome project currently underway, the project of mapping the structure and function of every human gene, will undoubtedly increase our understanding by several orders of magnitude.

McGinn, I think, causes himself the problem of irremedial mystery that he is so awed by. The problem is caused by placing draconian restrictions on the inferential context, and in particular by prohibiting the introduction of the concept of consciousness in scientific contexts unless it can be shown to be needed to play some explanatory role relative to perceptible properties of the brain. But this is an unnecessary positivistic constraint. Introspective, phenomenological data should convince us that consciousness exists. Such functional deficits as profound amnesia, prosopagnosia, and blindsight as reported in the writings of Luria, Sacks, and Weiskrantz involve defects of consciousness. We need to refer to different types of consciousness to describe and explain what has gone wrong, and we need to refer to certain neurological facts to explain why various types of consciousness are present, absent, or deficient. Facts about consciousness, facts about the brain, and questions about the links between the two are all on the explanatory platter at once.

In the end, I think that the correct diagnosis of why the air of mystery can never be dispelled completely is the epistemological diagnosis McGinn rejects in premise 5. Indeed, he himself says as much when he lets it slip that "in reality, there is no metaphysical mind-body problem; there is no *ontological* anomaly, only an epistemic hiatus" (1991, 31). The homogeneity constraint only exacerbates the epistemic hiatus. We are never allowed, according to the homogeneity constraint, to move from the subjective to the objective or from the objective to the subjective. Inferentially speaking, we are locked on whichever side of the subjective-objective divide we start. In effect, the homogeneity constraint takes the natural epistemic hiatus between the subjective and the objective and turns it into a principled methodological obstacle. We are not allowed, according to the constraint, to draw the subjective and the objective into the same inferential space.

To see that the epistemological diagnosis is correct, consider again Thomas Nagel's well-known arguments for the impossibility of capturing the subjective point of view in any completely objective analysis (1974, 1986). Nagel is right that no description cast in the language of neuroscience can *capture* what it is like to be me. The question is what follows from this concession?

If mental processes are physical processes, why won't the true story of how my brain works *capture* what it is like to be me? The answer is simple and far from mysterious. The objective story of my brain life does not capture what it is like to be me because it is a description. Imagine a third party, an omniscient neuroscientist, watching my brain operate in real time. What the omniscient neuroscientist experiences and what I experience, owing to the way I am hooked up to myself, are utterly different. The omniscient neuroscientist sees certain patterns of neural activity and says such things as "There he goes, experiencing red again." But I experience red, not he. There is no temptation to think that my conscious states, indescribable as they are from the omniscient neuroscientist's point of view, are not realized in the very hookups he observes. Nor is there any temptation to infer from the fact that my subjective point of view gives me no clue about the nature of the processes that subserve my conscious states, that my subjective mental life is not in fact realized in my brain states. Cartesians are notoriously prone to make this inferential error. A better inference is that I am simply not in touch with the "braininess" of my conscious states in the first person. The situation is somewhat analogous to the perceptual case where I see light but perceptually know absolutely nothing about its nature. I see light as light. The nature of the mechanisms

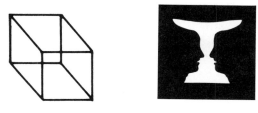

Figure 6.1
Face-vase illusion and Necker cube.

that subserve my perception of light tell me nothing at all about whether light involves waves or particles, about whether it has a speed, let alone what its speed is, and so on.

The epistemological diagnosis seems just right in this case. Consider the analogy with Gestalt illusions, for example, the image that produces the vase-face illusion or a Necker cube reversal (figure 6.1). Strictly speaking, there is just one physical configuration before one's eyes, but it can be seen in either of two ways, as a vase or as a pair of faces in one case, as a cube with reversed foreground and background in the other case. Gestalt illusions such as these show that something metaphysically unproblematic (they are just solid figures and lines) may be seen, known, or described in two different ways. Gestalt illusions have a further important property: when one is seeing the image in one way, one cannot at the same time also see it in the other way. But remember that Gestalt illusions *are* illusions. There is just one thing there. It has two aspects that are epistemically irreducible to each other, but not irreducible to the whole they compose, not irreducible in some venerable metaphysical sense.

The alleged mystery of consciousness has its source in biological facts that underwrite the different kinds of epistemic access we have to brain facts and to what it is like to be each one of us. We grasp facts about the brain through our sensory organs, typically with the help of sensory prostheses: MRI, CAT, and PET scanners. On the other hand, we are acquainted with consciousness by way of direct, internal, reflexive biological hookups to our own nervous systems. To this point in human history, all such hookups have been limited to the first person. The nature of our access to what we are made of and to how we function as complex biological systems is different in kind and provides different information than does our first-person, on-line hookup to our selves. The biological fact that each one of us possesses a direct, first-person, reflexive hookup to one and only one body explains how the most complete explanation from the physical point of view does not capture what it is like to be me. Only I can capture that. Only I am hooked up to myself in the right sort of way. Dewey's insight is worth repeating. "Given that consciousness exists at all, there is no mystery in its being connected with what it is connected with" (1922, 62).

The important point is that we possess a good naturalistic explanation of our inability to capture the phenomenology of what it is like to be each one of us from the objective point of view. The hookups, the epistemic access relations, are essentially different in the first person and in the third person. The fact that we possess this explanation of the dual aspect means that even though the third-person or impersonal point of view fails to capture the relevant first-person phenomenology, this does not undermine the naturalist's hope of isolating the specific properties that subserve first-person experience.

4   Some Further Objections and Replies

McGinn requires us to go either from the top down or from the bottom up, but never both ways at once. This methodological requirement is at least part of the source of the irremedial mystery he claims to find. McGinn relishes pointing out the poverty of either approach taken by itself, but curiously he fails to explore the prospects of mutual coordination. It is a credible inference to be drawn from the failure of a pure top-down or pure bottom-up approach that, although neither introspection alone nor perception alone can give rise to a theory of consciousness, both taken together, plus our general science-forming capacities, can give rise to such a theory. McGinn virtually acknowledges this much when he writes, "Perception is indispensable to arriving at a knowledge of the brain. More exactly, introspective data alone, even when combined with a general science-forming capacity, will never lead to the kind of understanding of the physical correlates and causes of consciousness that we now have" (1991, 75). Where could the "understanding of the physical correlates and causes of consciousness that we now have" have come from if not from coordinated efforts to draw the phenomenological and neurological analyses together? If we now possess some "understanding of the correlates and causes of consciousness," apparently consciousness is not a complete mystery. We know some things about its correlates and causes. Where does the principled impenetrability begin? What correlates and causes lie eternally out of reach, and why?

McGinn does not answer this question directly, but one can anticipate two replies congenial to his overall approach. The first reply says something like this: "Correlates and causes? Sure we have some knowledge of them. But everyone knows, thanks to Hume, that correlates and causes don't *really* explain anything. Correlates are a dime a dozen and get at nothing deep. Furthermore, we lack an understanding of the nature of causality. Whatever 'causal' regularities we detect today might, for all we can know, cease to obtain tomorrow."

The reason to expect this sort of reply has to do with the fact that McGinn requires of an acceptable theory of consciousness that it "fully explains" consciousness (1991, 6). Does the fact that water is H_2O "fully explain" the nature of water? The reply I have just put in McGinn's mouth suggests that he should say it does *not* "fully explain" what water is or make the nature of water "perfectly intelligible." But then we can start to see a troublesome pattern. Nothing can satisfy the explanatory demands set by McGinn, and so everything is really a mystery! Consciousness is no worse off than anything else. But viewed in this way, the argument really is not, as advertised, an argument stemming from a special case of cognitive closure with respect to the nature of consciousness. It is an argument steeped in skepticism. When McGinn writes that "nothing we can imagine perceiving in the brain would ever convince us that we have located the intelligible nexus we seek" (1991, 11), this is not because we might not have hit upon the intelligible nexus. It is because we could remain eternally unpersuaded even if we had hit upon it. No explanation, no matter how satisfactory, will satisfy the skeptic. It is telling that McGinn frames his argument in terms of every theory's failure to *satisfy* rather than in the failure of every theory to *be satisfactory*. "I think that honest reflection strongly suggests that nothing *we* could ever empirically discover about the brain *could* provide a fully satisfying account of consciousness" (1991, 28). The fact that water is H_2O, once spelled out, accounts fully for the properties of water. The account is fully satisfactory, even if not fully satisfying. Suppose that McGinn accepted the fact that water is H_2O fully explains the nature of water, in the sense that it provides a satisfactory analysis of the nature of water. If he accepted this much, it is hard to see how he could reject a well-motivated enumeration saying that consciousness (of different kinds) supervenes on neural states of such and such kind.

But here there is another sort of reply at the ready. The trouble with identifying consciousness with the brain states upon which it is discovered to supervene is "curiously brute and unperspicuous" (McGinn 1991, 20). Psychophysical correlations "have a brutish feel to them" (McGinn 1991, 118). But it is hard to see why the accounts of the nature of water in terms of its molecular structure, of life in terms of DNA, and so on, aren't also brute. If McGinn places higher demands on a theory of consciousness not to leave certain things brute, he needs to provide reasons why. He doesn't provide them. (For illuminating discussion of the issue of bruteness, see Levine 1983; Van Gulick, in press a.)

I have argued that there is no motivation for the homogeneity constraint that McGinn deploys to keep us from drawing links between concepts of two different kinds: physical on the one side and psychological and phenomenological on the other side. One possible motivation I have not explored is this. When two concepts are metaphysically at odds, they are heterogeneous and shouldn't be related in identity claims or functional theories. McGinn espouses this plausible principle (1991, 52). How could this principle apply to the present case? It could apply if one thinks that consciousness is a "nonnatural concept," while the concepts of neuroscience are "natural."

The trouble is that whether the concept of consciousness is natural or nonnatural depends on one's background metaphysic. If it seems nonnatural, this is because it is conceived nonnaturalistically, for example, in Cartesian terms. But there is no reason to think of the concept in that way. The concept of consciousness is natural or nonnatural according to one's background metaphysic. The naturalist has just as much right to the concept and can use it to pick out roughly the same set of phenomena as the nonnaturalist. So the homogeneity constraint can't be deployed to block the construction of a theory that links the phenomenological or psychological and the more canonically physical on grounds that the former is a metaphysical witches' brew. In any case, McGinn concedes all this in accepting that consciousness is a natural phenomenon. The prohibition on mixing metaphysical kinds simply does not apply to cases where naturalists are interweaving phenomenological, psychological, and neurophysiological concepts, because they are *all* natural.

5   The Second Argument: The Hidden Structure of Consciousness

The argument that the problem of consciousness is cognitively closed to us is repeated in the paper "Consciousness and the Natural Order" (McGinn 1991), but with the first explicit suggestion that P "is a property of the hidden structure of consciousness" (1991, 59). In the earlier rendition of the argument in "Can We Solve the Mind Body Problem?" (1989), P is characterized as a property (or set of properties) of the brain upon which consciousness supervenes. But in the later paper, P is depicted as a property that is neither a brain property nor a phenomenological property. P is the property that links, and thereby makes fully intelligible the connection between, the physical and the phenomenological. But alas, as before, P is as cognitively closed to our minds as the concept of an electron is to the mind of a cockroach.

Here is the second argument, the argument for the impenetrable hidden structure of consciousness:

> 1. The idea of hidden structure, of deep versus surface structure, has shown itself to be repeatedly useful in the history of science, for example, as with atomic structure and DNA.
> 2. However, the idea of a hidden structure of consciousness has not met with enthusiasm. We think that consciousness is transparent to itself, that "nothing about its intrinsic character lurks unseen.... Con-

sciousness has no secrets from introspection." "Nothing can be a property of consciousness unless the subject is conscious of that property" (1991, 90).

3. But we need to postulate a hidden structure for consciousness to explain features of consciousness like (a) the logical properties of conscious states, (b) the embodiment of consciousness, (c) and such empirical facts as blindsight.

4. Regarding (a), logical properties, logical analysis has revealed the necessity of distinguishing the surface structure from the "real logical" structure of sentences.

Explanation of (4). For example, 'Socrates is tall' involves the 'is' of predication, whereas 'Water is H_2O' involves the 'is' of identity. Sentences like 'The round square does not exist' and 'The present king of France is bald' look superficially as if they posit self-contradictory or nonexistent entities. Logical analysis reveals that the right glosses on these sentences are 'There exists no entity that is both round and square' and 'There exists an x such that x is the King of France, and for any y, if y is the King of France, then $x = y$ and x is bald' (1991, 97). Overall, logical analysis reveals that our sentences can be more ontologically noncommittal than they look on the surface.

5. In revealing the deep logical structure of language, logical analysis reveals an aspect of the hidden structure of consciousness.

Explanation of (5). The argument for interpreting logical analysis as having psychological significance proceeds thus: Although "thought is prior to language; language is the way it is, structurally, because thought is the way *it* is, structurally. Language externalizes the disguise consciousness throws over thought" (1991, 96). Because language and thought share a single disguise, logical analysis, by revealing the hidden structure of our sentences, simultaneously reveals the hidden structure of our conscious thoughts as well. "When the stream of consciousness ripples with thought there are patterns beneath the surface—patterns that are only imperfectly mirrored by the disturbances at the surface.... Consciousness, like language, disguises its underlying logical structure" (1991, 99).

6. The solution to (b), the problem of embodiment, the problem of how the brain gives rise to conscious experience, lies at neither the phenomenological nor the neural level. The solution requires us to accept that "conscious states possess a hidden natural (not logical) structure which mediates between their surface properties and the physical facts on which they constitutively depend" (1991, 100).

Explanation of (6). "Some properties *must* exist to link consciousness intelligibly to the brain, since it is so linked; my suggestion is that these properties belong to the hidden nature of consciousness" (1991,

100). "Nothing overt is up to the job" (1991, 100). "Neither phenomenological nor physical, this mediating level would not (by definition) be fashioned on the model of either side of the divide, and hence would not find itself unable to reach out to the other side. Its characterization would call for radical conceptual innovation" (1991, 103–104). "The operative properties would be neither at the phenomenal surface nor right down there with the physical hardware.... *Somehow they would make perfect sense of the psychophysical nexus* [my italics].... They really would *explain* how it is that chunks of matter can develop an inner life" (1991, 104).

7. Unfortunately, this radical conceptual innovation lies outside our cognitive powers. These deep properties are unknowable by us.

Explanation of (7). This "is because the required concepts need to straddle the gulf between matter and consciousness, but our concepts of matter and consciousness are constrained, respectively, by our faculties of perception and introspection—and concepts so constrained will not be capable of explaining the psychophysical link. Our perceptual access to material things, including the brain, sets limits on the way we can conceive of these things; and our introspective access to consciousness sets limits on the way we can conceive of it. We need a manner of conception that abstracts radically away from these two fundamental ways of apprehending the world, but we simply have no such manner at our cognitive disposal" (1991, 121). In effect, we know the form of a solution to (b), the problem of embodiment. But the actual details of the solution are closed to us, since we cannot form the concepts in terms of which such a solution must be expressed. "Our empirical faculties bypass the place in reality where the solution lies. They are wrongly targeted, so far as the true nature of the psychophysical nexus is concerned. That nature does not reside in the catchment-area of those faculties" (1991, 121).

8. Finally, (c), certain empirical facts suggest additional reason for positing a hidden structure of consciousness.

Explanation of (8). Consider blindsight. In blindsight, some of the causal properties associated with consciousness are preserved, even though the phenomenal features are not. "My proposed interpretation of these data is as follows: In cases of normal vision two sorts of (intrinsic) properties of conscious experience are causally operative in producing discriminative behaviour: surface properties, which are accessible to the subject introspectively; and deep properties, which are not so accessible.... In cases of blindsight we have a dissociation of the two sorts of properties" (1991, 111). There is reason to think that the discriminative abilities of blindsighted persons are subserved by the same hidden mechanisms that subserve conscious sight but are closed to introspection. This shows that the deep structure of ordinary visual discrimination is not introspectable.

9. However, hidden *neural* mechanisms are not up to the job of accounting for blindsight.

Explanation of (9). It will not do to say that normal visual consciousness supervenes on such and such neural mechanisms and blindsight involves these same mechanisms minus a certain few. As before, this is because claims linking the psychological and the neural levels are not fully satisfying; they never confer perfect intelligibility. "The puzzle of psychophysical supervenience infects the project of devising psychophysical laws, or accounting for psychophysical causation. Both require knowledge of the hidden structure of consciousness. Beyond this we shall not be able to progress much beyond crude psychophysical correlations." Psychophysical correlations "have a brutish feel to them" (1991, 118).

10. In sum, the mind-body problem cannot be given a constructive solution, the problem of consciousness cannot be given a constructive solution, and the science of the mind will forever lack depth. It will describe superficially brute links between consciousness and the brain and between mind and behavior. But it will leave "forever unquenched" our thirst to understand the deep structure of these phenomena. "There is no point in trying to make our concepts go deeper than our knowledge can extend." Consciousness has a hidden structure, but "that structure is too noumenal for them [our mental concepts] to get their talons into" (McGinn 1991, 124–125).

6   Critique of the Hidden-Structure Argument

Like the first argument, this one too is unsuccessful. Indeed, it is self-undermining. The seeds of destruction are contained in the very first premise. There we are told about the usefulness of the concept of hidden structure by being reminded of cases in which there turned out to be rich, formerly hidden, but now revealed properties of some phenomena. The premise is true. But the fact that the analogy with consciousness exploits cases in which what was once hidden is now revealed is bad for McGinn, since he wants the "hidden structure of consciousness" to be *terminally hidden*. Otherwise, the conclusion that the consciousness-brain problem is unsolvable has no force.

So the argument is off to an inauspicious start. The problem deepens at premise 2. It is doubtful that consciousness is fully transparent—self-luminous or phosphorescent. Naturalists reject the idea of full transparency, and they reject the idea that "nothing can be a property of consciousness unless the subject is conscious of that property" (1991, 90). Being realized in the brain is a property of consciousness, but it is not revealed to introspection. It is even possible that consciousness is not very good at detecting its own phenomenal properties. It is possible, after all, that conscious introspection depends on long-term memory and that many conscious experiences don't get into long-term memory. All the details about the causal role of the brain in giving rise to conscious mental life were unknown until recently. But insight into these details are beginning to be revealed, and so no longer hidden. Indeed, the imagined case of conscious experiences that are not loaded into long-term memory and that are therefore hidden from conscious introspection would require, at a minimum, that neuroscience revealed that certain brain states possessing the prototypical properties associated with being conscious did not load into long-term memory. Such a discovery and the inference that the states in question were (briefly) conscious despite not being introspectable could only be based on complex theoretical developments. The important point is that the imagined result shows that what is hidden from conscious introspection alone and what is hidden from looking in the brain alone are not necessarily hidden from a methodologically sophisticated science of the mind. Overall, the idea of the hidden structure of consciousness, developed on an analogy with genetic or atomic structure in premises 1 to 3, is plausible. The trouble is that this sort of hidden structure is not terminally hidden.

Things unravel further in step 4, where McGinn starts to unpack the rationale for postulating *unknowable* hidden structure in the case of consciousness. In the first place, one might wonder how McGinn can feel comfortable in telling us that the hidden structure of consciousness is not to be discovered when he himself seems so able to tell us certain things about it. Indeed, the argument is unstable, because the rationale for believing in a terminally hidden structure of consciousness depends on various revelations about this unknowable structure.

For example, in steps 4 and 5 we are told that the logical analysis of sentences reveals the deep structure of our sentential thoughts. But this is a very controversial point. Many think that logical analysis is analysis according to the principle of charity. That is, it is an attempt to interpret what we mean so that we turn out not to be speaking nonsense. But it doesn't necessarily reveal our thoughts as we think them. It is by no means obvious that logical form captures the real psychological structure of thought. If it doesn't, understanding logical form teaches us nothing about the hidden structure of consciousness. But if it does, McGinn again loses, since we would again have dispelled some mystery by revealing some of the hidden structure of consciousness.

Step 5 gives the argument for thinking that logical form captures the psychological reality of our thoughts. But step 5 is dubious at best.

Why think that "language externalizes the disguise that consciousness throws over thought"? Where does this idea that consciousness "disguises" thought come from? A simpler idea is that thinking is one of the heterogeneous forms of consciousness, not that it is something transformed by consciousness. Claiming that consciousness disguises thoughts, and that language is simply the surfacing of these disguised thoughts brings credibility and urgency to the project of removing the disguise and getting at the real thing. But why should anyone buy the disguise theory except to gain this result? I see absolutely no other reason.

In steps 6 and 7 the claim is made explicit that the hidden structure of consciousness cannot be understood in either physical or phenomenological terms. The reasons for this presumably go back to the first argument. No examination from the physical point of view will make the connection to the phenomenological fully intelligible, nor will scrutiny of the phenomenological mind make its connection to the brain fully intelligible. If an intelligible link between the physical and the phenomenological is to be drawn, it will have to be done with concepts lying at a "mediating level" between the two levels. If we did possess such concepts, they would make "perfect sense of the psychophysical nexus." The trouble is we do not possess, and cannot create concepts at this level. McGinn thus claims that there is terminal mystery.

I've already provided reasons for rejecting the requirement of perfect intelligibility in my discussion of the first argument. And I tried to show that once one is relieved of such impossible explanatory demands, very detailed links between the physical and phenomenological levels will be found illuminating, possibly satisfactory. The curious thing about the second argument is that McGinn no sooner repeats the ominous announcement that intelligibility cannot be created from any interweaving of physical and phenomenological cloth than he produces evidence against it. The problem is clearest in the discussion in steps 8 and 9 of the one empirical example he offers: blindsight.

The case of blindsight powerfully undermines the argument that the hidden structure of consciousness is noumenal and that the problem of embodiment is in principle unsolvable. There are two ways to think about blindsight, and both are bad for McGinn. On one interpretation, the phenomenon of blindsight undermines the argument that we need a mediating property that is neither phenomenological nor neurological but that we can never discover this mediating property. The fact is that we possess a fairly good grip of the exact brain locations damaged in cases of blindsight. McGinn claims that in the cases of atomic structure or DNA "we can actually specify aspects of the hidden structure in question: we can say what kinds of properties are instantiated at the hidden level" (1991, 119). He denies that this can be done for the hidden structure of consciousness.

Oddly, the very case he discusses is one in which we "can actually specify aspects of the hidden structure." That is, people with damage at area V1 of the striate cortex report no visual phenomenology in the blindfield. Nonetheless, in well-controlled experiments they show evidence of having picked up some information about what is in the blind field; that is, they do better than chance if prompted to make guesses about certain stimuli in the blindfield. How can this be? The best answer is that "the retina projects not only to striate cortex, but independently to another five or six, perhaps even more, other targets in the brain by routes that bypass the striate cortex" (Weiskrantz 1988, 187). The upshot is that we have a discovery in hand. Part of the hidden structure of consciousness essentially involves intact neural structures in area V1. Area V1 needs to be intact for conscious visual experience to occur.

This first way of thinking about blindsight undermines the claim that hidden structure would be revealed, if it could be revealed (which it can't), at a level that is neither phenomenological nor physical. The hidden structure is revealed, and it is revealed in straightforward neurophysiological terms. How physical can concepts get?

One can imagine hearing the reply, "Well, all that stuff about V1 and visual consciousness just points to brute correlations. Nothing is fully explained or made perfectly intelligible by drawing our attention to those sorts of links!" I have already tried to disarm this sort of response by pointing out that it rests on making impossibly high demands on explanation.

Nonetheless, this pressure to explain more fully how consciousness works and is realized points to a second way of thinking about blindsight, one that does posit a mediating level that is (part of) the hidden structure of consciousness. Imagine that someone is puzzled by the explanation of blindsight sketched so far. How might one respond? One way would be to start to explain how visual processing works with a theory, for example, like David Marr's (1982). Explaining how visual processing works involves deploying design-stance concepts (Dennett 1971). We would need to explain that the retina consists of over 120 million cells that process light waves of different lengths. An image from an object is cast and then dispersed into a two-dimensional array of dots of varying intensities. The retinal image is transformed into a two-dimensional "primal sketch" by processors that compute where light intensity changes from one set of dots to the next. This set of computations results in a rough delineation of the edges and contours of the object. Next, other processors analyze various saliencies, including shading and motion, and compute the $2\frac{1}{2}$-dimensional sketch. The $2\frac{1}{2}$-dimensional sketch makes "explicit the orientation and rough depth of the visible surfaces, and contours of discontinuities in a viewer centered coordinate frame" (Marr 1982, 37). Finally, other processors enter in to perform the most exotic computation of all. These processors take the $2\frac{1}{2}$-dimensional sketch and look for its "basic pattern of symmetry" about an axis. Humans and other mammals have one principle line of symmetry running through the center of the face and body, as well as subsidiary lines running through the limbs. Once the axes of symmetry are divined from the $2\frac{1}{2}$-dimensional sketch, the contours already computed are transposed onto these lines, and the three-dimensional image we see is produced.

Nothing depends on whether Marr's specific story is the right one. The essential point is that the account operates in terms that are neither straightforwardly physical nor straightforwardly phenomenological. All the goings-on are, of course, presumed to be done by certain brain processors, but the focus is on *what is getting done* and *how it is getting done*, not on what is doing it. This is what makes it a design-stance account rather than a physical-stance account. The reason the account is not phenomenological is obvious. All the processing—the computations of light intensities, the sketching, the projection of depth onto the sketch—is done without any phenomenological accompaniments whatsoever.

Functional, design-stance, and software concepts akin to those used in this explanation sketch abound in cognitive psychology and cognitive neuroscience (Dennett 1991b). Such concepts are neither physical nor phenomenological, since they are not typed by appeals to the neural substrata nor by the way things seem. Insofar as such concepts are concepts of "the mediating level," they are just what McGinn claims are needed but can't be found because they require capacities to abstract from the straightforwardly phenomenological or physical, which we lack. These concepts exist, they can be found, we possess the capacities to form them, and they illuminate the hidden structure of consciousness. They don't, of course, "make perfect sense of the psychophysical nexus." Nothing can do that—"make perfect sense." But they certainly dispel the aura of eternal mystery.

This last point blocks one closing move, the move of suggesting that these sorts of middle-level concepts aren't the right ones, since if they were, they would make all the links perfectly intelligible. Besides begging the question, this sort of response rests once again on the impossible ideal of perfect intelligibility. We are asked to think that the right concepts, whatever they are, will provide perfect intelligibility. That is the conjurer's trick. Don't believe it.

So McGinn is right that consciousness has a hidden structure. But he fails to provide a convincing argument for thinking that this hidden structure is noumenal. The first argument fails primarily because it places impossible demands, demands for perfect intelligibility, on relations drawn between the physical, psychological, and phenomenological levels. The second argument fails for this same reason, as well as for additional reasons. The argument is that explaining consciousness requires concepts that are neither physical nor phenomenological and that cannot be found because they lie beyond our capacities to abstract from either the physical or the phenomenological. But such concepts abound in cognitive psychology, cognitive science, and cognitive neuroscience. Furthermore, the argument is inherently unstable from its first step to its last. This is because it tries to convince us that there is unknowable hidden structure by convincing us that there is reason to believe in knowable hidden structure. This instability causes the argument to implode by the time the empirical example of blindsight is discussed. By that point there is no credible argument left from which to step onto the high ground from which one can claim simultaneously to see a mystery and to see that it will eternally elude us. The problem of consciousness is very, very hard. But no naturalist needs to think it is terminally hard. New mysterianism, or noumenal naturalism, is a coherent view, but the arguments offered so far on its behalf are, despite being clever, unconvincing. It will be better to get on with the project of seeing how far we can make the problem of consciousness yield. Only the future history of the science of the mind knows how far this will be. But there will be no future to the science of the mind at all if we are lulled into not trying to understand mind, because we can allegedly never plumb its depths.

Chapter 7

Conscious Inessentialism and the Epiphenomenalist Suspicion

Consciousness did not have to evolve. It is conceivable that evolutionary processes could have worked to build creatures as efficient and intelligent as we are, even more efficient and intelligent, without those creatures being subjects of experience. Consciousness is not essential to highly evolved intelligent life. This claim is true and important. However, from the fact that consciousness is inessential to highly evolved intelligent life, it does not follow that it is inessential to our particular type of intelligent life.

Conscious inessentialism is the view that for any intelligent activity *i* performed in any cognitive domain *d*, even if *we* do *i* consciously, *i* can in principle be done nonconsciously. Conscious inessentialism does not follow from the true claim about the possibility of intelligent life absent consciousness. It does not follow because there are certain intelligent activities that would not be the intelligent activities they are if they were not done consciously. Consciousness is partly constitutive of these intelligent activities. Take an action like lying. Telling a lie essentially involves a conscious intention to mislead. The intelligent activity called "misleading" could be done by a well-programmed robot. But misleading is not lying. Lying is an intelligent activity that requires consciousness. Not all our intelligent actions essentially involve consciousness, but many do—telling the truth, lying, thinking in words, and self-reflection come to mind as examples. The same point holds on the input side. Greeting a friend requires that one consciously perceives a particular human individual as that friend. Prosopagnosiacs don't see faces as faces and thus don't visually recognize friends as friends. When a prosopagnosiac greets a friend, it is because he has recognized that individual as a friend through a nonvisual modality, usually hearing.

One might agree that consciousness enters essentially into the characterization of some kinds of perception and action but still wonder whether consciousness does any work in these cases where it is partly constitutive of the intelligent activity in question. So what that some perception is conscious or that some types of actions are the actions they are only if done consciously. Perhaps the intelligent kernel involved in conscious perception and conscious action can occur without consciousness. Or to put the point differently, consciousness might be essential to how we characterize and individuate the exercise of certain human capacities without playing any interesting causal role in the exercise of these very capacities. Having an appendix is an essential property of *Homo sapiens*. We cannot give a true and complete characterization of human anatomy without bringing in the appendix. But the appendix plays no functional, causal role in human life (it can, however, play a dysfunctional role). Perhaps conscious inessentialism can be defeated as a claim about how intelligent mental activity must be described. But its falsehood is compatible with the truth of a different claim, the claim that consciousness lacks causal power.

2   The Epiphenomenalist Suspicion

The thesis of conscious inessentialism is not the only source of trouble. There is also the epiphenomenalist suspicion, the suspicion that although consciousness exists and enters into the characterization of some human actions, it plays a relatively inconsequential role in mental life, akin to the ineffectual, often misled, and ever belatedly informed public-relations officer for a large organization. The analogy with the public-relations officer is significant. It suggests that consciousness is not the proverbial ghost in the machine but rather a dispensable cog in the machine.

I take the epiphenomenalist suspicion seriously. Consciousness might be essential to our natures without being centrally involved in the causal fray. I have suggested at several points that we take seriously the idea that conscious experience involves neuronal groups locking into synchronous or semisynchronous oscillatory patterns in the 40-hertz range (Crick and Koch 1990). Seeing a red square involves a 40-hertz lock on the spiking patterns in the visual areas subserving color and shape detection. There may be no place where the patterns meet up, marry, and bind. Getting the right neuronal groups into synchrony and keeping them in synchrony for a short time may be sufficient for the experience.

This hypothesis, attractive as it may be, is fully compatible with epiphenomenalism. Consider this analogy. Seeing a red square is to the brain as the whistling pot is to the water boiling within it. Immediately after the brain detects a red square and gets on with whatever it intends to do with the information that a red square is there, it goes into this funny oscillatory state that persists for a few seconds and subserves the experience of seeing a red square. This oscillatory pattern does nothing useful. It is so smooth and predictable that the brain is able more or less to ignore it. Eventually it disappears into outer space. Likewise, immediately after the water starts boiling, the pot whistles. The whistling is a set of sound waves caused by the boiling. The whistling indicates that boiling is taking place, but it has no (interesting) effect on the boiling. When the boiling stops, the whistling rapidly, but not simultaneously, dissipates. The sound waves that constitute the whistling spread into sounds of silence.

The likening of consciousness to escaping steam—both are real, but both are relatively inconsequential—is an epiphenomenalist favorite. William James (1890, 135) quotes Thomas Huxley's startling version of epiphenomenalism:

> The consciousness of brutes would appear to be related to the mechanism of their body simply as a collateral product of its working, and to be completely without any power of modifying that working, as the steam-whistle which accompanies the work of a locomotive engine is without influence upon its machinery. Their volition, if they have any, is an emotion indicative of physical changes, not a cause of such changes.... The soul stands to the body as the bell of a clock to the works, and consciousness answers to the sound which the bell gives out when it is struck.... To the best of my judgment, the argumentation which applies to brutes holds equally good of men.... We are conscious automata.

James aptly refers to the epiphenomenalist position as the "inert spectator" view of the mind or the "conscious automaton" theory. The steam whistle is a physical effect of the work of the steam engine. Furthermore, it has physical effects. It adds moisture to the surrounding air and sound waves escape. But these effects are minor and of no consequence as far as the subsequent states of the steam engine go. Epiphenomenalism is the thesis that conscious experience has the same incidental relation to the whole person as the steam whistle has to the locomotive engine. To be sure, consciousness, like the whistle, makes itself noticed. But being noticeable, or even noisy, are different from being effectively involved in the real action. Or, so the epiphenomenalist suggests.

To James, as to most contemporary philosophers, psychologists, and laypersons, such a view seems preposterous. Consciousness is more like the steam engine that powers the locomotive and produces the steam than like the quaint but terminal toot. James calls epiphenomenalism an "unwarrantable impertinence." Against the epiphenomenalist he musters the commonsense evidence that we often bring about what we in fact mentally intend. He then joins this evidence to evolutionary theory, arguing that it is "inconceivable that consciousness should have nothing to do with a business [to] which it so faithfully attends." According to James, Darwin taught us that species-specific characteristics are selected for because they confer some survival advantage on the organisms that possess them. But consciousness cannot enhance an individual's survival advantage "without being in some way efficacious and influencing the course of his bodily history."

This sort of argument is now viewed with skepticism. Selection works over populations of genes. Species survive and proliferate when their members possess genes that lead to differential reproductive success. To be sure, well-adapted organisms make it. But being well adapted is not the same as being optimally adapted. Furthermore, selection isn't fussy about every single trait. Traits that are neutral and even some that marginally reduce reproductive success can sneak in as free riders in satisfactorily designed species (Gould and Lewontin 1979). The color of blood is widely thought to be an example of a trait that was not directly selected for, as is the structure of the human chin.

Could consciousness, despite its faithful attention to the life of the organism that houses it, be more like the nosey housekeeper who keeps an overzealous eye on the goings-on in the mansion and gossips about those goings-on to outsiders than like the master of the mansion who really runs the show? Maybe. Neo-Darwinian theory does not rule the possibility out of court. We need some arguments against epiphenomenalism.

3   Some Arguments from Design

It is possible, even on the neo-Darwinian picture I have recommended, that consciousness does little work, or at least that it does less work than we standardly give it credit for. To be sure, our species would not have survived if we had not been quick to respond to harmful stimuli. The natural temptation, therefore, is to think that conscious sensitivity to painful and dangerous things was directly selected for. The trouble with this sort of facile adaptationism is that some species that have survived much longer than we have detect when danger lurks but are conscious of nothing. Scallops, for example, get out of the way of potential predators without experiencing them as such, and when they fail to do so, they get eaten alive, quite possibly without experiencing pain.

It is possible that we survived as a species because we were unconsciously responsive (informationally sensitive) to harmful and useful stimuli, for example, the appearance of a predator or a mate. And it is possible that the capacities to *experience* fear and lust, pleasure and pain simply came on board as free riders at some later time and play no important psychological role even now, save whatever role is played by letting ourselves and others know how we feel. The standard view is this:

(1)   hot stimulus on hand ⟶ feeling of pain ⟶ withdrawal of hand

The epiphenomenalist suggests that the real picture is this:

feeling of pain

(2)   Hot stimulus on hand

withdrawal of hand

I will not try to allay all the fears that motivate the epiphenomenalist suspicion. In part, this is because I think that the causal role of consciousness has been overrated, and thus that the suspicion is healthy to a degree. Furthermore, the epiphenomenalist suspicion is extraordinarily hard to dispel. Take the case of pain. The usual hypothesis is that the experience of pain plays a functional role mediating a response to a potentially harmful stimulus. The epiphenomenalist hypothesis is that the experience of pain is just a very noticeable added attraction of the causal fray—all sparkle, glitter, and noise—that in fact does no useful work. One might think that the first hypothesis easily defeats the second, since individuals who are otherwise normal but who lack pain receptors on their skin are in constant danger of being scalded, of hemorrhaging, of losing fingers, limbs, and life. It can be argued, however, that these people are dysfunctional not because they do not experience pain but because they lack the receptors that, besides getting people to remove their hands, etc., from harmful objects, also typically give rise to feelings of a certain sort. The idea that conscious experiences are all sparkle, glitter, and noise is not crazy. I think it is false, but it is not *obviously* false.

The epiphenomenalist suspicion, even if untenable in its extreme form, is a useful corrective to views that overstate the role of consciousness in mental life. It is only in the last century that the idea that consciousness is definitive of the mental has yielded. Even if we no longer believe that consciousness is involved in all mental activity, we tend to think that when it is involved, it is centrally involved. Consciousness itself impels us to overestimate its causal role in mental life. That said, I want to allay worries about epiphenomenalism somewhat.

One credible way to argue for the claim that some trait has been directly selected for because of its adaptive value is to show that it occurs in different species that are not closely related. The force of this sort of argument comes from the idea that "really useful features tend to be re-invented by evolution. Photoreceptors have been independently invented over 40 times in various invertebrate lineages: partway out a branch on the tree of species, photoreception will appear and persist. Powered flight was invented at least three times after the insects did it: by the flying dinosaurs, by the bats, and by the birds (not to mention all the jumping spiders, gliding mammals, 'flying' fish, even a snake that glides between tropical treetops)" (Calvin 1991, 30). If one believes that there is something it is like to be a snake, a salamander, a fish, a bird, a bat, a dolphin, and that these creatures lie in different lineages from *Homo sapiens*, then there is some gain to the idea that endowing subjective consciousness is a matter of good evolutionary design.

Even if one is unwilling to impute consciousness to creatures other than *Homo sapiens* or thinks that the bloodlines of all these creatures have a single common source, there is still an opening based on properties of our own species design. Subjective consciousness is well connected to certain mental processors. This is why one can have a isolated deficit in subjective consciousness. For example, one can be blind or color blind or deaf or unable to recognize faces, and so on (you name a possible defect of consciousness and it seems to exist; see Shallice 1988).

This provides the basis for the following argument from design. Just as frequent appearance of a trait in many different species is evidence that the trait is a good solution to certain engineering problems faced again and again by Nature, so too the fact that a trait or capacity has been hooked onto many distinct mental systems in one species is evidence that the trait or capacity serves a purpose.

Memory is functional. One view is that we have one general-purpose memory system that stores information from a variety of processors. Another view is that there are multiple memory systems, with each memory system suited for remembering events processed by the system, the sensory modality, to which it is attached. Like memory, consciousness is depicted in two main ways by mind scientists. Often consciousness is portrayed as a single integrative, domain-nonspecific "faculty" that receives input from all the sensory modules and from the declarative memory system (the system that retains propositional information about facts and events). At other times, consciousness is viewed as the name for all the different types of awareness attached, as it were, to each distinct sensory module and to the declarative memory system. In the first case, Nature had to invent the faculty and then work at wiring it to the sensory modules and to memory. In the second case, Nature had to do for consciousness what it did for wings and photoreceptors. It invented consciousness time and again for many distinct modules. In either case, consciousness has been hooked onto many distinct mental systems. Furthermore, the hook-ups are not random. Most of what goes on in our head is consciously inaccessible. What is consciously accessible is primarily just what we have the most need to know about: conditions in the sensory environment, and past facts, and events. This gives some support to the idea that our conscious capacities were selected for because of their adaptive value. The argument is not decisive, but it has some credibility and provides some argumentative leverage against the suspicious epiphenomenalist.

A different sort of argument from design comes less from evolutionary considerations than from consideration of certain phenomenological features of consciousness and the types of neural structures that might subserve these phenomenological features. Coordinating the phenomenological and neural considerations helps us see that the brain, in being designed to display conscious states, is also designed in a way that quite possibly endows these states with a functional role. What are the phenomenological features I have in mind? Consciousness is multimodal, involving the discrimination of many different types of states, things, and events, and it is loud and noisy. It broadcasts what it knows. In the first instance, these broadcasts are to the system itself, for one's self only. What consciousness knows or represents at any given time often consists of disparate kinds of information. I am now aware of the computer on which I am writing, I hear its buzz, I hear music in the background, I smell and taste my coffee, and I see the trees in autumn colors outside my window. What the conscious mind knows is presented in "a connected and orderly flow ... which represents the myriad connections within the represented world. If we consider what sort of pattern of brain activity would be required as the neural substrate for such representations and their interactions, it would seem that of necessity it would also have to satisfy the conditions of broadcasting information. Conscious phenomenal representations because of their highly integrated and multimodal content require rich associative networks of activation as their basis" (Van Gulick, in press b).

The epiphenomenalist thinks that the noisy broadcasts of consciousness are like the noisy work of the printer that produces the text already written and filed away in the computer. The alternative is that broadcasting is internal to the ongoing activity of the brain. Since many conscious states are global in the sense that they involve synthesis of many different types of contents, the most plausible inference is that these states involve interpenetrating and/or synchronous processing in many different neural areas (Smolensky 1988). If that is right, then the broadcasts are realized in the system and available to it as it modifies, coordinates, and plans its next moves (Baars 1988). To be sure, we broadcast what we know to the outside when we say what is on our mind. Furthermore, speaking is always conscious (Rosenthal 1990). But we are conscious when we do not emit external broadcasts. The suspicious epiphenomenalist must explain how such consciousness can be realized in myriad brain structures without its content also being available to the brain structures it interacts with for subsequent information processing. The brain hardly seems like a system that doesn't listen to itself.

4   *An Experiment in Epiphenomenalism*

Whether epiphenomenalism is true is ultimately an empirical question, although it is notoriously hard to think of decisive tests for or against it. In regard to the epiphenomenalist suspicion, consider this widely discussed experiment of Benjamin Libet (1985). Libet's experiment has been thought by some to prove dualism and by others to secure the case for materialism. I am interested in it only as it relates to the issue of epiphenomenalism. The experiment works as follows: First, subjects are hooked up to electroencephalographs, which measure "the readiness potential" in the cortical area thought to subserve hand movement, and to electromyographs, which measure onset of activity in the hand muscles. Second, subjects are told to spontaneously flex their right hand whenever they feel like it. They are also told "to pay close introspective attention to the instant of the onset of the urge, desire, or decision to perform each such act and to the correlated position of a revolving spot on a clock face (indicating 'clock time'). The subject is also instructed to allow such acts to arise 'spontaneously,' without deliberately planning or paying attention to the 'prospect' of acting in advance" (Libet 1985, 530).

The findings were these: First, in cases where subjects experience no preplanning, the consciousness of an intention to flex occurs about 350 milliseconds after the onset of the readiness potential and about 200 milliseconds before muscle activation. Second, in cases where the subjects reported a feeling of preplanning, of getting ready to spontaneously flex a few seconds before they flexed, the subjects still were able to distinguish this preplanning stage from the immediately following urge to flex. The finding that the readiness potential precedes conscious intention or urge, which precedes muscle movement, was confirmed. Libet writes, "Onsets of RP regularly begin at least several hundred ms before reported times for awareness of any intention to act in the case of acts performed ad lib. It would appear, therefore, that some neuronal activity associated with the eventual performance of the act occurs before any (recallable) conscious initiation or intervention.... This leads to the conclusion that cerebral initiation of the kind studied ... can and does usually begin *unconsciously*" (1985, 536). Libet asks, "If the brain can initiate a voluntary act before the appearance of conscious intention, that is, if the initiation of the specific performance of the act is by unconscious processes, is there any role for conscious function?" He answers, "Conscious control can be exerted before the final motor outflow to select or control volitional outcome. The volitional process, initiated unconsciously, can either be consciously permitted to proceed to consummation in the motor act or be consciously 'vetoed'" (1985, 536–537).

Libet argues that so long as there is veto power, conscious triggering would be redundant. That is, the mind allows the action to proceed to consummation unless it has reason to stop it. So long as it can stop a motor movement before it occurs, it does not need to actively trigger it.

This experiment is interesting, but one wonders why it generates such surprise and why it is taken by many to be so deflationary, so bad for consciousness. In the first place, the strong evidence that subjects can consciously veto flexion in the 200 ms between the urge or intention to flex and the response indicates that consciousness can play an important functional role in this particular motor routine. So consciousness is hardly shown to be epiphenomenal by this experiment. Second, it is hard to see what causes surprise at the fact that brain processes precede conscious experience, unless it is, as I suspect, a lurking Cartesian intuition that in voluntary action our conscious intentions are prime movers, themselves unmoved (except possibly by prior intentions).

From a naturalistic perspective, this intuition, familiar as it is, gives rise to a set of deep illusions to be avoided at all costs. According to the naturalist, only some neural activity is conscious. All conscious processes occur in complex causal networks in which they both supervene on certain neural processes and are caused by and cause other mental processes (also supervenient on the neural), some of which are conscious but most of which are not. It would be completely unexpected if all the causal anteced-ents of conscious mental processes were themselves conscious. In other words, conscious mental processes emerge out of the neural processes that give rise to them. It would be absurd to expect these emergent conscious neural processes to precede the neural processes they arise from. (See the responses of Wood [1985] and Van Gulick [1985] to Libet's target article 1985 for related points.)

Analogously, frozen water supervenes on collections of water mole-cules whose mean molecular kinetic energy has slowed to 32 degrees Fahrenheit. Freezing is caused by water reaching that temperature. But getting to that temperature involves a process of cooling, and it would be absurd to expect the frozen water to antedate the process that brings it about.

In addition to misunderstanding the nature of emergent properties, the picture of the mind as conscious of all that goes on in it falls prey to a further difficulty. It involves a very inefficient design. The "buzzing confu-sion" that James (probably incorrectly) thought constituted the experiential world of the infant would be our lot for life if we were aware of everything happening in our nervous system!

Third, there is a problem with the interpretation of the experiment. The experiment and most of the discussion about it ask us to picture the experiment this way (Libet 1985 and accompanying commentary):

(3)   Readiness potential (500 ms) $\longrightarrow$
conscious awareness of urge to flex (200 ms) $\longrightarrow$ flexion

The trouble with this way of conceptualizing things is that it leaves out of view the fact that the subjects are first asked *to make a conscious effort* to let flexion occur spontaneously. To do so, the subjects have to load from conscious awareness an instruction to perform a certain complex task. Perhaps the instruction could be given subliminally to comatose patients or to normal persons in deep sleep. The fact is that in the actual experiment the instructions are given to fully conscious individuals who agree to comply with the experimental instructions and who make an effort to do so. How we load such instructions and get ourselves to do such things is completely closed off to introspection (to mine, anyway). But the power of complex intentions or plans to be carried out once the initial steps have been taken is made vivid in cases where individuals suffer petit mal seizures while driving to some destination and then, while unconscious, complete the drive to that destination! Once they have reached the destination, they just stop, unless they come out of the seizure-induced sleeplike state.

It is a matter of utmost importance that Libet's experiment begins with a discussion of the task and the conscious agreement on the part of the subject to perform as instructed. The right picture, then, is this:

(4)   Conscious awareness of instructions $\longrightarrow$
conscious self-instruction to comply (minutes later) $\longrightarrow$
readiness potential (500 ms) $\longrightarrow$
conscious awareness of urge to flex (200 ms) $\longrightarrow$ flexion

The upshot is that conscious processes are not epiphenomenal, even on (3), the narrow description of the experimental situation. Conscious processes serve as the middle link in a three-term chain, and they have the power to inhibit (or veto) the motor response being readied, if the agent so desires. It may be that occurrence of the awareness of the urge to flex 200 ms before flexion is not part of the cause of flexion in the case where flexion is allowed to go forward. But the fact that flexion can be stopped by a conscious veto strongly suggests that awareness of the impending flexion plays the role of broadcasting information about the system that the system can then use to change its course. On (4), the wide description, conscious processes appear at two different stages: first, when instructions are given and the effort to comply is made; second, when the instructions loaded at the first step are actually carried out.

I conclude that Libet's results, far from offering solace to the suspicious epiphenomenalist, are precisely the sort of results one would expect if one believes that conscious processes are subserved by nonconscious neural activity, and that conscious processes play variable but significant causal roles at various points in different cognitive domains.

5   *Teleological Functionalism, Epiphenomenalism, and Defects of Consciousness*

Teleological functionalism conceives of most mental capacities, both conscious and unconscious, as typically playing some adaptive role for the systems that have them (Lycan 1981, 1987; Van Gulick 1988, 1990). The words 'most' and 'typically' are important. The biological functions of objectless moods, especially bad ones, are fairly obscure. Perhaps they never had any. It is easier to tell a story about the emergence of emotions that gives them a role in enhancing fitness. This is compatible with certain emotional displays being less functional now than they were originally. Further, much of what we are conscious of is culturally transmitted. The learning capacities that subserve the acquisition of knowledge are clearly adaptive. But the details of what we learn and how we use the information we acquire, e.g., about how to make weapons, may or may not be functional in the short or long run. Finally, many of our conscious capacities, for example, to do arithmetic or geometry, were probably not directly selected for. They are the fortuitous outgrowths of combining our linguistic capacities and our capacities for abstraction with our abilities to individuate objects, estimate quantities, and display spatial savvy in manipulating objects and moving about the world.

In any case, there is evidence from both normal individuals and individuals with certain defects of consciousness that this hypothesis that consciousness has a function, that it generally serves a purpose, is true. Max Velmans (in press) argues for epiphenomenalism by arguing that there are cases in which choice, memory, learning, and novel responses occur without consciousness. But the fact that consciousness is not necessary for certain capacities to be exercised does not remotely imply that it serves no function when it is involved. There is ample evidence that consciousness facilitates performance on many activities, despite being not absolutely necessary for these activities (see Van Gulick, in press b, for an effective response to Velmans).

There are two main ways that information gets into our head and becomes available for reasoning, action guidance, and reporting. First, there are episodes of experiential sensitivity. I learned about the governmental system of checks and balances in third grade. The nun who taught and tested me on this made me vividly aware of how the system works. Since then I have often used that information in reasoning, acting (e.g., voting), and reporting, but usually only as implicit background. Second, there are cases of subliminal or implicit learning. In these cases, knowledge is acquired, but normal phenomenal awareness is prevented or for some other reason fails to occur (Schacter 1989, 359). The latter sort of cases require the postulation of modes of knowledge acquisition that do not require phenomenal consciousness. We really do gain information unaware.

It is worth emphasizing that many experiments indicate that knowledge *acquired* without awareness is accessed and deployed somewhat less well than knowledge acquired with awareness (Dixon 1987, 752–754; Schacter 1989, 359). One explanation is that phenomenal awareness involves attention, and attention secures better treatment by the keepers of the gates of memory.

Even if some knowledge can be acquired without awareness, it remains an open question as to how much is acquired without awareness and how well it can be acquired without awareness. It is useful to distinguish between the role of phenomenal awareness in acquiring knowledge and in deploying that knowledge. There is a sense in which well-honed activities, like the tennis stroke of a proficient player, are automatic. But it is important to watch the slide from automatic to unconscious. Activities, such as sports play by proficient players, driving, eating, and the like, are not performed unconsciously, as is sometimes suggested. It is a commonplace that excellent athletes were once coached. While being coached, they were phenomenally aware of the instructions they received, as well as the visual trajectory of the ball, the feel of the racquet, and so on. Once the body learns to do what has been described and subtle adjustments are made on the basis of experience, the instructions appropriately recede into the cognitive background (if they didn't recede from occurrent consciousness, they would actually interfere with performance). Reaching a stage of proficiency in tennis involves continuous phenomenologically robust experience of the ball's trajectory, of the visual surround, of the racquet's feel, and so on. The true idea that one eventually goes on "automatic pilot" can give rise to the mistaken thought that one consciously disassociates oneself from the play. The mistaken thought arises from the fact that the experiences are eventually mostly sensory and tactile-kinaesthetic, not verbal or thoughtlike.

One could try gaining all the information a good coach gives via techniques of subliminal perception. But there is good reason to think that to the extent that consciousness is kept out of the learning environment, acquisition and performance will suffer somewhat, although it is notoriously difficult to control consciousness in subjects who are not brain damaged, especially if the task is something like listening to tennis tapes while asleep. Let me and twin me receive instruction from the same coach, twin me subliminally, me in the normal way, and let us both practice the same amount. Bet on me in the match. If learning many tasks is superior when there is conscious loading of information and instruction about how to perform the task, relative to when the information and instructions are given subliminally, then the case for a functional role for consciousness scores some points.

There are other results relevant to the function of consciousness that come from persons with brain damage. The neurologically impaired individuals I now consider have inner lives, but their inner lives differ from those of normal persons in a variety of ways. These differences in conscious mental life cause certain functional deficits, and permit certain inferences about the role of consciousness in normal persons. Consider the following cases.

First, there are the blindsighted persons I have mentioned several times. Blindsighted persons have damage to the striate cortex (area V1) and therefore claim not to see objects in certain portions of the visual field, usually on one side. The evidence indicates that although such individuals are consciously insensitive to stimuli in the blind field, they are informationally sensitive to these stimuli. This shows up in a variety of ways. If blindsighted persons hear an ambiguous word (for example, 'bank' or 'palm') and have been primed in the blind field with another word relevant to the interpretation of the heard word ('money'/'river' or 'hand'/'tree'), they favor the interpretation tied to the word shown in the blind field. Blindsighted persons do far less well at this task than sighted people, but their responses are better than the chance level one would expect with the truly blind.

Furthermore, if a blindsighted individual is asked to say what object is on her blind side, she says she does not know. But if told to reach for what is there "preparatory adjustments of the wrist, fingers, and arm are suited much better than chance to the shape, orientation, size, location, and distance of the objects" (Marcel 1988, 136).

The evidence of semantic disambiguation and preparatory hand movements indicates that blindsighted persons are informationally sensitive to things they are not conscious of. Their being in certain unconscious intentional states—unconsciously knowing that there is a glass of water rather than a ball to their right or knowing that 'money' was flashed in the blind field—best explains their better than chance performance.

The fact remains that blindsighted persons claim to know nothing about the goings-on in their blindfield. They are wrong in this. But we have to press them to get them to show what they know. The case is altogether different with normal persons, and this difference is crucial from a functional point of view. Conscious awareness of a word that favors a particular interpretation, e.g., *river* bank over money *bank*, leads to better performance on disambiguation tasks than does mere informational sensitivity to the helpful clue. Conscious awareness of a water fountain to my right will lead me to drink from it if I am thirsty. But the thirsty blindsighted person will make no move toward the fountain unless pressed to do so. The inference to the best explanation is that conscious awareness of the environment facilitates semantic comprehension and adaptive motor actions in creatures like us.

In his brief on behalf of epiphenomenalism, Velmans (in press) cites impressive performance rates of blindsighted persons in tasks involving guessing whether Xs or Os are appearing in the blindfield. As impressive as rates of 27 out of 30 are for blindsighted persons, they are not impressive compared to normal subjects, who will never make mistakes detecting Xs or Os.

Persons with memory deficits provide a different sort of example. Sadly, amnesiacs are commonplace. Some have a good grasp of their life before some time but lack the capacity to remember new things. Victims of Korsakoff's syndrome, advanced Alzheimer patients, and persons who have suffered certain kinds of traumatic brain injury cannot remember anything from one second to the next. Often people who can't remember what has happened to them or what they did in the near or distant past still comprehend language, can speak, and have no trouble with routinized motor tasks, such as walking, reaching successfully for things, cooking a meal, and using bathroom facilities.

Depending on the nature and extent of the amnesia, amnesiacs are functionally impaired in different ways. One well-studied amnesiac, H.M., has acquired certain skills. H.M. can mirror read, and he knows how to do the Tower of Hanoi puzzle. However, H.M. is not aware that he knows how to do the Tower of Hanoi puzzle. Each time the puzzle is brought to him, he claims never to have seen it before. But his performance has improved over the years from that of a normal beginner to that of a fairly proficient player. Each time H.M. does the puzzle, his performance starts close to the level he previously reached. He does not begin at the point of someone his age who truly does not know how to do the puzzle. H.M. is epistemically impaired with respect to the Tower of Hanoi puzzle but less so than a patient who not only said he never saw the puzzle before but also always returned to a beginner's performance level. Such a patient would be both experientially insensitive and informationally insensitive. He might work on the Tower of Hanoi puzzle, but the information about how to do it would not sink in or it would not stick. In H.M.'s case the knowledge sinks in and sticks. But he believes certain falsehoods, namely, that he has never seen the puzzle before and that he has no idea of how to do it. H.M.'s epistemic impairment involves an inability to consciously remember certain things.

H.M.'s problems are more than epistemic, of course. He belongs to a class of persons who have identity disorders. There are identity disorders (such as multiple personality disorder) that, as best as we can now determine, have nothing directly to do with neurological deficits. But I will concentrate here on identity disorders linked to neurologically based amnesia, since these are best suited to displaying the multifarious types and roles of subjective consciousness. Cases of severe loss of autobiographical memory involve incapacities to constitute and reconstitute one's sense of identity, of who one is, of where one is coming from and where one is going. John Locke, in the second edition of his *An Essay Concerning Human Understanding* (1694), most famously linked the first-person sense of identity with conscious memory: "As far as this consciousness can be extended backwards to any past action or thought, so far reaches the identity of that person." From a subjective point of view, I am who I remember myself being.

In *The Man with the Shattered World: The History of a Brain Wound* (1972), A. R. Luria, the great Russian neuropsychologist, tells the story of Zazetsky, a soldier who suffered massive damage to the left occipito-parietal region of his brain. Subsequent to being shot, Zazetsky lived in a visually chaotic world, the right side of both his body and the external world were not there for him. He suffered profound incapacities to understand and produce language, and he had lost his memory. Most of his past was a blank.

Zazetsky eventually showed clear evidence of possessing an enormous amount of information about his own past. His first problem was acessing the information about himself and his life. He had to figure out a way to express the information he had inside himself so that he himself could see it again. His second problem was to consciously reappropriate this information, to recover it as the right description of his self. Zazetsky succeeded in many respects at solving the first problem. But the second remained in large measure intractable. That is, despite his possession of a great deal of information about his life and success at experiencing certain "memories *as memories*" at the moment of recollection (Marcel 1988, 125), Zazetsky's brain damage prevented him from drawing this information together into an experientially robust sense of his self. This inability appears in turn to have been at the root of his difficulty in carrying out a normal life plan after his tragic injury.

There are cases in which the loss of autobiographical memory involves the complete destruction or erasure of all the relevant information. There is nothing there—no permanent file, no well-honed set of distributed neural activity—to gain access to or to reactivate. The memories constitutive of one's past self and deeds are gone, never to return. Zazetsky's case, like H.M.'s on the Tower of Hanoi puzzle, was not like this. The information was still in there, and Zazetsky each day for almost three decades tried to get it out and thereby regain his identity.

How did he do this? Well, especially in the early stages, conscious effort was to no avail. The breakthrough came when Zazetsky made a fortuitous discovery. Luria writes,

A discovery he made one day proved to be the turning point: writing could be very simple. At first he proceeded just as little children do when they first learn to write—he had tried to visualize each letter in order to form it. Yet he had been writing for almost twenty years and as such did not need to employ the same methods as a child, to think about each letter and consider what strokes to use. For adults, writing is an automatic skill, a series of built-in movements, which I call "kinetic melodies."   (1972, 72)

The next step was to convince Zazetsky to let his writing flow automatically, to let the "kinetic melodies" emerge, not worrying about what he was writing or whether it made sense. In fact, it did make sense, and gradually over the course of twenty-five years, Zazetsky produced what Luria called an "archeological study of his memory."

Once the wound had healed, Zazetsky was able to remember his childhood fairly well. But the years after that were not there for him. As Zazetsky wrote automatically but with extreme difficulty, a life began to appear on paper. Zazetsky was able to recognize certain things he wrote as true of himself, and he was able with extreme effort to order the narrative into something approximating its right temporal sequence. The saddest irony is that although each piece of Zazetsky's autobiography was consciously reappropriated by him each time he hit upon a veridical memory in writing, he himself was never able to fully reappropriate, to keep in clear and continuous view, to live with, the self he reconstructed in the three thousand pages he wrote. His memory impairment was deep and abiding. Furthermore, many grammatical constructions, including many of those he himself was able to produce on paper, were exceedingly hard for him to decipher, and even harder to keep in mind over time. Tragically, Zazetsky, to some significant degree, was kept from regaining himself and from reconstituting himself in the first-person way that Locke thought was necessary if one is to have an identity.

Cases like Zazetsky's provide further evidence for functional deficits that are deficits of consciousness in some important respects and are rooted in underlying neurological problems. Zazetsky is at loose ends, he feels aimless, and his life lacks meaning. He cannot find his self. Much of the information about his self is inside Zazetsky. Indeed, he has externalized many of the most salient parts of his self in his monumental autobiography. He is simply unable to consciously reappropriate the whole story and own it. He has problems of identity and meaning, and these are rooted in problems of self-consciousness.

Zazetsky's quest to reconstruct and reappropriate his self—to locate an identity constituted by a particular history, a direction, and a set of identity-conferring likes, dislikes, roles, and commitments—is a universal one. Formulating complex intentions and life plans and carrying them out require the capacity to hold in subjective consciousness certain salient aspects (but obviously not every aspect) of one's past, character, and plans. Zazetsky can access information about all these things. What he cannot do is to hold this information in subjective view and, with this sense of where he is coming from and where he is going, move forward in living his life.

Zazetsky's tragedy consists in part in the fact that he knows what is wrong. His knowledge of his disability and his intact frontal lobes enable him to formulate an unambiguous and straightforward plan. He will fight on and try to regain his self, but he will not succeed, because the damage he has suffered undermines his abilities to coordinate impressions and memories from different sensory modalities, to tap memory, to hold onto his memories as memories, and to deploy the linguistic system in reliable ways. Zazetsky's ability to hold himself and his experience together in a mindful way is a casualty to the shrapnel that has indifferently slashed the neuronal connections in the posterior occipitoparietal regions of his left cerebral hemisphere. Zazetsky's conscious capacities are (partly) maimed. His dysfunction is rooted in certain defects of consciousness.

6   Blocking Teleological Functionalism

For several years now I have been especially fond of arguments of the sort just produced as ways of dispelling the epiphenomenalist suspicion. There are all sorts of cases of neurological deficits linked with deficits in subjective consciousness, and in many of these cases the incapacitation of subjective consciousness seems to explain some further incapacity. Zazetsky can't get on with his life because, although he can in some sense reconstruct who he is, he cannot hold that image firmly in view and move on as *that* person. Blindsighted patients never initiate activity toward the blindfield because they lack subjective awareness of things in that field. Prosopagnosiacs don't consciously recognize familiar faces. Thus they don't rush to greet long-lost friends, even though their hearts go pitter-patter when they see them (Pascal was right: the heart often knows what the mind does not).

Recently Ned Block (1991) has caused me to worry about the form of the argument. Although Block thinks that epiphenomenalism is probably false, he does not think standard arguments based on cases like blindsight show it to be false. Block's argument goes like this:

> 1. We can distinguish between two kinds of consciousness: phenomenal, what-it-is-like, consciousness, (consciousness$_p$), and access consciousness (consciousness$_a$). Access consciousness "has to do with information flow not qualia. The idea is that some—but not all—of the information that gets into our heads becomes (1) in Stich's (1978)

sense 'inferentially promiscuous', i.e., easily available as premise in reasoning, and (2) available for guiding action and (3) available for reporting."

2. A person who is knocked unconscious by a blow to the head is not conscious$_a$, but if she is seeing stars or dreaming, she is conscious$_p$. Consciousness$_a$ without consciousness$_p$ is also conceptually possible, although there may be no actual cases of it. "However when people talk about robots being unconscious zombies, they mean [they lack] consciousness$_p$ rather than consciousness$_a$.... The robot zombies are envisioned to have mechanisms of reasoning and guiding action and reporting that process information about the world."

3. The distinction between consciousness$_p$ and consciousness$_a$ is useful in describing such syndromes as prosopagnosia. "We can give descriptions of prosopagnosia in both phenomenal terms and cognitive or intentional terms (related to access), and both get at something important about the syndrome. Phenomenally speaking, we can say that prosopagnosiacs fail to have a feeling of familiarity when looking at familiar faces.... We can also characterize the syndrome cognitively: they don't know just from looking at people which ones are familiar, or who they are. They lack the usual visual access to information about which people are their friends and relations."

4. We can apply the distinction between consciousness$_p$ and consciousness$_a$ to expose a fallacy in the "reasoning to the effect that since a thirsty blindsighter doesn't reach for the glass of water in his blind field, we can reasonably suppose that it is the lack of consciousness that is to blame. And thus the function of consciousness lies in part in its role in initiating behavior."

5. The problem is this: "If it is consciousness$_a$ we are talking about, this reasoning is trivially right. If the information that there is a glass of water in front of me is to be put together with the information that this water can be used to quench my thirst, so as to guide action, these items must be conscious$_a$. After all, being available for inference and guiding action are part of what makes information conscious$_a$.... And it is equally obvious that this reasoning *cannot* simply be *assumed* to apply to consciousness$_p$. True, the blindsight patient is not conscious$_p$ of the glass of water, but consciousness$_p$ of the glass of water would not help in initiating action unless it brought consciousness$_a$ of the glass with it. The blindsight patient has *neither* consciousness$_a$ nor consciousness$_p$ of the glass, whereas the normal person who sees the glass and drinks has *both* consciousness$_a$ and consciousness$_p$ of the glass. The obvious facts of the case tell us nothing about the relation between consciousness$_a$ of the glass and consciousness$_p$ of the glass, for example, whether one causes the other, and if so, which causes

which.... These points seem entirely obvious once one accepts the distinction between consciousness$_a$ and consciousness$_p$."

6. In sum, the argument for the causal efficacy of consciousness is an argument for the causal efficacy of consciousness$_p$. But cases such as blindsight do not show that consciousness$_p$ is causally efficacious. The sighted person has both consciousness$_p$ and consciousness$_a$, and the blindsighted person lacks both. It is entirely possible, therefore, that it is the lack of consciousness$_a$ that is at the root of the difference and that the lack of consciousness$_p$ is irrelevant.

Block's point is that arguments against epiphenomenalism fail to keep the two kinds of consciousness apart. Unless this is done, we won't be able to disentangle whether it is access consciousness or phenomenal consciousness (or neither or both) that accounts for the differences between sighted and blindsighted persons.

7   Phenomenal Access

My reply to Block's argument is based on the premise that we should not accept any sharp distinction between the two kinds of consciousness. This is not to deny that it is useful in cases such as prosopagnosia to distinguish between the feeling of the condition and the type of information not picked up because of the deficit. But from both a terminological point of view and from a point of view that tries to do justice to the relevant phenomena, we are better off with the distinction I have drawn between informational sensitivity, which involves access to information without phenomenal awareness, and experiential sensitivity, which involves both phenomenal feel and access to information, than we are with Block's distinction between the two kinds of consciousness. If I am right that the distinction is less credible than Block makes it out to be, then the points that "seem entirely obvious once one accepts the distinction between consciousness$_a$ and consciousness$_p$," will seem less obvious, and the arguments linking deficits in subjective awareness with action deficits will look less problematic than Block maintains.

According to my preferred distinction between experiential sensitivity and informational sensitivity, some states we go into have qualitative or phenomenal feel to them, and some labor in our minds without possessing such feel. Phenomenal feel necessarily involves access to whatever it is we feel. This access may be epistemically impoverished, as in the case of the prosopagnosiac or the case of Block's character who is seeing stars. But all cases of phenomenal awareness, even if the awareness has no propositional content, are cases in which the agent has access to information about what state he is in. If, for example, I am in a good mood, I am in a state that, strictly speaking, is not of or about anything. But I can report that I am in that state, it makes a difference to how I act, and so on. The prosopagnosiac may not be able to say that this person before him is his friend Jane, but he will have access to and be able to report on *whatever* is phenomenally available to him, for example, "There is a person in front of me." Phenomenal consciousness always involves access to whatever we are phenomenally aware of. We are experientially sensitive to what we are phenomenally aware of.

However, there are things to which we are informationally sensitive but not experientially sensitive. It happens that things we barely notice or do not notice at all sometimes have detectable impacts on thought and behavior. Knowledge without awareness is a well-known phenomenon. I think it best to think of knowledge without awareness as unconscious, period. But if one insists on Block's distinction, then knowledge without awareness is unconscious$_p$; it involves informational but not experiential sensitivity. Block thinks that knowledge without awareness is unconscious$_a$, but I don't see how Block can avoid construing knowledge without awareness as conscious$_a$. After all, such knowledge involves access to information, and this information plays a role in inference, reporting, and action. States that can be shown to play a significant cognitive role without making a phenomenal appearance should be conscious$_a$ on Block's view, unless he implicitly assumes that conscious$_a$ events must *also* be conscious$_p$.

Block wants implicit or subliminal learning, what I call informational sensitivity and contrast with experiential sensitivity, to be unconscious$_a$, not conscious$_a$. However, if we adopt Block's terminology, we are better off thinking of the blindsighted person as unconscious$_p$ but conscious$_a$, since he has some access to the information in his blind field. The same is true of the prosopagnosiac; remember, the prosopagnosiac's heart goes pitter-patter when his beloved appears. My next move is predictable. Since the blindsighted person is conscious$_a$ in the blindfield but unconscious$_p$, it is his lack of phenomenal access that explains the problem. Actually, the situation is more complicated than this. Strictly speaking, I should say something like this: The information the blindsighted person has may be degraded. This may be part of the reason that the information does not reach phenomenal awareness. Or it may be that the information is not degraded but simply untransmissible due to the nature of the lesion in V1. In either case the inference to the best explanation is that if the information were to become phenomenally conscious, performance would improve.

In effect, the case isn't one where because both consciousness$_p$ and consciousness$_a$ are lacking, and we can't tell which one causes the problem. Only consciousness$_p$ is clearly lacking; consciousness$_a$, in Block's sense, is not. That is, the most natural way to describe the case in Block's terminology is to say that the blindsighted person possesses zero subjective awareness and is therefore unconscious$_p$ but conscious$_a$ to some degree. The task is to explain why being conscious$_a$, in the ways he is conscious$_a$, is insufficient to generate the normal sorts of linguistic identifications and bodily movements. If this is the right way to think about matters, then the idea that phenomenal consciousness is what helps explain the case looks more promising, for contrary to what Block says, the blindsighted person is not correctly characterized as unconscious$_a$. By what we know from the knowledge-without-awareness literature and about what the blindsighted person has access to, there is some plausibility in inferring that the lack of phenomenal awareness of the blindfield at every stage of processing partly explains the inability to bring the knowledge the system possesses into awareness and into normal, high-quality play in inference, reporting, and action. In a telling remark Block says that consciousness$_a$ without consciousness$_p$ is "conceptually possible" but "perhaps not actual." My suggestion is that it is actual. His imaginary case of a zombie shows the conceptual possibility, the case of blindsight shows its actuality.

8   Can the Epiphenomenalist Explain Everything That the Teleological Functionalist Can Explain?

Block is attracted to a general view that posits a consciousness$_p$ module that feeds the executive system responsible for issuing high-quality reports and sensibly guiding actions. The blindsighted person has some information about the blindfield, but this information is stuck in the peripheral modules. Forced guesses can tune in the executive because the person hears her own guesses and receives reports about how she is doing. But by and large the information is locked up in the peripheral modules. For people with normal sight, the information from the peripheral modules passes through the consciousness$_p$ module and into the executive. Thus normal reasoning, reporting, and action can occur.

According to this model, it is not the absence of consciousness$_p$ that directly causes poor performance or its presence that directly causes good performance. Good performance depends on whether or not information gets into the executive system, and it gets into the executive system only if it goes through the consciousness$_p$ module. The absence of consciousness$_p$ is an indication that the executive is not able to play its executive role, and the presence of consciousness$_p$ is an indication that it is able to play its executive role.

It would not be profitable to get embroiled in a debate over this specific theoretical model. The point I want to emphasize is that if the model is true, it would help the argument against epiphenomenalism. The support comes from the fact that on the proposed model, the consciousness$_p$ module plays a role in driving the executive. The model implies that the blindsighted person is dysfunctional because information is locked in the peripheral modules. If the information about the visual field were to get to the executive, it would be routed first through the consciousness$_p$ module, and consciousness$_p$ would thereby play an important causal role in the complex process that gives rise to reasoning, reporting, and action.

The suspicious epiphenomenalist has a counterproposal at the ready. The consciousness$_p$ module does feed not the executive. Rather, the executive informs the consciousness$_p$ module about what it has been up to. (See Velmans, in press, for a version of this hypothesis where focal attentive processing takes the role of the executive.) In the cases of blindsight the executive hasn't been up to anything, so phenomenal consciousness receives no reports.

The suspicious epiphenomenalist can also give an account of why I beat twin me at tennis, even though we have received identical coaching, I while fully conscious, my twin subliminally. The reason I beat twin me is that my executive system was properly tapped and that of twin me wasn't. The evidence for this is straightforward. According to the epiphenomenalist, executive activity causes (but is not caused by) phenomenal awareness (which causes nothing else). I can report the coaching techniques I have been taught because my executive system was activated and caused me to be aware of what I was taught. My twin lacks phenomenal awareness about how to play tennis (although he does many of the right things). This shows that subliminal coaching did not activate his executive system. Had it been activated, his executive system would have issued a phenomenal report, a report as inconsequential to the ability to play tennis well as the toot of the train's whistle is to its ability to continue full steam ahead, but a report nonetheless.

The epiphenomenalist is most resourceful. But the fact that the epiphenomenalist can explain certain data with a model that endows nonconscious parts of the system with executive powers and depicts phenomenal consciousness as a mental cul de sac does not mean that the view is credible overall. Epiphenomenalism is a coherent view. But it lacks credibility when considered in light of plausible theoretical commitments discussed earlier that emanate from neuroscience and evolutionary biology.

The biggest problem the epiphenomenalist faces is explaining how, given the massive connectivity of the brain, *any* feature as common, well-structured, and multimodal as phenomenal consciousness could supervene on certain neural processes without having interesting and important causal effects in other parts of the neural network. We know that different kinds of phenomenal experiences are processed in different parts of the brain. The epiphenomenalist will need to show that there is a cul de sac in each of the relevant areas where phenomenal consciousness is stopped dead in its tracks so that it makes no causal contribution to other neural events. This,

I suggest, is a research program destined to fail. The brain doesn't work that way.

The second problem the epiphenomenalist faces is explaining why phenomenal consciousness is out of touch with so much of what goes on in the brain but is hooked up to the sensory modules and to declarative memory, that is, memory for facts and events. Our species' success and our personal survival depend on successful commerce with the external world. This requires being in touch with the present state of the environment and drawing inductive inferences based on the past. In theory, we could have evolved so as to succeed in being in touch and drawing the right inferences without phenomenal consciousness. But the fact is that we did evolve with phenomenal consciousness. Furthermore, phenomenal consciousness is hooked up to exactly the systems processing the information that, from the point of view of wise evolutionary design, it has most need to know about if it is to make a significant contribution to the life of the organism in which it occurs.

The experiments and data discussed in this chapter must be considered in light of a general theoretical commitment to massive neural connectivity, to a picture of consciousness as distributed (a single faculty might be locked up and do no interesting work, but it is extremely implausible that widely distributed conscious activity plays no significant causal role at any of the distributed sites), and to the evolutionary rationale for the structure and function of consciousness. In light of these credible theoretical commitments, the experiments and data discussed in this chapter weigh on the side of conceiving of phenomenal consciousness as playing multifarious causal roles.

I conclude that subjective awareness plays a role in our mental lives. But exactly what role it plays, how important it is in fixing informational content, in what domains it is important, how it figures in remembering, what its relation is to attention (possibly it is a species of attention, or attention is a species of it), whether it is constitutive of certain kinds of sensation and memory, or whether it receives output from the sensory modules and memory—all these are unsettled questions. Until they are settled, the precise roles of subjective awareness will remain unclear, as will its relative importance in the multifarious domains of mental life. This will leave the suspicious epiphenomenalist with many openings to raise his skeptical questions. But, as far as I can see, all current and potential disputes between the epiphenomenalist and his opponents are matters to be settled in empirical court. I have shown how we already possess some theory and evidence that, taken together, bears on the question of the role of subjective consciousness. At this point in a five-set tennis match, the teleological functionalist leads the suspicious epiphenomenalist two games to one, up 15-love in the fourth game of the first set. There is still a long way to go, the day is hot, and both players have their strengths. I can't see the epiphenomenalist winning. But it will be a good fight, and there are lessons to be learned by those overzealous fans of consciousness who have historically overrated its power and ability to get to every place on the court.

Chapter 8

The Stream of Consciousness

1   What Is It Like to Have a Normal Consciousness?

What is it like to have a normal conscious life? This is a bold question. It assumes that beneath the noise and clatter of the multifarious ways of experiencing things, there is a universal way consciousness seems. Because of this presupposition, the question might be ill advised. But there is some evidence that the question can be answered in its own terms. William James thought so. James believed that "adult consciousness," regardless of time and place, has a certain universal phenomenological structure (1892, 18).

This chapter is a meditation and defense of the analysis of consciousness offered by James in his famous "Stream of Thought" chapter in *The Principles of Psychology* (1890) and in the chapter entitled "The Stream of Consciousness" in *Psychology: The Briefer Course* (1892). These two chapters are respectively followed by chapters entitled "The Consciousness of Self" and "The Self." James first provides an analysis of ordinary first-order consciousness. Then he provides an analysis of self-consciousness. Taken together, the pairs of chapters propose a radical idea. The phenomenology, the way that consciousness and self-consciousness seem, stands in no need of the posit of a Self that does the thinking, stands behind all experience as the very ground of its possibility, and appears as object when consciousness takes a reflexive turn. The stream of consciousness can flow, just as it seems to, without the implausible prop of a "mind's 'I'." In this chapter, I explore the idea of the stream of consciousness, for it is controversial in its own right. Then in the next chapter, I discuss the illusion of the mind's "I" and defend the alternative James proposes, that "the thoughts themselves are the thinkers."

2   Phenomenology

I am committed to an overall strategy of drawing the phenomenological, the psychological, and the neuroscientific analyses of consciousness together. James's analysis is largely, but not exclusively, phenomenological. Some philosophers think that the phenomenology is fundamentally irrelevant. There are multifarious reasons why they think this, but two reasons are dominant. First, there is no necessary connection between how things seem and how they are. Second, we are often mistaken in our self-reporting, including in our reporting about how things seem. Both points can be conceded without abandoning phenomenology. Furthermore, two factors stand very much in favor of doing phenomenology. First, how things seem, even if this is revisable upon reflection, is interesting in its own right. Minimally, it will tell us what things seem like at the phenomenological surface. Second, even if our deepest hope is to provide the right neuroscientific account of consciousness, it will be to some significant degree a theory of how states with multifarious phenomenological character are realized in the brain. A PET scan that detects lots of activity in the amygdala when people are led to anticipate a shock (and say that this is what they anticipate) says something interesting across many subjects about the brain states upon which states of anticipatory fear supervene. Likewise, inducing states of panic disorder in patients already victimized by the disorder, and seeking cure, by injecting these patients with sodium lactate and observing temporal-lobe activity (rather than the expected lower brain activity) is an ingenious way of drawing the phenomenological and neurological stories into reflective equilibrium (personal conversation with Marcus Raichle). Unless we accept a certain amount of first-person phenomenology, the complete story of the brain will stand independent of, and aloof from, any link with the story of conscious mental life, which we initially sought deeper understanding of.

That said, phenomenology is no easy business. James is quick to point out that the empiricist philosophers who depicted ideas (for example, the idea of a red ball) as made up of mental atoms (the simple ideas of round, extended, and red) could not have been speaking phenomenologically. We might analyze the idea of a red ball as logically composed of these more elementary ideas, but surely experience does not seem to involve putting together ideas of round, extended, and red to form the perception of a red ball. The trouble with empiricism as phenomenology is that it trades on the dubious idea that experiences are built from simple conscious atoms. The awareness of a red, round ball may in fact be built from simpler components computed in different parts of the brain. Indeed, recent evidence from cognitive neuroscience suggests that this is exactly how the awareness emerges. There are separate neural processors responsible for color, edge, motion, and depth detection. This lends credence to empiricism as a theory of the origin of experiences. But it is unclear that acceptance of this as the true story of how things *are* will make them *seem* that way. Indeed, it is not clear that empiricism should affect how things seem at all. After all, the idea that our simple perceptions are in fact generated by the binding of even simpler units is compatible with these simpler units making no phenomenological appearance whatsoever. We need to beware of imposing our views about how experiences are generated onto the phenomenological surface.

James proposes that we avoid being corrupted by abstract theoretical views by starting "with the most concrete facts, those with which [the ordinary person] has a daily acquaintance in his own inner life" (1892, 18–19). In a sense, James is not interested in the "most concrete facts," as we understand that phrase. He is not interested (at least not for purposes of this exercise) in having people tell the multifarious stories of how things seem to them or what their inner lives are like. Such stories will be too individualistic and too concrete with regard to the aims James has for phenomenology. He believes that there is something conscious mental life is like when we abstract from all the particularities of our own experience. Possibly he is right in this belief, but it is nowhere defended. James is not interested in what it is like to be a particular individual or type of individual—an African-American woman or a gay male or an analytic philosopher—he is interested in what it is generally like to have a conscious mental life. He presumes that *there is a universal way conscious mental life seems* that all individual persons can locate beneath the noise and clatter of their own particularities.

The master metaphor is that of a stream. Individuality is the rule. But all individual consciousnesses are streamlike. This is true even for persons with disorders of consciousness. Such disorders are abundant (see Shallice 1988 for a recent review). But most disorders of consciousness do not dry up one's personal stream. When this happens, personhood is in jeopardy, soul loss occurs. Short-term memory is normally sufficient to keep up the feel of the streamlike flow, no matter how weird the contents of consciousness are and no matter how disabled long-term memory is. Indeed, short-term memory may be the sole necessary and sufficient condition for having a minimal streamlike consciousness (see Calvin 1990, 82; Crick and Koch 1990, 270; Minsky 1985). If one has only short-term memory and has lost long-term memory, one's sense of personal identity in the rich thick sense of knowing who one is and where one is coming from will be greatly diminished. But so long as one has short-term memory one will possess a sense of oneself as a continuous subject of experience—a bare, pathetic, thin subject, perhaps; a mere conduit for briefly connected happenings, perhaps; but a continuous subject in some minimal sense, enough to constitute a sorry stream, but a stream nonetheless.

If there is some universal streamlike phenomenology, getting at these phenomenological features will require great abstraction, and it will require theory at least in the following sort of respect: we will need to count on our fellow phenomenologists as sharing a conceptual world on which notions like consciousness, mental state, continuity, stream, fringe, and so on, have a hold. There is always the suspicion that when concepts have a hold, even in the simple sense of being understood, they bring a whole set of theoretical assumptions with them. This raises the possibility that far from getting at the ways things seem independently of our theories of how things seem, we are simply getting at the way our folk theory conceives things in its most deeply settled places. But it is a commonplace in philosophy that what is settled may have things wildly wrong. We need to be open to this possibility.

3   Are We Ever Wholly Unconscious?

In the chapter before the "Stream of Thought," James makes sure to mark the following important fact.

> The life of the *individual* consciousness in time seems ... to be an interrupted one, so that the question: *Are we ever wholly unconscious?* becomes one which must be discussed. Sleep, fainting, coma, epilepsy, and other "unconscious" conditions are apt to break in upon and occupy large durations of what we nevertheless consider the mental history of a single man. And, the fact of interruption being admitted, is it not possible that it may exist where we do not suspect it, and perhaps in an incessant and fine-grained form? ... Is consciousness really discontinuous, incessantly interrupted and recommencing (from the psychologist's point of view)? and does it only seem continuous to itself by an illusion analogous to that of the zoetrope [a turning toy that makes an inanimate figure seem alive]? Or is it at most times as continuous outwardly as it inwardly seems?   (1890, 199–200)

James's answer is that "we can give no rigorous answer to this question" (1890, 200). He writes that some of the evidence suggests that the "view that thought and feeling may at times wholly disappear seems the more plausible. As glands cease to secrete and muscles to contract, so the brain should sometimes cease to carry currents, and with this minimum of its activity might well coexist a minimum of consciousness" (1890, 213). Nonetheless, James decides, "On the whole it is best to abstain from a conclusion. The science of the near future will doubtless answer this question more wisely than we can now" (1890, 213).

Here we are a full century down the road. Do we have an answer to this question of whether we are ever "wholly unconscious"? Before I answer, notice how James puts the point. He suggests an analogy between the way in which glands and muscles can shut down altogether and the way in which brain activity becomes minimal. The trouble is that no activity and minimal activity are very different; achieving some minimum is not the same as wholly disappearing. Perhaps glands and muscles can and do shut down temporarily, but when the brain shuts down, the person is dead. So the question is really whether a person stays conscious, in any interesting sense of the term, when the brain changes its type of activity or becomes less active. James was well aware that the answer to this question is not resolved in the first person: *"We must never take a person's testimony, however sincere, that he has felt nothing, as proof positive that no feeling has been there"* (1890, 211). James is open to the possibility that persons with multiple personalities or blindsight may in fact possess "secondary consciousness," which does not link up to primary consciousness. These people feel things in a certain way in secondary consciousness, they simply can't report what they feel or feel it in primary consciousness (these being different). James is also thinking of uncontroversial cases in which a person experiences, but fails to tune into, a commonplace visual scene or noise, or she experiences it but quickly forgets that she has experienced it. James is impressed by our "insensibility to habitual noises, etc, whilst awake" and thinks that this insensitivity "proves that we can neglect to attend to what we nevertheless feel" (1890, 201).

What wise answer does science "of the near future" give to the question of whether we are ever wholly unconscious? Unfortunately, it is not entirely clear, but the shape of an answer is emerging. "It seems likely that the essential features of consciousness are probably not usually present in slow wave sleep, nor under a deep anaesthetic. Rapid Eye Movement (REM) or dreaming sleep is another matter. It seems that a limited form of consciousness occurs in REM sleep" (Crick and Koch 1990, 265; also see Hobson 1988 on dream consciousness). There is also some evidence that the oscillatory patterns associated with consciousness occur under light anaesthesia (Crick and Koch 1990, 271).

So despite the fact that the brain never altogether shuts down, the neural states that subserve subjective consciousness may well not occur in deep sleep. Long ago John Locke recognized that deep sleep was a problem. Although he believed that consciousness grounds the sense of identity, he rejected the Cartesian idea that consciousness constitutes our essence. This is because consciousness is absent during deep sleep, and the essence of an entity is something that the entity cannot lack without ceasing to be that entity.

What should we think, given that consciousness appears to be interrupted, or at least in principle interruptable? In what sense is an interrupted individual consciousness a single stream? James's likening consciousness to a stream is jeopardized by his own honest admission that we might indeed sometimes be wholly unconscious. A stream, then dry land, followed by another stream do not a single stream make. What kind of stream is this? The key is to understand that what is subjectively or "inwardly" streamlike may objectively or "outwardly" be nonstreamlike, at least in certain respects.

4   The Stream

When James engages in the "introspective study of adult consciousness itself," he is primarily after how conscious mental life considered as a process occurring over time seems (1892, 18). He has less to say about how the conscious stream is at each moment, and there is even less attention to the phenomenology of individual conscious mental states. This is important to recognize. Just as the properties of the overall process of consciousness subjectively conceived might differ from the same process objectively considered, so too the properties of the overall process subjectively considered might differ dramatically from the properties of particular mental states also subjectively conceived. For example, a single thought lacks the streamlike property that James thinks is the essential feature of the process, and particular states might be objectless or noncontentful—as with a pain, itch, or yucky mood—without the stream itself being contentless.

So what exactly is universal, normal, adult conscious mental life like? "The Fundamental Fact" is that "consciousness of some sort goes on. 'States of mind' succeed each other.... Thought goes on" (James 1892, 18–19). The process of succession has four important characteristics.

Every state is part of a personal consciousness

> In this room—this lecture-room, say—there are a multitude of thoughts, yours and mine, some of which cohere mutually, and some not. They are as little each-for-itself and reciprocally independent as they are all-belonging-together. They are neither: no one of them is separate, but each belongs with certain others and none beside. My thought belongs with *my* other thoughts, and your thought with *your* other thoughts. Whether anywhere in the room there be a *mere* thought, which is nobody's thought, we have no means of ascertaining, for we have no experience of its like. The only states of consciousness that we naturally deal with are found in personal consciousnesses, minds, selves, concrete particular I's and you's.   (James 1892, 20)

So "thought goes on." But "so long as *something* corresponding to the term 'personal mind' is all that is insisted on, without any particular view of its nature being implied, ... the personal self rather than thought might be treated as the immediate datum in psychology. The universal fact is not 'feelings and thoughts exist' but 'I think' and 'I feel'" (1892, 20). The "thoughts that we actually know to exist do not fly about loose, but seem each to belong to some thinker and not to another" (1892, 68). Each thought is owned (1892, 20).

Furthermore, conscious ownership is private. There are no mergers and acquisitions when it comes to personal consciousness and its contents. "No thought ever comes into the direct *sight* of a thought in another personal consciousness than its own. Absolute insulation, irreducible pluralism, is the law" (1892, 20). Thoughts can be shared. That is not at issue. It is just that you cannot have my thoughts. Only I am hooked up to myself in the right way to directly experience my own mental states. In a thought experiment befitting a modern cognitive scientist, James asks us to "take a sentence of a dozen words, and take twelve men and tell to each one word. Then stand the men in a row or jam them in a bunch, and let each think of his word as intently as he will; nowhere will there be consciousness of the whole sentence" (1890, 160). Each one of us has only our own thoughts and feelings and no one else's. From the first-person point of view, the great divide is between what is me and what is not me.

Consciousness is in constant change
Within each personal consciousness, states are always changing (1892, 19, 21). On this point James appeals both to the way things seem and to theoretical considerations. Consciousness seems constantly in flux. It changes and flows, and novel states abound. Indeed, we are always in a new state of mind.

But one might object that this is not right. We sometimes seem to be in exactly the same state we were in before. For example, my sense impression of the greenness of my lawn now is the same as my impression of its greenness five minutes ago. But here James challenges us to reflect more carefully. "The grass out the window now looks to me of the same green in the sun as in the shade, and yet a painter would have to paint one part of it dark green, another part yellow, to give it its real sensational effect. We take no heed, as a rule, of the different way in which the same things look and sound and smell at different distances and under different circumstances" (1892, 21–22). We are concerned to establish the sameness of things—that is the same lawn I was looking at five minutes ago—"and any sensations that assure us of that will probably be considered in a rough way to be the same with each other" (1892, 22). The illusion that the green of this lawn now is the same as the green of five minutes ago, or that the taste of this beer is just like its taste yesterday, is caused by a certain similarity in the sensations sufficient to judge that the lawn is the same lawn I saw before, that the beer is the kind I always drink. Judging two objects of perception to be the same or of exactly the same kind is not remotely the same as judging two perceptions or feelings to be the same, even if these perceptions or feelings subserve the judgment that the objects are the same.

The physical, neurological, and phenomenological evidence suggests that *"no state once gone can recur and be identical with what it was before"* (1892, 21). Variability in external conditions and small changes in external objects produce changes in "incoming current." Our criteria for two things being the same object or same thing never require absolute sameness or identity of thought; otherwise there would be no objects or things to reidentify as the same. "*What is got twice is the same* OBJECT," and we in "our carelessness" suppose that our ideas of these things are exactly the same (1892, 21). But this is not so. Reflection reveals how disparate are the ideas that can give rise to the judgment of same object, and conversely how variable and interest-relative are our judgments of same object or same thing.

That said, it is an interesting question whether the more careful reflection needed to overcome the illusion that we often go into exactly the same conscious state as we were in before is more careful phenomenological reflection, testing seemings against other seemings, or whether it is simply more careful reflection broadly construed to include our best judgments about object and event identity. I think it is the latter rather than the former. If this is right, it follows that sometimes we allow nonphenomenological data to nudge the phenomenology in the right direction when it is ambivalent, when, for example, it fails to render a clear verdict about itself, as is the case with the question of whether certain experiences actually seem exactly the same as certain prior experiences or only seem very similar to those prior experiences.

Indeed, James makes much of a purely theoretical reason in his brief against the view that identical states of consciousness recur. This is the *network thesis*: "Every sensation corresponds to some cerebral action. For an identical sensation to recur it would have to occur the second time *in an unmodified brain*" (1892, 23). This, James tells us, is a "physiological impossibility." I call this the network thesis because the point is not merely the obvious one that small physiological changes occur in the brain over even short intervals of time. Rather, the point is that these changes rapidly accrue to constitute changes in the systematic network constitutive of thought and feeling that determines how incoming signals are experienced. "When the identical fact recurs, we *must* think of it in a fresh manner, see it under a somewhat different angle, apprehend it in different relations from those in which it last appeared.... The thought by which we cognize it is the thought of it-in-those-relations, a thought suffused with the consciousness of all that dim context" (1892, 23).

The network thesis expresses at once the ideas that the mind has a connectionist architecture, that we bring previously acquired experience as background to each new experience, and that neural connectivity is global, or potentially so. That is, there is no change in one part of the system that does not (or cannot) have some effect on some other part of the system. Furthermore, every neural change produces a modification at the level of consciousness.

This last assumption—"For to every brain-modification, however small, we may suppose that there must correspond a change of equal amount in the consciousness which the brain subserves" (1890, 233; 1892, 23)—is much too strong. James expresses the core idea in a way that is amusing to the contemporary ear: "As the total neurosis changes, so does the total psychosis change" (1890, 243). There are almost certainly neural changes that do not affect either nonconscious or conscious mental functioning (in any interesting way). James is right about holism and constant change, but he is wrong about supervenience. Any change at the level of consciousness must be explicable in terms of changes at the neural level. But the converse does not hold. There can be changes at the neural level that do not make themselves felt at the level of consciousness.

Each personal consciousness is sensibly continuous and has a fringe
With the third and fourth features of consciousness we enter the waters of the stream itself. In the discussion of the previous point, it emerged that it is possible to try to capture the phenomenal features of consciousness from a purely subjective point of view, straightforwardly in terms of how things seem, or alternatively, when the subjective point of view is indeterminate in its deliverances, to shape the phenomenology, or at least to cast our pronouncements about the character of experience, in terms of knowledge arrived at objectively. We can use the knowledge of the fact that we are more interested in object sameness than sensation sameness to explain how we make the slide from judgments of object sameness, based in part on sensation similarity, to mistaken judgments that we are having the exact same sensation. Or we can bring knowledge about the connectionist structure of the brain to weigh in against the thought that sensations or ideas or feelings can recur identically.

The point is that the analysis of consciousness does not rest simply on how things seem on first pass. How things seem bears reflective scrutiny. Sometimes reflection will shift the seemings, so we will admit that indeed what first seemed like an identical sensation is simply a similar one. At other times the seeming will not shift. But we will have powerful theoretical reason to judge that the experiences aren't exactly the same. Despite powerful feelings that this beer tastes exactly the same now as it did last week, it probably just isn't so.

This tension between the subjective and objective perspectives also emerges as we examine the idea of the stream. James emphasizes that "consciousness feels continuous" (1892, 25). The question arises as to whether it *is* continuous. The answer seems to depend exclusively on whether one is taking the subjective or objective point of view. The claim that consciousness feels continuous means two things: "(a) That even where there is a time-gap the consciousness after it feels as if it belonged together with the consciousness before it, as another part of the same self; (b) That the changes from one moment to another in the quality of the consciousness are never absolutely abrupt" (1890, 237; 1892, 25).

When two people wake up together in bed, "each one of them mentally reaches back and makes connection with but *one* of the two streams of thought which were broken by the sleeping hours." Each consciousness reconnects to its past and "never by mistake knits itself" onto that of another. We remember who we are and what we are like, whereas we conceive of the mental life of others.

> Remembrance is like direct feeling; its object is suffused with a warmth and intimacy to which no object of mere conception ever attains.... So sure as this present is me, is mine, it says, so sure is anything else that comes with the same warmth and intimacy and immediacy, me and mine. What the qualities called warmth and intimacy may in themselves be will have to be a matter for future consideration. But whatever past states appear with those qualities must be admitted to receive the greeting of the present mental state, to be owned by it, and accepted as belonging with it in a common self.   (1890, 239; 1892, 26)

Even if in sleep, consciousness is not simply turned way down but is turned off altogether, and even if I accept this, my present consciousness will nonetheless feel continuous. On this point objective knowledge can't nudge the subjective point of view into conformity. To be sure, we accept that we in fact are not always subjectively conscious. We simply do not have any phenomenology associated with these nonconscious periods; that is, after all, what makes them nonconscious. We can believe that we are not always conscious, but this true belief is not enough to give us a feel for what it is like to be wholly unconscious.

"This community of self is what the time-gap cannot break in twain, and is why a present thought, although not ignorant of the time-gap, can still regard itself as continuous with certain chosen portions of the past" (1890, 239; 1892, 26). James accepts that consciousness appears, or at least might appear, to be gappy from the third-person point of view. The fact remains that "whatever it be for the onlooking psychologist, [consciousness] is for itself unbroken. It *feels* unbroken" (1890, 238).

There is evidence that the feeling of connectedness to one's past can show complete insensitivity to even extremely long temporal gaps. In *Awakenings*, Oliver Sacks's moving story of the lives of patients in the grip of sleeping sickness, Sacks describes the victims of the terrible encephalitis as having "passed into a timeless state, an eventless stasis ... with their thoughts and feelings unchangingly fixed at the point where the long 'sleep' had closed in on them" (Sacks 1983, 22). When L-dopa treatment temporarily "awakened" many of these patients, sometimes after thirty years in their "timeless state," they experienced their long lost past "as present" (Sacks 1983, 75). Consciousness reconnects, as it were, to where it left off. Even first-person knowledge of a three-decade-long fugue state cannot defeat this feeling of connectedness to whatever experiences one last had, whenever these were.

These thoughts are tied together with James's master metaphor of the stream. "Consciousness, then, does not appear to itself chopped up in bits. Such words as 'chain' and 'train' do not describe it fitly as it presents itself in the first instance. It is nothing jointed; it flows. A 'river' or a 'stream' are the metaphors by which it is most naturally described. *In talking of it hereafter, let us call it the stream of thought, of consciousness, or of subjective life"* (1890, 239; 1892, 26). There are events—such as a sudden thunder clap, a fire alarm, a sudden explosion—that produce distinctive *"contrasts in quality."* But no matter how great the qualitative contrast is, it does not constitute a break in the stream: "Even into our awareness of the thunder the awareness of the previous silence creeps and continues; for what we hear when the thunder crashes is no thunder *pure*, but thunder-breaking-upon-silence-and-contrasting-with-it" (1892, 26). If, by any chance, we think that consciousness is broken into discrete parts, this is probably due to a confusion of the contents of consciousness with consciousness itself, which, of course, is partly constituted by its contents. The things of which we are aware "are discrete and discontinuous; they do pass before us in a train or chain.... But their comings and goings and contrasts no more break the flow of the thought that thinks them than they break the time and space in which they lie.... The transition between the thought of one object and the thought of another is no more a break in the *thought* than a joint in a bamboo is a break in the wood" (1890, 240).

A different kind of qualitative contrast has to do with the pace of consciousness. "Like a bird's life, it seems to be an alternation of flights and perchings" (1890, 243; 1892, 27). Occasionally, consciousness spends some time with an idea or an image, but usually consciousness is in transition between substantive resting places. The transitory flights can be especially long, as when someone is "spaced-out" or daydreams. There is a tendency to focus on the substantive perches and less on the transitory flow. This is probably due to the fact that the contents of consciousness, the information particular states bear, is ecologically most useful. The flow from one substantive thought to the next is typically due to the fact that the object of the next thought is worth paying attention to.

But a mistake can be fostered by focusing too resolutely on the resting places. We will not only miss the phenomenological reality of the flow; we will also fail to see the "penumbra," the "fringe," the "halo of relations" that is carried in the flow and is partly constitutive of the substantive state, that frames or washes over the contents of consciousness. James introduces the idea of the fringe of consciousness in this way:

> The traditional psychology talks like one who should say a river consists of nothing but pailsful, spoonsful, quartpotsful, barrelsful, and other moulded forms of water. Even were the pails and pots actually standing in the stream, still between them the free water would continue to flow. It is just this free water of consciousness that psychologists resolutely overlook. Every definite image in the mind is steeped and dyed in the free water that flows round it. With it goes the sense of its relations, near and remote, the dying echo of whence it came to us, the dawning sense of whither it is to lead. The significance, the value, of the image is all in this halo or penumbra that surrounds and escorts it.... *Let us call the consciousness of this halo of relations around the image by the name of 'psychic overtone' or 'fringe'.* (1892, 33)

The fringe of consciousness often accounts for why and how some situation is experienced differently by different persons (simple differences of perspective sometimes independently account for why I see this table as oval and you see it as round). The fringe suffuses the present thought with the resonating feel of past thoughts, and it is the carrier of the network of memories already acquired and of expectations about the future. The idea of a conscious fringe or halo or penumbra is intended to explain the idiosyncratic features of thought and to "reinstate the vague and inarticulate to its proper place in our mental life" (1892, 32). The tip-of-the-tongue phenomenon, anticipating the next word in a passage we are reading, differentially attending to several things at once, sensing that some conclusion is rational and fitting (or misplaced), feeling that we have just said what we want to say without ever having vividly formulated it—all these are cases where the fringe of consciousness makes itself felt and plays an explanatory role. James writes that a "good third of our psychic life" consists in "premonitory perspectives"—in vague anticipations, in feelings of affinity or discord among thoughts. These must be explained relationally in terms of the halo of relations that do not merely accompany each thought but in a sense, constitute it as the thought that it is.

It is not quite right to think, as we do, that two people can have the same thought of a dog, one suffused with warm and tender accompaniments, the other with disdain. Two people can think of the same dog, but their thoughts are different. Likewise, we say that two people think the same thing, when they reach the same conclusion. When we say this and focus only on the "halting places," we disguise two genuine possibilities. First, there is the possibility that two persons who assent to the same sentence or judgment may have gotten to the thought in such different ways that

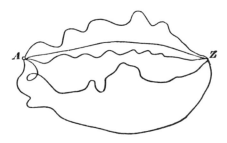

Figure 8.1
William James's picture of three minds starting from the same premises and reaching the same conclusion but traversing radically different mental terrain along the way. (Reprinted with permission from James 1890, 269.)

they really do not share exactly the same conclusion. Second and relatedly, this difference in conclusion may come out when one person suggests the natural next thought, what he thinks follows from the accepted conclusion, and the other person balks. How is this possible? How is the natural inference for me not natural for you, who accept the very same thought from which I start? The answer has to do with the fact that the halting places for people are "steeped and dyed" in the unique waters of their conscious streams: one full of eddies, another smooth with occasional waterfalls; one murky, another clear; one straight and narrow, another curvy; one with a branch stream that reenters the main stream, another with a branch stream that comes to an abrupt end. With reference to figure 8.1, James describes the situation this way:

> Let *A* be some experience from which a number of thinkers start. Let Z be the practical conclusion rationally inferrible from it. One gets to this conclusion by one line, another by another; one follows a course of English, another of German, verbal imagery. With one, verbal images predominate; with another, tactile. Some trains are tinged with emotions, others not; some are very abridged, synthetic and rapid; others hesitating and broken into many steps. But when the penulti-mate terms of all the trains, however differing *inter se*, finally shoot into the same conclusion, we say, and rightly say, that all the thinkers have had substantially the same thought. It would probably astound each of them beyond measure to be led into his neighbor's mind and to find out how different the scenery there was from that in his own.   (James 1890, 269–270)

The idea of the stream is a powerful one. A stream has length and breadth. It appropriates its past as it moves forward. Furthermore, streams come in multifarious kinds, and the character of the flow is determined by the character of the stream bed, as well as what lies beneath and beside it. This last point is crucial. The stream of consciousness is not all of mental life. We have already seen that James wants to distinguish the vivid states of the conscious stream from the more dim and inarticulate states of the stream, while at the same time insisting on a causal role for both. In addition, there are all sorts of nonconscious brain events that, like the stream bed and bank, have an enormous effect on the properties of the stream itself.

5   The Function of the Stream

There are many theories about the function of a streamlike personal consciousness. James's own view is that the personal conscious stream evolved because it enabled adaptive response to novelty and more flexible action guidance in novel situations in which nonhabitual action was necessary. If consciousness is effective, it must be because it is capable of "increasing the efficiency of the brain by loading its dice. . . . Loading its dice would mean bringing a more or less constant pressure to bear in favor of *those* of its performances which make for the most permanent interests of the brain's owner; it would mean a constant inhibition of the tendencies to stray aside. . . . Every actually existing consciousness seems to itself at any rate to be a *fighter for ends*, of which many, but for its presence, would not be ends at all" (James 1890, 140–141). Consciousness is useful. It evolved to fight for the ends of the system that houses it (James 1890, 143–144). Why couldn't the system fight for and achieve its ends absent consciousness? It can and does much of the time. Consciousness is involved in only some, possibly very little, of mental life. Novel situations, situations requiring attention, planning, goal setting, and watching out for "permanent interests" are especially prominent in calling on its good offices. "The *distribution* of consciousness shows it to be exactly what we might expect in an organ added for the sake of steering a nervous system grown too complex to regulate itself" (James 1890, 144; see Baars 1988 for an approving elaboration of James's views on the function of consciousness). When the mind wants to "load the dice" and fight for its ends and permanent interests, it distributes or broadcasts what it knows and wants throughout the brain. Important broadcasts intended for wide distribution are often conscious. In this way the broadcasts get the whole system's attention and prepare it for quick and efficient action.

6   Nonstandard Phenomenologies

James's phenomenology is intended to get at the universal features of human consciousness. These features are partly constitutive of personhood. The senses of identity, direction, agency, and a life plan are all grounded in the memorable connections of the stream. It follows that certain extreme defects of consciousness should have effects on our ascriptions of personhood. This is exactly so. Some defects of consciousness are insufficient in degree or kind to affect our ascriptions of personhood, but others are severe enough to cause us to remove or withold the ascription of personhood. The lack of particular types of conscious experience, for example, the loss of the capacity to experience faces as faces or to see words as words or to feel one's limbs as one's own, do not diminish one bit our sense that another is a person. However, certain sorts of brain damage can eliminate the conscious stream altogether. Such brain damage takes the person away, but not perhaps his living body. Final-stage Alzheimer patients may be like this.

Even without severe brain damage, the loss of the sense of identity, of personal sameness, can undermine our ascriptions of personhood. Erik Erikson writes,

> The term 'identity crisis' was first used, if I remember correctly, for a specific clinical purpose in the Mt. Zion Veterans' Rehabilitation Clinic during the Second World War. . . . Most of our patients, so we concluded at that time, had neither been "shellshocked" nor become malingerers, but had through the exigencies of war lost a sense of personal sameness and historical continuity. They were impaired in that central control over themselves for which, in the psychoanalytic scheme, only the "inner agency" of the ego could be held responsible. Therefore I spoke of loss of "ego identity." (1968, 16–17)

Individuals in identity crises are persons in one sense. They normally experience themselves as the locus of a set of subjectively linked events, as a conduit in which a certain bland and low-level sameness and continuity subsists. What they lack, which horrifies us and immobilizes them, is any sense of coherent and authoritative me-ness, of "personal sameness"—any sense that these subjectively linked events occurring to and in them constitute a bona fide person, a self, a life. Erikson asks what "identity feels like when you become aware of the fact that you undoubtedly *have* one," and he answers that it consists of "a *subjective sense* of an *invigorating sameness and continuity*" (1968, 19). Without the invigorating sense of self, there is no person and thus no coherent cognitive and motivational core from which the individual can generate purposes or in which he can find the energy required to sustain them were he able to find any in the first place. There is, in effect, a ubiquitous linkage between a firm sense of identity and the capacities to formulate goals and sustain effort. Emptied of the subjective sense of an "invigorating sameness and continuity," there is no role for consciousness to play in moving one's life in a certain direction. A sense of direction is lost whenever, and to roughly the same degree that, the sense of sameness and continuity is lost.

Individuals in identity crises have memories. Their memories simply don't feel like *their* memories. In other sorts of cases, memories feel owned but are of such short duration that they can hardly constitute a self. Jimmie, Oliver Sacks's "lost mariner," lost his long-term memory to alcoholism. Jimmie's impairment, Korsakoff's disease, the destruction of the mammillary bodies in the brain by drink, left him in a state in which "whatever was said or done to him was apt to be forgotten in a few seconds' time" (Sacks 1985, 25). Jimmie was "isolated in a single moment of being, with a moat or lacuna of forgetting all round him.... He is a man without past (or future) stuck in a constantly changing, meaningless moment" (Sacks 1985, 28).

Jimmie is conscious. He has short-term memory. No person has ever existed who was conscious but lacked short-term memory, this being necessary, and possibly sufficient, for holding an experience long enough to have it, as it were (Crick and Koch 1990, 271). But his short-term memory is *very* short. This is why Sacks has trouble attributing enough overlap to his short-term memories to start a streamlike flow. His inner life seems choppy—"a sort of Humean drivel, a mere succession of unrelated impressions and events" (Sacks 1985, 34). Indeed, Jimmie, when asked, denies that he feels alive. He is neither miserable nor happy. His experiences don't connect in a way that constitute a self that could be any way at all.

Amazingly, Jimmie discovered a way to reconstitute his identity, to reappropriate a sense of himself. First in chapel and then in art, music, and gardening, Jimmie's attention was held. What sustained him and his activity in these contexts was not so much a stream of his own bound by contentful memories but a stream of his own bound by affect, by mood, and by aesthetic, dramatic, and religious resonances. In these self-reconstituting moments it was almost as if Jimmie's conscious stream (which lacks substantive memory connections, lacks epistemic connectedness, and is normally an inconsequential dribble) bursts forth into a thick and rich flow that is Jimmie's own. When mood and affect, rather than memory, reconstitute Jimmie's stream, he feels alive, acts alive, and seems happy. The reemergence of a personal stream coincides with the reemergence of a person, a bona fide self. The Humean drivel disappears for a time. His consciousness becomes more like a stream than like islands in the sea.

Jimmie's case and those of individuals in identity crises show how consciousness and personhood are connected. Persons experience their experiences as their own. Normally, experiences are bound together in a sensibly continuous stream in which the past is appropriated by present consciousness, which is itself poised to move into the future. The sort of identity constituted by remembering who one is over time and carrying out complex intentions and plans that fit one's self is undermined whenever the personal stream of consciousness is seriously impaired. This can happen because of major life traumas, as in Erikson's cases, or because of brain damage, as in a case such as Jimmie's.

7 Phenomenal Competition

Can the way consciousness seems withstand pressure from theorizing about the way it really is, its underlying causal structure, its place in the mind as a whole, and its place in nature? Is the phenomenology in competition with the facts?

One might think that the phenomenology is true as phenomenology, as a description of how things seem from a point of view that tries to be both naive, in the sense of not bringing a load of theory to bear, but also reflective enough to notice things, like the network features of consciousness, as well as the fringe and its role, that do not reveal themselves in any simple and straightforward way in experience. One might nonetheless think that phenomenology does more harm than good when it comes to developing a proper theory of consciousness, since it fosters certain illusions about the nature of consciousness. I will focus my discussion by reflecting briefly on three issues: the continuity question, the binding problem, and the idea that mind is massively parallel rather than serial.

Continuity

One alleged illusion that the phenomenology might be accused of fostering is the idea that consciousness is continuous, when in fact it is not. Daniel Dennett, ever the gadfly, thinks that it is a "crashing mistake" to think that one of the most striking features of consciousness is its continuity. "This is utterly wrong. One of the most striking features of consciousness is its *dis*continuity—as revealed in the blind spot, and saccadic gaps, to take the simplest examples. The discontinuity of consciousness is surprising because of the *apparent* continuity of consciousness.... Consciousness may in general be a very gappy phenomenon, and as long as the temporal edges of the gaps are not positively perceived, there will be no sense of the gappiness of the 'stream' of consciousness" (Dennett 1991a, 356).

Here is a good place to focus again on the tension between the subjective and the objective and on a certain ambiguity in the idea of the nature of consciousness. Dennett accepts that consciousness is apparently continuous, despite the existence of temporal gaps, changes in focus within and between modalities, and so on. So consciousness feels like a stream. This is its subjective side. But objectively, there is evidence of gaps and qualitative contrast. James acknowledged this. Viewed subjectively, consciousness is streamlike. Viewed objectively, it is less streamlike. Which is the truth? James thought that both can be true. I think he is right.

Both can be true because they have points of view built in. Phenomeno-logically, consciousness is a stream. Objectively, it is less streamlike. Interesting research problems fall out of the apparent tension between the two stories. Suppose that neuroscientists discover that consciousness is in fact realized like a movie reel consisting of individual images, the moments of consciousness, with small separations between them, the gaps. It is not clear that this would or should have any impact on what we say about how consciousness seems from a first-person point of view. What we have is the interesting problem of explaining how the streamlike quality so dominates ordinary awareness when the brain processes subserving it are so gappy. It isn't that we have an illusion to be explained. There is no mistake or illusion involved in claiming that consciousness feels streamlike. Again, the point of view is built in. The interesting question is why subjective consciousness is insensitive, if it is, to certain things about itself, objectively construed. Eventually we want a fine-grained answer of the sort we can give for how other discrete things, e.g., movies, give a continuous impression. Giving a continuous impression may well be what the system is designed to do. In that case there is no mistake in thinking that consciousness seems streamlike. It does because it is designed to feel that way.

Relatedly, consider the cascading saccadic eye movements. It is very impressive that the brain smooths over and ignores the visual leaping about of our eyes, and we will want a fine-grained explanation of how the brain does this. The mood at the start of inquiry should not be one of disappointment in the powerlessness of consciousness to reveal the way the brain works. Given the role of consciousness in "steering a nervous system grown too complex to regulate itself," it would be bad evolutionary design if consciousness were an accurate detector of all the neural goings-on. Its job is not to do neuroscience!

So we can accept that consciousness is not a sensitive detector of nonstreamlike features of brain processes without abandoning the idea that it is subjectively streamlike. We can also accept that our consciousness of the external world is gappy without doing harm to the claim that consciousness has a subjective streamlike character. Consciousness does not pick up all the information in the world. There are the visual blindspots, and there is much that we simply fail to consciously notice. But who would have thought otherwise? There are all sorts of interesting research questions about why we notice what we notice, about the architecture and baseline sensitivities of the sensory modalities, and about sensory compensation. But the fact that there are things in the world we miss at each and every moment has no direct consequences for the streamlike quality of consciousness. We must be careful, as James says, not to infer gaps in the conscious stream from gaps in what we know about things in the world.

That said, it is a very interesting question how we ought to conceive of cases of divided consciousness. William James was impressed by our ability to split consciousness and to attend to two different things and perform two different acts at once, though we are unaware at the time that we are doing so. Consciousness *"may be split into parts which coexist but mutually ignore each other"* (James 1890, 206). Are such cases, cases in which there are two distinct streams running simultaneously in parallel, or is there simply a single complex stream? One possibility is that a single attentional mechanism switches back and forth between two tasks at blazing speed. The mind somehow sequesters each task-solving sequence so that each seems to take place in a stream of its own, running in apparent parallel with the other stream, when in fact there is an objectively choppy serial switchback mechanism at work. The development of better theories about brain structure and function, about attention, perception, and motor activity, will help us to answer questions about apparent split streams. This is a case where the phenomenology is unclear in its deliverances and where we can imagine discoveries about underlying processes changing what we are inclined to say about the way things seem from a first person point of view.

In sum, I don't see that the phenomenological stream needs to foster any illusions. The National Science Foundation should not fund neuroscientists who want to use expensive equipment to find the stream. But they should fund researchers who want to explain the various discrepancies between the way consciousness seems and the way it is from the objective point of view. There is at this point in time no objective phenomena that warrants giving up the streamlike phenomenology.

Binding

The stream of consciousness is, among other things, a stream of perceptions. I see the yellow tennis ball. I see your face and hear what you say. I see and smell the bouquet of roses. The binding problem arises by paying attention to how these coherent perceptions arise. There are specialized sets of neurons that detect different aspects of objects in the visual field. The color and motion of the ball are detected by different sets of neurons in different areas of the visual cortex (the medial temporal lobe and V4, respectively). Binding seeing and hearing, or seeing and smelling, is even more complex, since multimodal perception involves labor in different areas of the cortex, and when audition is involved, in areas of the paleocortex as well. The problem is how all this individually processed information can give rise to a unified percept. The answer would be simple if there were a place where all the outputs of all the processors involved delivered their computations at the same time, a faculty of consciousness, as it were. But the evidence suggests that there is no such place. There is simply lots of activity in the relevant areas, with resonance spreading near and far.

The binding problem is a puzzle, a deep problem, in cognitive neuroscience. But I don't see that it touches the claim that consciousness is a stream. (Wundt discovered in the 1880s that the *felt* simultaneity of seeing and smelling a rose are sometimes detectably sequential, even by the very person who feels them to be simultaneous!) Indeed, the facts that consciousness is streamlike and that its contents are unified perceptions make the binding problem a problem. Binding occurs. The question is whether it occurs by all the computations of special purpose processors finding a path to some yet to be discovered central headquarters (see Baars 1988 for an argument for a central "blackboard," a global workplace, realized in the extended reticular-thalamic activating system) or whether a certain level of synchronous oscillatory patterns in the relevant pathways simply produces perceptual binding without ever joining up, so that "timing is binding." Rather than standing in the way of this research, the phenomenology of the stream motivates explanatory work designed to explain how disparate processors can give rise to felt perceptual unity.

Parallelism
Daniel Dennett, we have seen, accepts that consciousness seems streamlike or continuous but thinks that it is a crashing mistake to think that it really is so. I tried above to show how we could save the truth of a streamlike phenomenology from Dennett's challenge. Consciousness is streamlike, and it is an important research problem to explain how and why it is this way phenomenologically, despite the fact that the physiological and brain processes that subserve consciousness are not streamlike in many respects.

One argument against the stream metaphor that I have not considered directly is based on the idea that the architecture of mind is massively parallel and that consciousness itself involves "parallel pandemoniums." Without even being sure what parallel pandemoniums are, it seems pretty clear that if 'parallel pandemoniums' is the right metaphor for consciousness, the metaphor of the stream must go. The two metaphors are not compatible.

Dennett provides a thumbnail sketch of his theory of consciousness in these words:

> There is no single, definitive "stream of consciousness," because there is no central Headquarters, no Cartesian Theater where "it all comes together" for the perusal of a Central Meaner. Instead of such a single stream (however wide) there are multiple channels in which specialist circuits try, in parallel pandemoniums, to do their various things, creating Multiple Drafts as they go. Most of these fragmentary drafts of "narrative" play short-lived roles in the modulation of current activity but some get promoted to further functional roles, in swift succession, by the activity of a virtual machine in the brain. The seriality of this machine (its "von Neumannesque" character) is not a

"hard-wired" design feature, but rather the upshot of a succession of coalitions of these specialists.   (1991a, 253–254)

There is a lot going on in this passage. Indeed, this passage is an attempt to sketch Dennett's whole theory of consciousness. It deserves the treatment of a Talmudic exegete, whereas I can offer only some brief remarks on the main point of controversy: whether parallel architecture spells doom for the idea of a conscious stream. My view is that is does not.

First, notice that the quote ends with an acknowledgment of the seriality of consciousness, "its 'von Neumannesque' character," whereas it begins with a denial that there is a "single, definitive 'stream of consciousness.'" The quote is largely given over to defending a theory of mind in which most of the processing is carried out by a system of specialized processors often working in parallel. On Dennett's view, the system of "specialist circuits" are involved in the never ending process of performing "micro takes" on various matters that call on their powers. Only some takes become conscious. This idea is widely accepted (Calvin 1990, 1991; Baars 1988; Johnson-Laird 1983, 1988; Rumelhart and McClelland 1986). There is agreement that most mental processing is unconscious and occurs in parallel. There is also agreement that consciousness is serial or streamlike in quality (this despite our insensitivity to certain nonstreamlike features of the physiological processes that subserve consciousness, the saccades of the eye, for example). What there is disagreement about is whether the qualitative seriality, the streamlike feel of consciousness, is supported by an architectural feature of mind that is in fact really serial or whether the system consists of parallel processors from top to bottom that nonetheless have the capacity to produce the streamlike phenomenology. This is an interesting and complicated empirical question, as yet unsolved. But the main point is that the parties to this debate accept the same first-person phenomenology and treat it as a feature of our mental life in need of explanation.

Second and relatedly, since Dennett accepts that consciousness seems serial and streamlike, the complaint in the opening sentence that "there is no single, definitive 'stream of consciousness'" must rest exclusively on the "no single, definitive" part of the sentence, since the streamlike, von Neumannesque character of consciousness—what Dennett elsewhere refers to as its "Joycean character"—is accepted as a legitimate characterization at the end of the passage.

Third, the reason offered for doubting the existence of a single and definitive stream is dubious at best. It is "because there is no central Headquarters, no Cartesian Theater where 'it all comes together' for the perusal of a Central Meaner." But the advocate of the Jamesian or Joycean stream has no need for such weird homunculi. The idea that consciousness has a streamlike quality is unfairly linked to these weird homunculi, and is dragged into the battle designed to destroy the ideas of a Cartesian theater, a central headquarters, and a central meaner. The aim is to defend the multiple-drafts model of mind. This is a credible model of mental processing. But it endangers the idea of the conscious stream not one bit.

Imagine a tailor fitting you for a new suit. He circles you. At what point in his perusal does the tailor achieve a single, definitive grasp of how you look in the suit? The right answer is at no point. The tailor looks, looks again, sizes you up, and forms an opinion about how you look, what needs adjustment, and so on. The tailor is creating drafts as he circles. Each step results in a revision of the previous draft. This continues until he is finished marking fabric and tells you to change back to your street clothes. So far, so good.

However, there being no single, definitive image of what you look like to the tailor is compatible with there being a single, definitive stream-of-consciousness segment for the tailor as he fits you. This single, definitive stream segment is constituted by whatever phenomenal events occurred to the tailor as he circled you (these needn't even mostly have been about you and the suit). To be sure, if the phone had rung or another customer had asked the whereabouts of the tie rack during your fitting, the tailor's stream segment would have been different (the phone and the customer correspond to different probes that change the character of the stream [see Dennett 1991a, 113]). But these counterfactual possibilities weigh not a bit against the idea of a single and definitive stream. They simply show that what character a stream has is incredibly sensitive to small perturbations.

It may well be that the various nonconscious parallel processors involved in giving rise to the conscious stream "are multiple channels in which specialist circuits try, in parallel pandemoniums, to do their various things, creating Multiple Drafts as they go." But all the drafts that reach awareness become part of the singular, definitive stream of consciousness. Still, most of the representations and contents created in the pandemonium of nonconscious information processing never make phenomenal appearances.

The idea of multiple drafts is useful as a metaphor for the nonconscious information processing of mind. It is also useful as a way of describing how thinking, sizing things up, occurs *within* the stream of consciousness. However, when it is used as a metaphor for the conscious stream, it is fully consistent with the idea that there is a singular, definitive stream. The singular, definitive stream is the stream of phenomenal experience that the person actually has, realizes, or undergoes (whether she can remember each and every awareness is irrelevant). When the idea of multiple drafts is used to describe nonconscious parallel processing, the issue of the stream does not arise, so neither does the question of whether the stream is singular and definitive.

In sum, the phenomenology of the stream is robust. The reality of a conscious stream is not incompatible with anything that the science of the mind thus far needs to say. Discontinuities in the neural underpinnings of conscious awareness, the binding problem, and massive parallelism neither undermine nor compete with the description of consciousness as a stream. They make more compelling the need for an explanation of how the stream emerges from neural processes that are anything but streamlike, at least at certain levels. But no one ever thought that consciousness was diaphanous, that we could see right through to its underlying nature and causal structure.

Chapter 9
The Illusion of the Mind's "I"

---

1   The Mind's "I"

In this chapter, I discuss a tempting idea: that there must be an "I" that stands behind all conscious experience as the very condition of its possibility. Thinking that there must be an "I" that stands behind all conscious experience can give rise to the closely related thought that this "I" shadows all experience and thus that all consciousness is self-conscious, that "I think" accompanies all experience. These tempting ideas, taken together, constitute the illusion of the "mind's 'I'." This chapter is designed to show how to avoid the illusion of the mind's "I"—how to avoid being an *egoist*. An egoist is prone to a variety of mistakes: the belief that each individual starts life with a self; the belief that development or enhancement of a preexisting self is possible, but that self-emergence is not; the belief that this original self constitutes the core of the self, our conscious control center, the source of all action plans, and the agent for whom all experiences accrue before being filed for future reference or discarded.

I exploit James's idea that the self is a construct, a model, a product of conceiving of our organically connected mental life in a certain way. My consciousness is mine. It is uniquely personal. But this is not because some mind's "I" shadows my experience. It is because of my nature as an organic thinking thing; it is because of the way thoughts hang together in evolved humans beings. Self-emergence occurs, and self-control is real. But this is not because some antecedent self is filled out or because some inner agent controls what one does. Self-emergence occurs as a person develops. Self-control occurs when an agent initiates action. Sometimes this is done by entering a certain representation of one's self into the motivational circuits and guiding action accordingly. No small-sized but very powerful ego is needed to explain how this happens.

2   The Illusion of Ego

How can one argue that the mind's "I" is an illusion? One tactic is to argue that the alleged fact that the "I" is designed to explain, namely the unity of consciousness, is itself an illusion, and thus not in need of an explanation at all. If conscious experience lacks unity, there is no need to postulate a unifier, an "I" for which it all comes together or that brings it all together. On this view, we have fallen prey to two illusions: the unity of mind and the need for a unifier to explain this unity.

This tactic is unavailable and unappealing to me. There is an important sense in which consciousness is a unity. Furthermore, this unity is in need of explanation. But the explanation that turns on the "I" fosters an illusion. The illusion is that there are two things: on one side, a self, an ego, an "I," that organizes experience, originates action, and accounts for our unchanging identity as persons and, on the other side, the stream of experience. If this view is misleading, what is the better view? The better view is that what there is, and all there is, is the stream of experience. "Preposterous! What then does the thinking?" comes the response. The answer is that "the thoughts themselves are the thinkers" (James, 1892, 83). "Ridiculous! What accounts for my ongoing sense that I am the same person over time?" I hear you say. What account for your ongoing sense of self are the facts that you are constituted by a unique and distinctive stream, that thought can create complex models of the course of the stream in which it occurs, and that you are an insensitive detector of the great changes that accrue to you over time and thus miss how much you do in fact change over time.

We are egoless. This, of course, sounds crazy, so I have a fair amount of explaining and comforting to do. Egolessness is such a chilling thought, but we shall see that it needn't be (Minsky 1985; Varela, Thompson, Rosch 1991; Dennett 1991a).

The main idea is that the self emerges as experience accrues, and it is constructed as the organism actively engages the external world. The self develops. In this sense the ego is an after-the-fact construction, not a before-the-fact condition for the possibility of experience (James 1892, 68–70, 72). Self-representation involves thinking of our dynamic, ever-changing, but organically connected mental life in either of two modes: in the active agent mode or in the passive object mode—as seer or as seen. The first-person pronoun points to an active moment during which the speaker is thinking, possibly about himself. 'I' points to me, or some aspect of me, in the act of thinking or doing something in my capacity as agent or thinker. 'Me' is an objective designation. This is not to say that 'me' gets at or captures the way some individual really is. It is not objective in that sense. 'Me' is objective in that it involves taking some person or aspect of a person's mental life as the content of a thought. 'Me' is objective in that it involves thinking about mental or bodily life. This is less deflationary than it might seem. Although we begin life without a self, one emerges. We develop a character, a personality, a set of aims and ideals. Some aspects constitute a self without being well known to the system that houses them. For example, a person's self might display a stubborn streak without the person seeing herself as such. On the other hand, especially for reflective persons in reflective cultures, many aspects of character and personality become known by the system and utilized by it in initiating action, in self-control, in further self-development, and in self-transformation.

By playing a little phenomenology, showing how this radical view can leave things mostly as they *seem*, we can make things more congenial for this idea that there is no mind's "I" but only organisms with mental capacities to think thoughts, some of which possess self-representational content. By being clearer on what is not being challenged, we will clearly delimit the idea that is being challenged, and we will find less threatening the alternative expressed in William James's motto that "the thoughts themselves are the thinkers" (1892, 83).

3   Me: The Self as Known

To understand the first-person pronoun 'I', we must understand what I mean by 'the self as known', or 'the "*me*"'. Then we will be in a better position to understand the self as knower, the "I." Here is what James writes:

> The consciousness of Self involves a stream of thought, each part of which as "I" can remember those which went before, know the things they knew, and care paramountly for certain ones among them as "*Me*," and *appropriate to these* the rest. This Me is an empirical aggregate of things objectively known. The *I* which knows them ... need [not] ... be an unchanging metaphysical entity like the Soul or a principle like the transcendental Ego, viewed as "out of time." It is a *thought*, at each moment different from that of the last moment, but *appropriative* of the latter, together with all that the latter called its own. All the experiential facts find their place in this description, unencumbered with any hypothesis save that of the existence of passing thoughts or states of mind.   (1892, 82)

There are two key ideas here. First, that what counts as "me" is largely an interest-relative matter. What counts as "me" or "myself" depends on my drawing together into one more or less unified model those events in my personal stream that I "care paramountly" about. What it is like to be me depends in an important sense on what aspects of my self I appropriate at a given time. Second, the "I" that thinks need not be conceived as an unchanging soul or transcendental ego. It doesn't seem like one, after all. It is sufficient to think of the thinking "I" as a thought thickened with an appropriation of a model of the self. When I act, I do what makes sense for my self. This is because the thought that is, so to speak, the proximate cause of my action draws on or appropriates the relevant information about what kind of person I am, what I care about, and so on.

In an expanded version of the same passage in *The Principles*, James adds,

> The nucleus of the *"me"* is always the bodily existence felt to be present at the time. Whatever remembered-past-feelings *resemble* this present feeling are deemed to belong to the same *me* with it. Whatever other things are perceived to be *associated* with this feeling are deemed to form part of that me's *experience*; and of them certain ones (which fluctuate more or less) are reckoned to be themselves *constituents* of the me in a larger sense,—such are the clothes, the material possessions, the friends, the honors and esteem which the person receives or may receive.   (1890, 400)

And earlier in the same chapter he writes, *"The words* ME, *then, and* SELF, *so far as they arouse feeling and connote emotional worth, are* OBJECTIVE *designations, meaning* ALL THE THINGS *which have the power to produce in a stream of consciousness excitement of a certain peculiar sort"* (1890, 319). James points out that the distinction between me and mine is variable. My self, objectively understood, consists of "all the things" that produce the right sort of appropriative feelings. What does this will vary. For an especially acquisitive person, his wealth will constitute an essential part of his self, and the loss of that wealth will undo him. To capture the range of things that can be appropriated into the "me," into one's self-conception, into the thought or set of thoughts that constitute the model of one's self, James distinguishes among a "material me," a "social me," and a "spiritual me."

The material "me" consists first and foremost of one's bodily being, how one experiences one's body, and how one thinks one looks and moves. The sense of what it is like to be "me" normally depends in some important way on the experience of one's bodily being. The material "me" often extends to include one's close relations and friends, whose weal and woe, joys and accomplishments, are felt almost as if they were one's own. The beloved, Aristotle said, is another self. The material "me" might incorporate one's home and other important places to which one's identity is tied and in which it is fostered. "Me," as I have said, is an interest-relative construct; what it contains or fails to contain is determined by what the individual sees as of paramount importance to him.

The social "me" is constituted by the patterns of thought and behavior that one deploys with different groups and on whose successful deployment one understands one's image with that group to depend. James writes, *"Properly speaking, a man has as many social selves as there are individuals who recognize him* and carry an image of him in their mind. To wound any one of these images is to wound him.... We may practically say that he has as many different social selves as there are distinct *groups* of persons about whose opinion he cares" (1892, 46). As with the material "me," the social "me" involves identification and care. This is why one's social self can be wounded.

But we should be wary of accepting James's claim that a person "has as many different social selves as there are distinct *groups* of persons about whose opinion he cares." The self is a very complex construct. Nonetheless, there are pressures to coordinate and to bring into reflective equilibrium the different ways of conceiving the self. I will speak of the model of the self to refer to the highest-order model of the self that contains the various components of the material, social, and spiritual "me" as proper parts or aspects. Tactically, this allows me to side with James on the important point of the self being a construct without advancing the dubious idea of self-proliferation. Different *aspects* of the self can explain everything that several different selves can explain without undermining the sense of phenomenological self-coherence that most people experience.

The spiritual self is not spiritual in any hoary metaphysical sense. It too belongs to the empirical self. It refers to the "entire collection of my states of consciousness, my psychic faculties and dispositions taken concretely.... When we *think of ourselves as thinkers*, all the other ingredients of our Me seem relatively external possessions." We think of ourselves as spiritual selves when we think of the "active-feeling" states of consciousness, when we think of ourselves as possessing the capacities of sensation and will, the capacities to desire and to experience emotions. This "me" is spiritual in the sense that there is a "peculiar *internality* of whatever states possess this quality of seeming to be active" (James 1892, 48). When turned into its active mode, this spiritual self is the "I." The fact that when we "think of ourselves as thinkers, all the other ingredients of our Me seem relatively external possessions" does not mean that we do not in fact bring our thick and complex models of our selves, or the relevant aspects of them, to the active-feeling episodes of our lives. When we think and act, certain aspects of the great historical legacy of who and what we are, are appropriated by the very thought that does the thinking. Each conscious thought is suffused by a "psychic overtone," which carries the resonances of various aspects of the stream's own past (James 1890, 258). Minimally, each new thought or thinking episode appropriates the sense that it occurs in *this* stream.

The interplay among, reflection on, and social feedback about various aspects of our empirical self are the source of self-respect, self-esteem, self-satisfaction, and self-despair. Furthermore, each "me" (the material, social, and spiritual "me") has a past, a current form, and certain unfulfilled potentials. A reflective person, and even an unreflective person bothered by a sense of dissonance, draws these analytically distinct "me"s into coordinated play in the processes of living, planning, self-comprehending, and self-improving. The "me" thoughts that are worked over in attempts at reducing dissonance can be vividly conscious, inchoate, or unconscious. But, you ask, what in the world is this talk about self-comprehension and self-improvement if there is no self to orchestrate the comprehending and carry out the transformation? The critic will remind us that I have recommended egolessness!

4   The Seduction

Thinking about the empirical self seems to make the rationale for positing a real self, an antecedent "I," a transcendental ego, more rather than less warranted. We can think we have captured the mind's "I" when we locate the active spiritual self and bind it to the identity-constitutive aspects of the material and social selfs. We can be seduced into thinking that in having the thoughts that we have powers of perception and agency and that certain things we care about constitute our identities, we have isolated some internal ego, a self from which these powers of perception and will emanate and in which our identity-constitutive commitments are held.

The mistake here is small but significant. Each of us is an agent. Each of us has an identity. But there is no small, more-powerful agent inside each of us. There is no need to posit a "'sanctuary within the citadel' of our personal life" (James 1890, 303).

The posit of a mind's "I" is unnecessary. First, whatever is captured is an object, a model, a thing thought of or represented. The spiritual me, the material me, and the social me, even when integrated in thought, are things seen, not the seer. The obvious questions arise. What does the seeing? Who is the seer? The answer is that a whole organism, with its functional nervous system, is the seer. To be sure, we detect the active capacities of our self and the identity-constitutive components of our self. We detect these things as thinkers, and we frame our self-comprehension by mustering thoughts that carry rich information about the past course of the stream and the direction in which it is headed. Thoughts, whether turned toward the external world or to the organism itself, are enriched with complex anticipatory models of the nature of what we are about to meet, and they are steeped and dyed in waters rich with information about the self and past agency (Johnson-Laird 1983, 1988; Lakoff 1987; Baars 1988).

But we never detect an immutable self, a transcendental ego, or a mind's "I." Nor do we need to posit that such is brought to experience. Thoughts that contain images of an evolving self are enough to explain the sense of self. And the complexity and organismic integrity of the nervous system are enough to explain how a continuous stream of connected experiences accrues. Furthermore, whatever we detect when we detect ourselves thinking causally efficacious thoughts hardly includes the detection of these thoughts as incorporeal. "*Whenever my introspective glance succeeds in turning around quickly enough to catch one of these manifestations of spontaneity in the act, all it can ever feel distinctly is some bodily process, for the most part taking place within the head*" (James 1890, 300). James puzzles over feelings of sensations, emotions, acts of spontaneous will, and he concludes that *"our entire feeling of spiritual activity, or what commonly passes by that name is really a feeling of bodily activities whose exact nature is by most men overlooked"* (1892, 302).

The upshot is that we can be egoless without vaporizing. Some egoless beings are embodied persons. Personal selves abound. We are examples. But it is an illusion to think that these personal selves contain an inner agent, an ego, a mind's "I." So you get to keep yourself. Nothing changes.

5   I: The Self as Knower

When James finishes his discussion of the empirical self, he tells us that he has said all that there is to say about "the phenomenal self" (1890, 329–330). Since James is no friend of a noumenal self, a transcendentally real self about whose nature we cannot speak (1890, 342–350, 360–370), all that needs to be said about the "I" is contained in, or can be derived from, what has been said about the phenomenal self. 'I' is first and foremost a grammatical construction. It is an indexical that denotes either the organism that is doing the thinking or some model of the self, one of James's empirical "me"s, that is now judged to be controlling the motivational circuits, loading the dice of thought and action. So when I say, "I intend to start Van Wert as catcher," my coach self is indexed and dominates the motivational circuits. When I say, "I reject immaterialism," my philosopher self is indexed and involved in what I add to the claim by way of explanation. 'I' marks my self in its agent role. According to the circumstances, 'I' marks my self narrowly, as when it picks out aspects of my overall self (my coach self, my philosopher self), or broadly, as when it simply picks out *this* subject of experience.

> The words *I* and *me* signify nothing mysterious and unexampled— they are at bottom only names of *emphasis*; and Thought is always emphasizing something.... It contrasts a *here* with a *there*, ... a *now* with a *then*: of a pair of things it calls one *this*, the other *that*. *I* and *thou*, *I* and *it*, are distinctions exactly on a par with these— distinctions possible within an exclusively *objective* field of knowledge, the 'I' meaning for the Thought nothing but the bodily life which it momentarily feels.... All appropriations *may* be made *to* it by a Thought not immediately cognized by itself.   (James 1890, 341; see Rosenthal 1989 for development of the idea that consciousness involves thoughts, which are not immediately cognized themselves, cognizing other thoughts.)

There are two points I want to emphasize. First, the words 'I' and 'me' are ordinary grammatical constructions, designed like other grammatical constructions to pick out things worth picking out. Second, 'I' normally emphasizes the thought of myself as agent rather than patient—it marks this person, this bodily life, being active. Nothing here is mysterious.

James writes,

> The I, or 'pure ego,' is a very much more difficult subject of inquiry that the Me. It is that which at any given moment *is* conscious, whereas the Me is only one of the things which it is conscious *of.*... [The I] is the *Thinker*; and the question immediately comes up *what* is the thinker? Is it the passing state of consciousness itself, or is it something deeper and less mutable? The passing state we have seen to be the very embodiment of change. Yet each of us spontaneously considers that by 'I,' he means something always the same.   (1892, 63)

James rejects the postulation of both the substantial 'I' of Cartesianism and the transcendental, noumenal self of Kant. Both are antinaturalistic: the first removes the self from space, the second from time. Neither an incorporeal soul nor a ubiquitous accompanying ego about which we cannot speak "explains anything" (1890, 350).

> *If there were no passing states of consciousness*, then indeed we might suppose an abiding principle, absolutely one with itself, to be the ceaseless thinker in each one of us. But if the states of consciousness be accorded as realities, no such "substantial" identity in the thinker need be supposed. Yesterday's and to-day's states of consciousness have no *substantial* identity, for when one is here the other is irrevocably dead and gone. But they have *functional* identity, for both know the same objects, and so far as the by-gone me is one of those objects, they react upon it in an identical way, greeting it and calling it *mine*, and opposing it to all the other things we know. This functional identity seems really the only sort of identity in the thinker which the facts require us to suppose. Successive thinkers, numerically distinct, but all aware of the same past in the same way, form an adequate vehicle for all the experience of personal unity and sameness which we actually have. And just such a train of successive thinkers is the stream of mental states.... The logical conclusion seems then to be that *the states of consciousness are all that psychology needs to do her work with.... For psychology the hypothesis of ... a substantial principle of unity is superfluous.* (James 1892, 69–70)

The "successive thinkers" of which James speaks here are the successive thoughts in the stream.

A natural question arises: "*Why* should each successive mental state appropriate the same past Me?" (James 1890, 70). The answer is that my organic constitution, the way my central nervous system works, guarantees that my own past psychic history is drawn into the present moment with a certain "warmth and intimacy."

It is tempting to think that I am in a boat drifting along on a stream. The warmth and intimacy of my experience is accounted for by the fact that I am there at every point of the journey enjoying the scenery. But that is not the metaphor. There is just the stream. There is no person in a boat adrift on it.

We might try to meddle with the metaphor and make room for an immutable self-comprehending mind's "I" in a different way. Perhaps I am the stream bed. The warmth and intimacy of my experience is explained by the fact that I am the welcoming container in which the flow happens. I contain all the experiences. The idea is of an arch-ego that contains "the entire stream of thought and all the selves that may be represented in it" (James 1890, 338–339). But this is not the metaphor either. To be sure, the streambed constrains and effects what happens in the stream. Furthermore, focusing on the stream bed is useful in thinking about the depth and breadth, ebb and flow, murk and clarity, of the stream. But it is not a particularly plausible metaphor for an arch-ego. Stream beds are mutable, quirky, and finite. The arch-ego is immutable. Stream beds constrain, contain, and have effects, but they are complete know-nothings. The arch-ego knows most everything. James is drawn again to the conclusion that we let the embedded stream do all the work:

> For how would it be if the Thought, the present judging Thought, instead of being in any way substantially or transcendentally identical with the former owner of the past self, merely inherited his title.... It would then, if its birth coincided exactly with the death of another owner, *find* the past self already its own as soon as it found it at all, and thus the past self would thus never be wild, but always owned, by a title that never lapsed. We can imagine a long succession of herdsmen coming rapidly into possession of the same cattle by transmission of an original title by bequest. May not the "title" of a collective self be passed from one Thought to another in some analogous way? ... It is a patent fact of consciousness that a transmission like this actually occurs. Each pulse of consciousness, each Thought, dies away and is replaced by another. The other, among the things it knows, knows its own predecessor, and finding it "warm," ... greets it, saying: "Thou art *mine*, and part of the same self with me." ... Each Thought is thus born an owner, and dies owned, transmitting whatever it realizes as its Self to its own later proprietor.... It is this trick which the nascent thought has of immediately taking up the expiring thought and "adopting" it, which is the foundation of the appropria-

tion of most of the remoter constituents of the self. Who owns the last self owns the self before the last, for what possesses the possessor possesses the possessed.   (1890, 339–340)

James rightly asks the reader's natural question: "But *why* should each successive mental state adopt the same past Me?" James does not immediately give an answer. Rather, he alludes back to an earlier discussion of evolution. Nature needs to have endowed us with capacities for self-concern and self-preservation. Mechanisms for self-concern and self-preservation require memory capable of retaining information relevant to the idiosyncratic adaptive activity of persons in idiosyncratic environments. Memory for the particulars of one's life becomes crucial. Nature could have built a little but very powerful "I" inside each person to organize memory and orchestrate life, or she could have solved the design problem with the neat trick of endowing each nascent thought with the power to take up the expiring thought, to adopt it, and to appropriate the (relevant) memories about the remoter constituents of the self. In this way "who owns the last self owns the self before last, for what possesses the possessor possesses the possessed" (James 1890, 340; 1892, 72). The brain holds no evidence that it contains a conscious control faculty. Even if it did, it would be mutable, since everything natural is. It appears that nature adopted the streamlike design that James thought it had. Egolessness reigns.

I have insisted that this idea is credible. Still the idea that the "thoughts themselves are the thinkers" requires a bit more explaining. James says that we should *"use the words* ME *and* I *for the empirical person and judging thought"* (1890, 371). This is confusing. First, the idea of a single judging thought requires clarification. Here James's own idea of "appropriation" can help. Appropriation involves both finding and fashioning unity (Myers 1986, 349). Individual thoughts are the thinkers. But they carry the weight of tradition in thinking what they think. Having appropriated past thoughts, including thoughts about myself, the empirical person I am, acts of thinking are now capable of taking in new experiences in a way framed, indeed constituted, by all that has gone before. Using the word 'I' to refer to a judging thought simpliciter, needs to be interpreted in this way: 'I' is an indexical denoting the person as a whole in her thinking capacity. 'I' names this judging thought only insofar as this thought is appropriative, only insofar as it appropriates my life and brings to bear some appropriate model of who I am. James says, "Personality implies the incessant presence of two elements, an objective person, known by a passing subjective Thought and recognized as continuing in time" (1890, 371).

There is no antecedent metaphysical ego. But there is an important sense in which experiences are structured by whatever personality has developed and is in place at any given time. Furthermore, there is an important sense in which the passing subjective Thought that knows the objective person, the Thought marked by 'I', knows that person in advance as it thinks. It knows the objective self in advance because the occurrent thought emerges from a system with a certain history, a system that knows about that history and brings various aspects of that history to bear in thinking any new thought or generating any new action.

6 Personal Identity

For James, personal identity is a matter of degree. He is a continuity theorist in the tradition of John Locke, and he rejects the views of Immanuel Kant, Joseph Butler, and Thomas Reid, who in their different ways posit a problematic immutable ego. There is no such thing as a person, or a proper part of a person—her ego, self, or mind's "I"—that is exactly the same over time (James 1890, 332–334; 1892, 68). "*The sense of our own personal identity ... is exactly like any one of our other perceptions of sameness among phenomena. It is a conclusion grounded on the resemblance in a fundamental respect*" (James 1890, 334). "If in the sentence 'I am the same that I was yesterday', we take the 'I' broadly, it is evident that in many ways I am *not* the same.... The Me of now and the Me of then are *continuous*: the alterations were gradual and never affected the whole of me at once" (James 1892, 68).

The present thought in the stream of consciousness hugs to itself and adopts its own past. It thereby stands "as the *representative* of an entire past stream with which it is in no wise to be identified" (James 1892, 72). To say that the present state of the stream represents the entire past stream but is not to be identified with it is a way of emphasizing both that the past is experienced as past and that it is a variable matter whether any particular past experiences are actively remembered. My present state of consciousness is continuous with my past. The past determines the felt quality of the present, and many parts of my past (but not even remotely all) are recoverable as my memories. Past conscious thoughts make themselves felt in the process of appropriation, in the fringe, in the penumbra.

Yet it is a mistake to think that most, even many, of the past conscious thoughts that affect the here and now are themselves consciously present. Nothing in the phenomenology indicates their presence. Besides, it would be a terrible, noisy design that kept all memories active. Certain hallucinatory experiences might be fun, but all that noise wouldn't be fun. Most things are better forgotten.

> The Me, like every other aggregate, changes as it grows. The passing states of consciousness, which should preserve in their succession an identical knowledge of its past, wander from their duty, letting large

portions drop from out of their ken, and representing other portions wrong. The identity which we recognize as we survey the long progression can only be the relative identity of a slow shifting in which there is always some common ingredient maintained. The commonest element of all, the most uniform, is the possession of some common memories.... Thus the identity found by the *I* in its *Me* is only a loosely constructed thing, an identity "on the whole." (James 1892, 72; 1890, 371–372)

'I' is an indexical—it (typically) refers to "THIS subject of experience NOW," this concrete particular subject of experience, this "concrete person" (James 1892, 92). Because the "I" appropriates the contents of an ever changing stream and because it meets that stream with models of "me," of a complex self whose parts are undergoing constant revision, the "I" itself is continuously enriched and renewed. The system is dynamic. No part of the system resembles the soul, the ego, the self, or the "I" of traditional metaphysics. There is no mind's "I" that stands behind all experience as the condition of its possibility. This is because there is nothing that stands behind anything without something else standing behind it as the condition of its possibility. This is true even for the whole organism. A human organism is a thinker only if it possesses a functioning nervous system and is embedded in a world that sustains it. The "I" "is a *thought* at each moment different from that of the last moment but *appropriative* of the latter, together with all that the latter called its own. All the experiential facts find their place in this description, unencumbered with any hypothesis save that of the existence of passing thoughts or states of mind" (James 1892, 82).

Framed in this way, the seemingly radical idea that "the thoughts themselves are the thinkers" makes utter sense. As the stream flows and accrues a history, various models, including an ever changing model of the self, become part of the dynamic dispositional structure of the brain. We are brainy creatures who meet experience thinking. So Kant was half right. I am a cognitively enriched system with an identity and a character, and I do come to meet the world halfway. But there is nothing transcendental about this "I." There is only my empirical self, accrued over a lifetime and represented partly consciously and partly nonconsciously in my brain, and it is active on each occasion of thought, imagination, and action.

7   The Unbearable Lightness of Egolessness

The ideas that there is a real self, a transcendental ego, or a mind's "I" that accompanies all experience are variations on a fictional theme. This is not to deny that we have a higher-order self (or a set of self models). We do.

The self is the center of narrative gravity (Dennett 1989). This is the self that we posit when we say who we are, and it is the self that others posit in doing the same. When things go well, the two posits, the first-person self and the third-person self harmoniously coexist. We do not need to deny that the self plays a functional role in mental life. In fact, it plays several crucial roles. Most crucially, it plays the role of giving organization, meaning, and structure to a life that extends over a half dozen or more decades. Nonetheless, it is puzzling how a mere mental model can organize, guide, and give meaning to anything, especially to something as complex and profoundly important as a human life. The tug remains to posit something more substantial, a mind's "I."

The answer to the puzzle, in broad strokes, is that a person's higher-order self is one of the many models contained in her brain. There are also the multifarious models of the external natural world, of other selves, of social norms, of various motor routines, and so on. Whether a person's model of his self is grandly self-deceived or well grounded in the way he lives and whether it sets its sights on worthy aims or unworthy ideals, once acquired and in operation, it is part of the recurrent brain network causally responsible for the life he lives and how he thinks and feels. ⸜

It is tempting to think that mind *must* have a control center and that the conscious self must be *the* control center in the mind. James thought this idea was a nonstarter: "There is no one cell or group of cells in the brain of such anatomical or functional pre-eminence as to appear to be the keystone or centre of gravity of the whole system" (1890, 180). Despite such authoritative prescience in favor of a model of distributed consciousness, almost every picture of mind drawn during the heyday of functional flowcharts, that is, from the late 1960s to the beginning of the 1990s, contained a box whose job was conscious control (see, for example figure 9.1, from Dennett 1978, 155).

One reason for thinking that the mind must have a single central control device is that it seems that an efficient design will involve a "high level processor that monitors and controls the overall goals of lower-level processors, which in turn monitor and control the processors at a still lower level, and so on in a hierarchy of parallel processors, which at the lowest level govern sensory and motor interactions with the external world" (Johnson-Laird 1983, 463; see also Johnson-Laird 1988, 353–368). The phenomenology of the stream of consciousness, together with this sort of reasoning, has led many philosophers and cognitive scientists to posit consciousness as the operating system of the mind. It is implemented as a serial von Neumann device laid over the system of massively parallel processors.

The basic idea has considerable appeal. Consciousness has a serial quality. It has a heavily representational character. We typically do what we

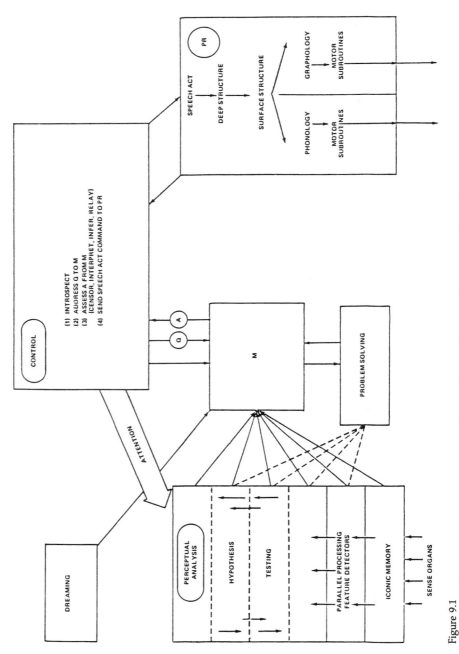

Figure 9.1
A picture of the mind with a conscious control center. (Reprinted with permission from Dennett 1978, 155.)

consciously intend, and so on. Johnson-Laird suggests a possible evolutionary scenario in which a serial conscious-control mechanism might have emerged: "A primal form of consciousness may originally have emerged from the web of parallel processors as a way of overriding deadlocks and other pathological interactions" (1983, 464; see also p. 477).

An alternative and underestimated possibility is that there is in fact no center of control, no von Neumann device laid over the system of parallel processors. What there is instead is a Darwin machine all the way down (more akin to a connectionist PDP device). The idea that there is a single serial control device might be a "user-illusion," to use Dennett's phrase. According to this alternative centerless view, conscious experience emerges seriatim, in a streamlike fashion, because the recurrent network of parallel processors declares one winner at a time in the competition among all its tracks (imagine the tracks to be like a multitude of students in a lecture hall raising their hands to gain the floor, though they can only do so one at a time). When there are lots of events worthy of one's attention, the brain queues them up in an orderly fashion. The winner of the competition for attention is the production of the overall state of the nervous system, which is due to certain wired in weightings (pain gets attention) and to the coordinated system of weighted models of the world and the self (it is therefore less arbitrary in its method of selection than most teachers are in the manner in which they call on questioners from a sea of enthusiastic flailing arms). On this model, we no longer need a box marked "control," although there may be something like a serial buffer (or many serial buffers only one of which can be operative at a time: if the pain buffer is on and registering excruciating pain, then the theorem-proving buffer cannot also be on). The idea that the brain is a Darwin machine, with many modular parallel processors working at once, helps us to understand both how consciousness can emerge without reaching any single central and unified faculty of consciousness and how control can emerge without any single center or processor (the Self) directing the entire show.

Apparently, many bird flocks operate according to this basic theme. It has been established that certain flocks maintain cohesion without depending on any single leader or even on a small cadre of leaders. Flocks paint the skies with the most amazing aesthetic patterns and with many different birds moving to the flock's leading edge at different times. "Birds of a feather are chaotic together" (Weiss 1990, 172). Actually, many birds that migrate long distances, Canadian geese, for example, depend on a cadre of leaders trading the leader's role to avoid exhaustion (Ken Winkler, personal conversation). They work more like a team of cyclists who trade the lead and tuck in behind the ever changing beacon to catch the vacuum he creates. But the fact remains that in neither the case of swarming starling or sparrow flocks nor the case of flocks of migrating geese or ducks does any single leader run the whole show. Teamwork is everything.

William Calvin compares the process whereby we come to display a particular personality and to experience ourself as unified as akin to the situation of a choir: "The population evolves, as the scattered group of novel individuals start coalescing into a synchronous chorus. The dominant version now becomes the one that won out in the competition, not the one written down on some preordained sheet of music" (1990, 269). The synchronous chorus is in one sense not really a serial processor. It might seem like one to the chorus and to the audience as it listens to the music produced. It is *virtually* serial, but strictly speaking, the choral performance is the straightforward emergent product of a system of parallel processors (the singers and players) working in synchrony.

> The narrator of our conscious experience arises from the current winner of a multitrack Darwin Machine competition. It isn't an explanation for everything that goes on in our head, but it is an explanation for that *virtual* executive that directs our attention, sometimes outward toward a real house, sometimes inward toward a remembered house or imagined doll's house, sometimes free-running to create our stream of consciousness. Directing sensory attention may seem unlike making movement plans, but the neural circuits seem analogous, all parts of that frontal lobe circuitry used in making preparations for action.   (Calvin 1990, 270, my italics)

Either way, whether consciousness is implemented in an *actual* serial brain processor or a *virtual* one, it has the phenomenological characteristics of a stream. Furthermore, the higher-order model of the self plays an important causal role in our overall psychological economy. Although the self may not be *the* control center, it, in setting out or broadcasting plans, aspirations, ideals, and so on, does give the rest of the cognitive system information about what subplans to implement when and what parts of the natural and social world to focus on in the effort to stay on course. But just as other conscious and unconscious models contained in the brain are responsive to the higher-order model of the self, so too the higher-order model of the self is responsive to new experiences. The self of narrative construction changes, sometimes radically, over the course of a life. The self of the conscious stream is fluid, qualitatively ebbs and flows, circles roundabout, runs deeply and shallowly, is at times stagnant and muddy and at times as swift and clear as a white river. The self is natural. And because it is natural, it is quirky in ways in which a mind's "I" or transcendental ego could never be.

Chapter 10
Consciousness and the Self

---

1 Weak and Strong Self-Consciousness

Some have thought that human consciousness is necessarily self-conscious and that this feature distinguishes our human consciousness from that of other conscious creatures. Is all human consciousness self-conscious? And if all human consciousness is self-conscious, what self or aspects of the self am I conscious of when I think?

There is a weak sense in which the idea that consciousness is self-conscious makes sense. Infants are subjects of experience. There is something it is like to be a newborn. But newborns have no concept of the self. It is credible nonetheless to describe what it is like to be an infant as involving an inchoate sense that something is happening here, where 'here' gestures elusively to what the newborn will some day come to designate in more transparently self-referential terms. Utterances deploying self-referential terms—'I', 'my', 'mine', 'me', 'myself', or the child's name with a verb ('Sam eats')—are absent until about 19 months but are common by 27 months (Kagan 1989, 233). Around the time of the second birthday, children are competent at locating them*selves* in the causal nexus, in relation to external objects, as sources of action and as fountains of desires. Even when self-referential capacities arrive—the result, I presume, of brain maturation, certain innate dispositions, and normal interaction with persons and things —nothing very exotic in relation to the self needs to be imputed. Most self-referential utterances serve simply to locate the agent and express her thoughts and desires as hers. Yet this is no small accomplishment. By this time the child does possess some sort of self concept. She can clearly mark off herself and her individual actions, beliefs, and desires from the rest of things. But the child is not telling us *who she is* or *what she is like* in any deep sense when she uses her name or words like 'I' and 'my'. In part, this is because one's name and words like 'I' and 'my' primarily serve indexical functions. They do not function to say who one is. That requires a narrative. Furthermore, when the child first acquires self-referential capacities, there is no deep way that she is, at least not yet (Stern 1985).

We can say that self-referential utterances express self-referential thoughts. But self-referential thoughts need not be about the self in any strong sense. Still one might think that all thoughts are (eventually) self-referential in the sense that they are explicitly marked in the child's mind as her own, as "*my*-thoughts." It is doubtful that this is the case. The facts that children consciously think and that they have self-referential capacities provide no warrant for the claim that "I think that" accompanies all thought. The thought that precedes the report "I see a red ball" is normally simply a perception of a red ball, a red-ball-there experience. Seeing a red ball is phenomenologically robust, and it involves being self-conscious in whatever weak sense having a phenomenologically robust experience does. But seeing a red ball requires no conscious marking on the subject's part, in language or in thought, of her own involvement in the seeing. Indeed, only 35 percent of two-year-olds' utterances involve self-reference of any sort (Kagan 1989, 233). Children say, "There is a red ball," more often than they say, "I see a red ball." It is unlikely that unverbalized thought involves appreciably more self-reference than verbalized thought. It is unlikely, that is, that after two years all perception and thought is an "I perceive that [_____]" perception or an "I think that [_____]" thought.

It is an illusion, fostered by reflection on experience, insofar as reflection requires that we be thinking about thought, that an "I think that" thought accompanies all experience. Furthermore, even when we do think or speak in self-referential terms, there is no warrant for the claim that we are thinking about our complex narrative self. We are not *that* self-conscious. The upshot is that all subjective experience is self-conscious in the weak sense that there is something it is like for the subject to have that experience. This involves a sense that the experience is the subject's experience, that it happens to her, occurs in her stream.

The low-level self-consciousness involved in experiencing my experiences as mine is, I think, what James had in mind when he wrote, "Whatever I may be thinking of, I am always at the same time more or less aware of *myself*, of *my personal existence*" (1892, 43). What James presumably did not mean is that we bring an explicit "I think that" thought, or even less plausibly that we bring some sort of rich narrative conception of our self, to each and every experience.

Sometimes, however, we are self-conscious in a deep way, for example, when we are engaged in figuring out who we are and where we are going with our lives. Being self-conscious in this way requires that we engage in a temporally extended soliloquy or in a temporally extended dialogue with others. There is no occurrent thought or linguistic expression that can accomplish or capture this sort of self-consciousness in a single stroke. When awareness of the self accompanies ordinary experience in the way it does in these episodes of intentional self-scrutiny, we think of the self as intrusive, and we speak of the person as overly self-absorbed and neurotic. The self can get in the way when a person, usually because of low self-esteem, is overly attentive to his self.

The self that is "the center of narrative gravity" (Dennett 1988a), the self that answers to questions about who we are, what we aim at, and what we care about, is a complex construct. It is both expressed and created in the process of self-representation. The self in this sense, what I call "self-represented identity," is a causally efficacious part of the whole system, and it affects both the cognitive content and the qualitative character of new experiences. The causal efficacy of self-representing is fairly obvious when we are actively engaged in representing our selves. It is also plausible to think that once a complex model of the self has been constructed and is in place, it exists as a complex dispositional structure in the brain and is often involved in structuring experience, albeit unconsciously. That is, the causal efficacy of the model of the self is compatible with its making only infrequent, and then only partial, appearances in consciousness and with its having differential effects in different situations from behind the phenomenological scenes.

In sum, at one end of the spectrum there is the self-consciousness involved in having a subjective experience. At the other end of the spectrum is the sort of self-consciousness involved in thinking about one's model of one's self, or as I shall say for simplicity, *the self*. Unlike the capacity to be self-conscious in the first sense, the self is not something that we are born with. Maturation, living in the world, being socialized in a life form, and acquiring certain ways of thinking are required before one can start to build the complex set of representations that, taken together, come to constitute the narrative self.

2   Actual and Self-Represented Identity

We represent our selves to answer certain questions of identity. Given that I am a person, what kind of person am I? Getting at identity in this sense requires more than being a good detector of the fact that one is the locus of a certain kind of psychological connectedness or is housed in an enduring body. It requires in addition that one have representational resources and cognitive abilities to access and issue reports about the various states, traits, dispositions, and behavioral patterns that make one the person one is.

When we represent our selves for the sake of gaining self-knowledge, we aim to detect and express truths about the dynamic integrated system of past and present identifications, desires, commitments, aspirations, beliefs, dispositions, temperaments, roles, acts, and actional patterns that constitute our "actual full identity" (Flanagan 1991a).

The posit of actual full identity is motivated by two main considerations. First, it is widely accepted that there is in fact a gap between the self we think we are and the self we "really" are. Aspirations to greater self-knowledge, as well as ascriptions of self-misapprehension, presuppose a targeted self that can be captured or missed. Second, the science of the mind is predicated on the view that there exists a set of true counterfactual generalizations about the human mind. These truths about the nature of mind, whatever they turn out to be, constrain and structure the construction of particular selves, and for the most part they are not transparent to the first person. Contemporary psychologists regularly analyze personality in terms of processes that are opaque from the first-person perspective, e.g., in terms of innate temperamental dispositions (Kagan 1989), underlying neurobiology (Eysenck 1967), and subtle situation sensitivities of various traits (Bandura 1986).

It will be useful to distinguish two different aims of self-representation, which in the end are deeply intertwined. First, there is self-representing for the sake of self-understanding. This is the story we tell to ourselves to understand ourselves for who we are. The ideal here is convergence between self-representation and an acceptable version of the story of our actual identity. Second, there is self-representing for public dissemination, whose aim is underwriting successful social interaction. I have been focusing so far on the first function of self-representation. But the two are closely connected. Indeed, the strategic requirements of the sort of self-representing needed for social interaction, together with our tendencies to seek congruence, explain how self-representation intended in the first instance for "one's eyes only," and thus which one might think more likely to be true, could start to conform to a false projected social image of the self, to a deeply fictional and farfetched account of the self.

Self-represented identity, when it gets things right, has actual identity (or some aspect of it) as its cognitive object. Because representing one's self is an activity internal to a complex but single system, it does not leave things unchanged. The activity of self-representation is partly constitutive of actual identity. This is true in two senses. First, even considered as a purely cognitive activity, representing one's self involves the activation of certain mental representations and cognitive structures. Once representing one's self becomes an ongoing activity, it realigns and recasts the representations and structures already in place. Second, the self as represented has motivational bearing and behavioral effects. Often this motivational bearing is congruent with motivational tendencies that the entire system already has. In such cases, the function of placing one's self-conception in the motivational circuits involves certain gains in ongoing conscious control and in the fine-tuning of action. Sometimes, especially in cases of severe self-deception, the self projected for both public and first-person consumption may be strangely and transparently out of kilter with what the agent is like. In such cases, the self as represented is linked with the activity of self-representation but with little else in the person's psychological or behavioral economy. Nonetheless, such misguided self-representation helps constitute, for reasons I have suggested, the misguided person's actual full identity.

One further point is worth emphasizing. Although self-represented identity is identity from the subjective point of view, it invariably draws on available theoretical models about the nature of the self in framing its reflexive self-portrait. We represent ourselves by way of various publicly available hermeneutic strategies. Psychoanalytically inspired self-description is most familiar in our culture. But genetic and neurobiological models are increasingly visible in the self-understandings of ordinary people. It is a variable matter—one dependent on the character of public discourse, the available models for self-comprehension, as well as on certain objective social facts—whether and to what degree self-comprehension involves seeing oneself essentially in terms of the social relations of which one partakes or whether the self is seen more individualistically and atomically (Flanagan 1991a).

3   The Narrative Structure of Self-Representation

Zazetsky, the brain-damaged soldier described by A. R. Luria in *The Man with the Shattered World* (1972), works tirelessly to recover his self by producing on paper a narrative in which he appears as the main character. Zazetsky had two worlds shattered at once by a single bullet. The external world is disjointed, gappy, and strangely textured. Zazetsky's inner life is also a mess. Zazetsky's life lacks wholeness, meaning, and direction. Zazetsky cannot find his self; he cannot relocate who he is. Zazetsky "fights on" to reconstitute his self by valiantly trying to uncover memories he still possesses but is out of touch with. Automatic writing, just letting his hand mark on paper what it wants to produce, has resulted in the production of a monumental three-thousand-page autobiography. Zazetsky has produced, or better, he has reproduced the objective story of who he is. Sadly, Zazetsky himself is impaired in ways that keep him, the very subject of the autobiography, from consciously reappropriating the self revealed in his tale. Still, Zazetsky sees that "fighting on" to get his story out and bring it into view is his only hope for eventually reentering his self, for eventually reclaiming his identity. This is why he writes tirelessly. Identity is that important.

No one can grasp the whole narrative of his or her life at once. Indeed, there is always more to our identity than what we can narratively capture or convey. For one thing, we are forgetful. Zazetsky's problems are extreme, largely because his memory is so bad and thwarts him from keeping in view, or making easily accessible, the snatches of narrative he is able to write about and briefly consciously reappropriate. But the fact that

Zazetsky cannot grasp his identity all at once distinguishes him from no one. Furthermore, no matter how successful Zazetsky became at regaining his self, in so doing, he would not capture his full identity. No finite, fallible, defensive creature can do that.

Zazetsky's quest is universal. Evidence strongly suggests that humans in all cultures come to cast their own identity in some sort of narrative form. We are inveterate story tellers. Many thinkers have converged on the insight that a narrative conception of the self is the "essential genre" of self-representation (Bruner 1983, 1986; Kermode 1967; MacIntyre 1981). A self is just a structured life, structured in part by its temporal components —its beginning, middle, and end—and by the relations among the various characters who play on the stage of our lives. Continuity, coherence, and comprehensiveness are the ideals of narrative explanation (Spence 1982, 22). "In what does the unity of an individual life consist? The answer is that its unity is the unity of a narrative embodied in a single life. To ask 'What is the good for me?' is to ask how best I might live out that unity and bring it to completion" (MacIntyre 1981, 203).

Although personal identity proper can be grounded in the thinnest thread of biological or psychological continuity, the connectedness that constitutes a normatively acceptable self or life is of the sort that makes for a contentful story, a story that involves an unfolding rationale for the shape it takes. Furthermore, because the story of any individual life is constituted by and embedded in some larger meaning-giving structure and because, in addition, only in terms of this larger structure does a life gain whatever rationale it has for unfolding in the way it does, it follows that a life is illuminated, for the person who lives it and for others, by seeing it against the background of this larger structure. But finally, no life is simply reducible to the larger meaning-giving structure of which it partakes and by which it is constituted. "I am the *subject* of a history that is my own and no one else's, that has its own particular meaning" (MacIntyre 1981, 202). It is "natural ... to think of the self in the narrative mode" (1981, 192).

Why is narrative structure natural? Several reasons come to mind. First, human life is experienced as lived in time. It is obscure whether this is because the stream of consciousness legislates temporal structure or because evolution endowed the mind with the capacity to coordinate itself with the temporal structure of reality. Second, our memories are powerful. We possess the capacity to appropriate our distant past and draw it into the present. Life and consciousness can be as streamlike as you want, but if memory is weak, if present thought is not powerful enough to appropriate what has gone before, no narrative can be constructed. There is simply the here and now. Third, as beings in time, we are also prospectors. We care how our lives go. Successful concern requires attention to the long term. We look toward the future, attentively planning insignificant things and making monumental life plans, and we do so with a grasp of our present beliefs and desires and of who we are, given our past (Bratman 1987). Fourth, we are social beings. We live lives in time and in predictable and unpredictable interaction with other people. Characters abound to fill out the complex story of our lives.

Although numerous characters appear in the story of a person's life, we cap the number of characters that constitute her self at one. With narrative selves, the basic principle is "one to a customer" (Dennett 1989). Multiple chapters, novel twists and turns, even radical self-transformations are allowed. But these have to be part of the life of a single self. A self can change, but the changes had better make sense, or so we prefer. I need to understand your conversion from hedonism to ascetic Buddhism in a way that locates *you* both before and after the conversion. In those rare cases where this is not possible, we say that some individual is no longer the same person. There may be different judgments rendered from the insider's and outsider's points of view about narrative flow and personal sameness. Despite my judgment that you are no longer there, you may well judge otherwise and see your radical transformation as part of a perfectly coherent narrative of your life.

Oneness reigns when it comes to selves. It makes sense to have one and only one inner "figurehead," given the complexities of rationally guiding action in a complex and ever changing social world (Dennett 1989, 171). It is normative for us that each person has one and only one self. Zazetsky has been robbed of his fair share: he lacks one full self. Jimmie, the Korsakoff patient who has lost the last 45 years and retains virtually nothing new, is even worse off. Some other kinds of identity disorders, for example, cases of multiple personality disorder (MPD), involve having too many selves. Normally, persons suffering multiple personality disorders can represent the self that is in the driver's seat. Since they are wholly or partly amnesiac of other personalities they house, they cannot represent these selves until they, so to speak, become them.

The sort of self that Zazetsky has too little of and MPD patients have too many of is the self that is "the center of narrative gravity" (Dennett 1988a). We start at one end of the continuum with the dim and inchoate self/nonself distinction, the awareness of what is me and mine and what is not me and not mine. Such awareness requires virtually nothing in the way of knowledge or awareness of my nature: birds, cats, and dogs are aware of the self/nonself distinction but are very unclued as to their natures across most every dimension. At the other end of the continuum we reach the weighty self that is the center of narrative gravity. This is the self that we present to ourselves (strictly, we present aspects of ourselves) for planning, self-scrutiny, and a sense of the whole of our lives and that we present to others for their recognition and approval of who we are.

It is important to emphasize that both Zazetsky's and Jimmie's life stories can be filled out from the outside. There are stories that tell who they are and what they were like, that incorporate what things seem like for them, and also that go beyond this and describe the acts, dispositions, moods, thoughts, abiding personality characteristics, even the activity in their brains that each in his different way lacks the capacity to see. The same is true for multiple personality disorders. Such facts show the usefulness of the distinction between self-represented identity and actual full identity.

4   Self-Emergence

On one traditional view, the self does not emerge. The self or ego is in place from the very start. Personality emerges. But that is a different thing altogether. The indivisible and unchanging Self houses personality. It is a condition for the very possibility of personality. According to the view I have been defending, this is misguided. The self emerges. The self is personality, broadly construed. To make my view more credible, more needs to be said about two perennial puzzles. (1) How does the self get constructed? (2) Once there is a self (whenever that is), who does it work for and answer to, if not the self itself? And if it does work for and answer to the self itself, how is that possible? Here I discuss the first question. The second question is taken up in the next section.

The first question, How does the self get constructed? is deeply puzzling only if one thinks that only something like a self is up to the task of making a self. This is a bad thought, one to get rid of.

The construction of a self begins in earliest childhood as parents try to shape the emerging character of the charges they love. Since we abide the "one self per customer" principle, we try to assist the child in building an integrated self that comprehends basic social norms and is equipped with a system of beliefs, desires, and values that will help it to live successfully and well. The "one self to a customer" principle is not just an arbitrary social construction. The Darwin Machine itself favors minimal cognitive dissonance and maximal integration at the level of conscious thought and action guidance (harmony at the top may well belie all sorts of disagreement and competition among lower-level processors). Indeed, the brain is designed to fully cooperate in the construction of one and only one self, although it is capable in extreme situations of cooperating in the construction of multiple selves. It is important to recognize that almost all MPD patients were sexually or otherwise physically abused as children (see Hacking 1991 for some questions about the data for this claim). They create additional selves to fend off the pain of abuse. Often the abuser helps in the construction, presumably to reduce his own dissonance at being so awful, by offering alters to the child as they play "Daddy games." It is unclear why there is such a proliferation of alters once the process starts, but it is easy to understand why a child would want not to be the self who was abused and who must see one or more of her caretakers as an abuser (Humphrey and Dennett 1989).

In both normal and abnormal cases, the process of constructing a self starts in interaction with elders, and it begins well before the child uses language. Indeed, the child may be innately disposed to develop a theory of mind, a theory of its own mind and those of others, given social interaction (Wellman 1990). The parents provide models for constructing the self in what they do and say and in how they express their own formed being. Rarely does a parent try to construct a child's self through direct linguistic instruction (and when they do try, they are almost always unsuccessful at getting what they want). Increasingly, as time proceeds, the child engages her parents with her own emerging self and modifies their attempts to shape her. With the onset of the ability to speak, she will be able to say things about herself and to articulate appeals about her own desires in a form which formerly could only be expressed through resistance or tears on the one hand and happy compliance on the other. There comes a day when the child's fussing and fidgeting as she is dressed and her hair is brushed yields to a complex theory of fashion, style, and cool, which is revealed in the articulate expression of very specific views about how she wants herself to look.

With language, time, maturity, autonomy, and elaborate and multifarious interactions with others, the self emerges. The construction and maintenance of the self involves many players. Whether I know it or not, "others made me, and in various ways continue to make me the person I am" (Sandel 1982, 143). Our selves are multiply authored. Lest this sound too deflationary, it is fair to say that normally we are one of the main authors of our identities. Once our characters are well formed and we have a good grasp of them, our powers of self-authorship increase dramatically. We gain the power to guide our lives more self-consciously in terms of our model of who we are. We can modify and adjust our self-conceptions unconsciously and effortlessly in response to social feedback, as well as consciously in response to our judgments of fit between who we are and who we aspire to be.

That said, there is wide agreement among psychologists and philosophers who have thought carefully about identity formation that it proceeds largely unconsciously and that many aspects of identity never come into view for the agent who has that identity (Erikson 1968; Kagan 1984, 1989; Sandel 1982; Stern 1985; Taylor 1989). Consciously coming to grasp one's self does not require, at least in the early stages, that there already is a Self in place. Erikson writes that the process of identity formation is "a process taking place on all levels of mental functioning.... This process is, luckily, and necessarily, for the most part unconscious except where inner conditions and outer circumstances combine to aggravate a painful, or elated, 'identity-consciousness'." (1968, 22–23). Furthermore, our innate temperamental traits (Kagan 1989), our differential natural intelligences (Gardner 1983), are productive generative forces in identity formation from the start. These aspects of our self may never be seen very clearly in self-representation from the first-person perspective, but they are indispensable pieces of the puzzle of who we are. They are causally efficacious aspects of our actual full identity.

The main point is that selves are just like most other things. They are complex effects that do not in any way precede their causes. They don't need to. They emerge naturally in complex interactions with the world and other persons. And they acquire autonomy and increased causal efficacy as they develop, ripen, and come to constitute character and personality.

I mentioned earlier the idea that the self is like a figurehead. Dennett writes, "There is in every country on earth a Head of State.... That is not to say that a nation lacking such a figurehead, would cease to function day-to-day. But it is to say that in the longer term it may function much better if it does have one.... The drift of the analogy is obvious. In short, a human being too may need an inner figurehead—especially given the complexities of human social life" (1989, 171). Figureheads differ dramatically in their power, but in no case do they remotely exhaust what the whole nation is or does. This is the first important point. Self-represented identity is emblematic of how I work. But it hardly represents much, let alone most, of who I am or what makes me tick. The second point that can be extracted from the analogy relates to the issue of autonomy and self-authorship. Some nations allow lots of individual freedom, others do not. Likewise, one culture, subculture, social environment, or particular family, might involve the dictatorial imposition of a kind of self, or the agent might be given multiple options and be called upon to truly participate in her own self-construction.

5 Whom the Self Plays For

I have explained how a Self can emerge without a Self already being in place. I now need to address the second puzzle posed above: Whom does the self work for and answer to? Or to put the question in slightly different terms: Whom does the self play for? Who orchestrates the self? If it plays for itself, that is, if it is self-orchestrating, that is puzzling. If it plays for a different self, a conductor self, then the question of who controls that self is repeated ad infinitum. The solution to this puzzle is contained at least in part in what has just been said about the emergence of the self. The self emerges from, and is subsequently controlled by, a complex of interacting forces. These include the social environment, the entire system that the model of the self serves, and the reflexive action of self-construction and narration. Let me elaborate.

The self "bubbles up," as Dennett likes to say, as it develops. And once formed, it, or better, different aspects of it, bubble up each day. Let me give a personal example. I identify in a compelling way with my role as father to my children. But I do not wake up each day and put on my father self. I am a self partly constituted by being a father. I did not self-consciously choose to be the kind of father I am or to be gripped by the self-constituting role of father. Nor, of course, did I have any choice whatsoever in the particular children I am father to. Like all parents, I often need to reflect on and make adjustments to the kind of father I am being. But that mainly seems to involve adjusting things I do more or less because of the way I am, because of the personality I have. I am fine-tuning who I am, not creating a new father in me from scratch.

Much of what I think about and say to others and how I am identified by others involves reference to a narrative essentially involving my family. I see myself as a husband and father uniquely related to three other unique selves, and I am known by all my friends as a character essentially embedded in that familial narrative. I know about this self, and I talk about it, as I am doing here. Did I consciously create this self? Do I consciously call up this self as needed? The best answer to both questions is no.

> We (unlike professional human storytellers) do not consciously and deliberately figure out what narratives to tell and how to tell them; like spider webs, our tales are spun by us.... Our narrative selfhood, is their product, not their source.... These strings or streams of narrative issue forth as if from a single source—not just in the obvious physical sense of flowing from just one mouth, or one pencil or pen, but in a more subtle sense: their effect on any audience or readers is to encourage them to (try to) posit a unified agent whose words they are: in short to posit ... a center of narrative gravity. (Dennett 1989, 169)

To some extent my familial self and my philosopher self are played for different audiences. Different audiences see who I am differently. Neither self is a self that I have the slightest sense of having labored on alone to create. This is true despite the fact that both selves required, as necessary conditions, certain conscious choices on my part. My two selves bubble up to the surface in different interpersonal ecological niches. Displaying either self and getting my audience (or myself) to posit one or the other as the center of my narrative gravity is, in a sense, to produce an illusion, since to me, these two selves are, from my first-person perspective, part of an integrated and unified narrative that contains, as proper parts, both of these selves, which I sometimes display in isolation. In fact, I have many other selves (or other aspects of my self) besides these two. What distinguishes me from a multiple personality is simply the fact that I am not amnesiac with respect to these selves; they permeate each other in ways that the selves of a multiple personality typically do not. Furthermore, I draw my selves together and comprehend my self in terms of a single narrative in which they all fit (somewhat uncomfortably) together.

So whom does my narrative, self-represented self play for? The answer should be pretty clear and painless by now. It plays for third parties, and it plays for one's self. The self plays for the self? How does that work? Here we need to beware of words making things seem more mysterious than they are. I produce in thought and words a narrative self. I do this largely, but not completely, unconsciously. My narrative self is not its own source, although, of course, past self-representing has a causal influence on subsequent self-representing. My narrative self is a product of complex social interaction and much mental processing, both conscious and unconscious, on my part. The phrase 'on my part' means all of me. All of me includes all past self-representations and their traces, but much more besides, even more than my self-represented identity and my actual full identity. It refers to all of me that thinks, the entire *res cogitans* (now naturalized), not just my conscious self or my unconscious self, but many parts and processors that are not "selfy" at all: my neurotransmitters, hormone levels, the idiosyncratic features of my eyes and ears that determine the quality of my vision and hearing, my language acquisition device, and so on.

So the "I" or self for which my narrative self plays is me, the whole information-processing system, from which the narrative self emerges and for which it plays a crucial role. Often I express and grasp snatches of my narrative self and utilize these representations in monitoring and guiding my life. This way of thinking about our reflexive powers makes matters fairly unmysterious. I am a system constituted in part by a certain narrative conception of self. Sometimes I hold that conception in view as I think about things. I, being more than my narrative self, can comprehend it, utilize it, and, in concert with outside forces, adjust it. What am I? This organism. This thinking thing.

6   The Self as Fiction

Dennett insists that the self that is the center of narrative gravity is a fiction, a useful fiction, but a fiction nonetheless. "Centres of gravity" are "fictional objects ... [that] have only the properties that the theory that constitutes them endowed them with" (1988a, 1016). What might this mean? If our highest-order self, the self in whose embrace we find identity and meaning, is a fiction, then the epiphenomenalist suspicion seems secure, at least as regards the self. This inference, however, would be a mistake. The idea that the self is a fiction is compatible with its being real and its playing a functional role in an individual's psychological economy and social life.

The idea that the self is a fiction is in part a way of expressing the fact that it is, for the reasons given, a construction. Mother Nature does not give us a robust self. She starts us off caring about homeostasis, and she equips us with the equipment to distinguish "me" from "not me." But she hardly wires in a personality or an identity. Identity is the joint production of many sources, including one's own evolving self. Michael Gazzaniga (1988) has suggested that evidence from split-brain patients indicates that the narration of this fictional self emanates from the left cerebral hemisphere in most people. The left brain loves to tell stories about the system of which it is a part, and it will spin fantastic tales if need be. So the self is a fiction because it is constructed and because the narrative in terms of which we construct and express it often ranges far from the facts.

The idea that the self is a fiction also captures a second feature of identity. The self I am is subject to constant revision. This is true in two senses. Not only do new things I do change the ongoing story; also, the past is sometimes reconstructed or filled out from the point of view of hindsight. Sometimes these reconstructions are self-serving ("I never really loved her anyway"). Other times they involve rendering various indeterminacies determinate, revising certain hypotheses about what we are like in light of new evidence, and answering questions that arise now, but didn't arise before. For example, one wonders in one's thirties why one cares so deeply about a certain worthless thing, and one reconstructs some story of one's distant past to explain to oneself, and possibly to others, why things are as they are. Most such reconstructions are uncorroborated; some are uncorroboratable.

So the self is fictional because it is a construction and because it involves all manner of revisitation to past indeterminacies and reconstruction post facto. Dennett has us imagine John Updike making the Rabbit trilogy into a quartet not by writing about a still older Rabbit Angstrom (this, in fact, Updike has now done) but by creating the story of a very young Rabbit Angstrom. The extant trilogy constrains what Updike can say about the Rabbit who existed before the Rabbit of *Rabbit Run*. But the indeterminacy of Rabbit's former life is vast, and thus there are numerous credible ways in which the story of the earlier years could be told. For certain parts of our lives we have similar degrees of freedom in how we tell the story of our selves.

There is a third way in which the picture of the self as a fiction is appropriate. A piece of fiction starts off from some narrative hook or set of hooks and pins a character and his story on those hooks. In the case of pure fiction, the author has complete freedom in choosing what hooks to pin a character on. But if she wants to sell copies, she had better make sure that there is something compelling about her characters and their stories. The same principles apply in the first-person case. A life is satisfying from the inside and respected from the outside when its central themes are built around worthy aims and values. But what are compelling to one's listeners and worth respecting vary temporally, culturally, and subculturally. Different kinds of narratives fly at different times and in different places. The book-buying and interpersonal markets create selection pressures favoring certain kinds of narratives and disfavoring others. We see these pressures at work in everyday life when one presents oneself primarily as a concerned parent in one context and as a professional philosopher in another. In each context there is almost a Gestalt effect. The features of one's identity that are dominant in one form of presentation recede in the other.

This brings me to a fourth way in which the self trades in fiction rather than fact. The self that is the center of narrative gravity is constructed not only out of real-life materials, out of things that really have happened to me; it is also constructed so that it holds, abides, and strives to maintain certain ideals not yet realized. The narrative is in many cases organized around a set of aims, ideals, and aspirations of the self. But since these have not yet been realized, they are fictions, albeit useful and necessary ones.

To conceive of the self as a fiction seems right for these four reasons:

- It is an open-ended construction.
- It is filled with vast indeterminate spaces, and a host of tentative hypotheses about what I am like, that can be filled out and revised post facto.
- It is pinned on culturally relative narrative hooks.
- It expresses ideals of what one wishes to be but is not yet.

But there are two important respects in which the analogy of the self with a piece of fiction can be misleading. First, there is the issue of constraints. The author of a true piece of fiction has many more degrees of freedom in creating her characters than we have in spinning the tale of our selves. Despite the indeterminacies operative in construction of the self and despite the fact that different narrative emphases will be reinforced in different communities, there are firmer and more visible epistemic constraints in the case of self-construction than in the case of ordinary fictional construction. There are, after all, the things we have done, what we have been through as embodied beings, and the characteristic dispositions we reveal in social life. Third parties will catch us if we take our stories too far afield. We may also catch ourselves. There are selection pressures to keep the story that one reveals to one's self and to others in some sort of harmony with the way one is living one's life.

Some people are, of course, massively self-deceived. Self-deception makes sense only if selves are not totally fictive, that is, only if there are some facts constraining what is permitted to go into our self narrative. Self-deceived individuals sequester certain facts from view, possibly totally unconsciously. In this way they keep these facts from entering the narrative. Some alcoholics know that they have a problem but try to keep their drinking a secret from others. They deceive others but not themselves. Other alcoholics display their alcoholism publicly but develop immunities to comprehending social feedback intended to challenge their self-conception that they have no drinking problem. They deceive themselves but not others.

So real selves are fictive. But they are less fictive than fictional selves because they are more answerable to the facts. The second way in which the idea that one's self is a fiction can be misleading is if it leads one to think that the self plays no functional role in mental life. In fact, it plays a pivotal role in giving organization and meaning to a life that will last on average three quarters of a century. But the question haunts: In what sense can a fiction organize or guide anything? And how can a fiction give *real* meaning to a life?

The answer, as I said earlier, is that a person's higher-order self is one of the many models contained in his brain. Once acquired and in operation, this model is part of the recurrent brain network causally responsible for the life a person lives and how he thinks and feels. This is true whether a person's model of his self is in touch or out of touch with his actual full identity, and it is true whether a person's self contains worthwhile or worthless aims and ideals. Even though the self is not *the* control center of the mind—the mind may well have no single control center—in setting out plans, aspirations, and ideals, it plays an important causal role in a person's overall psychological economy.

The self changes, evolves, and grows. It displays a certain continuity, and its home is the brain. The fact that my higher-order conception of my self is a model housed in my brain explains the first-person feel I have for my self (but not for your self), and it explains my special concern that my story go as I plan. If things go awry, if my plans don't materialize, if great pain befalls me, it will happen to this subject of experience, to the individual wrapped in this particular narrative. It is not surprising that I care so deeply that the story go the way in which I intend. It's my self that we're talking about, after all.

7   Real and Unreal Selves

Let me approach this issue of the fictional status of the self from a slightly different angle and at the same time block an objection to my distinction between actual full identity and self-represented identity.

Humphrey and Dennett claim that there are two main views on the self: a realist view and a nonrealist view.

> Two extreme views can be and have been taken. Ask a layman what he thinks a self is, and his unreflecting answer will probably be that a person's self is indeed some kind of *real* thing: a ghostly supervisor who lives inside his head, the thinker of his thoughts, the repository of his memories, the holder of his values, his conscious inner "I." Although he might be unlikely these days to use the term "soul," it would be very much the age-old conception that he would have in mind. A self (or soul) is an existent entity with executive powers over the body and its own enduring qualities. Let's call this realist picture of the self, the idea of a "proper self." ... Contrast it, however, with the revisionist picture of the self which has become popular among certain psychoanalysts and philosophers of mind. On this view, selves are not things at all but instead are explanatory fictions. No-body really has a soul-like agency inside them: we just find it useful to imagine the existence of this conscious inner "I" when we try to account for their behavior (and, in our own case, our private stream of consciousness). We might say indeed that the self is rather like the "center of narrative gravity" of a set of biographical events and tendencies; but, as with a center of physical gravity, there's really no such *thing* (with mass or shape or color). Let's call this nonrealist picture of the self, the idea of the "fictive-self." (Humphrey and Dennett 1989, 76)

The realist is motivated, according to the nonrealist, by a discomfort with the idea that the self could be just "a *concept* or an *organizing principle*" (Humphrey and Dennett 1989, 76). The realist, proper self view is described as involving belief in a real *incorporeal* "I," in a "ghostly supervisor." But it is important to see that the crucial thing that makes a view realist is not the belief in an incorporeal "I" but simply the belief that the self "is indeed some kind of real *thing*." The thing can be an incorporeal supervisor, as in the passage quoted, or it can be "a node or a module in the brain" (Dennett 1989, 163). The first kind of realist is an orthodox Cartesian; the second kind of realist is a "Cartesian materialist" (Dennett 1991a; Dennett and Kinsbourne 1992). Cartesian materialism is what you are left with when "you discard Descartes's dualism but fail to discard the imagery of a central (but material) Theater where 'it all comes together'" (Dennett 1991a, 107). So realism about the self involves several beliefs: the self is some sort of real thing; it has executive powers over the body; it is the originator of plans, intentions, and will; it holds all one's memory, values, and personality; and it is the place where all conscious events happen.

This is a bad view. But one wonders why rejecting this package makes one a nonrealist. The story I have told about the emergence and causal powers of the self involves no commitment whatsoever to any of the implausibilities just cited.

One can imagine the response (I have heard it) that what I call "actual full identity" is just like the "proper self" of the realist. But that is just false. First, actual full identity is not characterizable as a small yet powerful agent or, indeed, as any kind of "real thing." Actual full identity is a construct that draws on the best theories available to describe what a person actually does, as well as the dynamic system of traits, dispositions, identifications, including self-representations, that constitute character and help drive the system. Second, unlike the proper self, actual full identity is not the sort of thing that can be known, grasped, or otherwise apprehended in some simple act of self-consciousness. Third, actual full identity is not a place at all, so it cannot be the place where all conscious events happen. Fourth, there is no need to anthropomorphize actual full identity along the lines of a powerful CEO. Actual full identity is important in explaining what the system does, but it hardly supervises and orchestrates all happenings. Actual full identity is the self as described by the most enlightened version of the story of the self that emerges as science advances and first-person opacities and distortions are removed. It is described in abstract terms. But the actions, relations, and patterns depicted are real, not fictional. There is, to be sure, no proper self inside each of us. But this is compatible with the view that each of us possesses an actual full identity. Our actual full identities include what we have done, so it is not altogether inside us. Nonetheless because our actions may well leave traces inside us, it is legitimate to think of actual full identity as possessing some sort of basis in distributed brain activity. Indeed, we need to posit some sort of neural realization. Otherwise, the causal activity of actual full identity is inexplicable. Thinking of actual full identity as (mostly) supervenient on brain activity does not involve endowing this self with a specific location. The neural basis is presumably distributed and largely dispositional—most of one's memories and traits will not be turned on at all times.

The point is even more straightforward with self-represented identity. The self can be a construct or model, a "center of narrative gravity," a way of self-representing, without being a fiction in the problematic sense. Biographies and autobiographies are constructs. But if they are good biographies or autobiographies, they are nonfictional or only semifictional. For Dennett (1989), there are, it seems, only normal fictive selves and invasive fictive selves such as those suggested by abusive caretakers who posit imaginary selves for the abused child. One father gave his daughter biblical names, displaying at once his anti-Semitism and his need to sanctify his great sinfulness.

I want to hold out for a more moderate position between realism and nonrealism. First, self-representing can and often does correctly represent the person. The portrait it paints has many realistic properties. If it does not, we call the person self-deceived, a liar, or worse. Second, although the narrative self is "an organizing principle," it does have causal efficacy in the way any complex model or set of representations does. Since it has causal efficacy, there is no escaping the conclusion that it is supervenient on multifarious brain processes. Self-representation, even massively deceived self-representation, is causally efficacious—it causes the person to say wildly false things about himself. This is inexplicable unless the self-deceived thoughts that (sometimes) precede and prompt false self-descriptions are realized in the brain.

So there is a middle position between realism and nonrealism. Such a view involves denying the idea of a proper self while insisting on the legitimacy of the posits of both actual full identity and self-represented identity. Identities are things humans possess. There is no executive self that knows about and orchestrates all one thinks, does, and says. But there really are things we think, do, and say. And there are genuine patterns of thought, action, and speech that give sense to the posit of an actual full identity for each of us. Actual full identity is a theoretical construct, to be sure. But it is a well-motivated construct designed to get at genuine features of mental organization and action. Insofar as the posited identities capture features of what we are like, what makes us tick, and what we have done, they get at real phenomena. Self-representing is partly dedicated to the task of deep self-description, a task it is not in the end up to on its own. It too is real. Self-representation supervenes on certain neural processes. It has causal efficacy. Furthermore, we sometimes accurately represent who we are, and when we do, we are privy to more fact than fiction.

The question of the reality of the self is separate from the question of whether self-representation trades in fact or fiction. The realism/nonrealism issue and the fiction/nonfiction issue need to be kept apart. The first involves taking a stand on matters ontological, on the sort of thing a self is (if indeed it is anything at all), on whether there are different levels of the self, different kinds, different aspects, and so on. The second question concerns epistemic matters, in particular, whether the narrative self accurately or inaccurately represents who and what we are. One can be a "nonrealist" (in Dennett's sense) or a moderate realist about the self, and a nonfictionalist at the same time. That is, one can reject both Cartesian immaterialism and Cartesian materialism and yet think that there are selves and that we are capable of saying true things about selves in both the first- and third-person. To be sure, there is no shadowy supervisor that is your CEO, and there is no nonshadowy central headquarters either. You are a complex system. Much of what makes you tick is neither "selfy" nor transparent from the subjective point of view. But there are ways that you are. That is for real. Some of these ways you know about. Some of these ways you don't know about. Common public wisdom in unison with emerging knowledge from the sciences of the mind can help both you and the rest of us see who and what you are more clearly and deeply. Meanwhile, keep the story of who you are on track. There is a good chance that with effort you can see many things about yourself clearly. Your life will go best when this is so.

Chapter 11

A Unified Theory of Consciousness?

1   *Prospects for a Theory of Consciousness*

Some naturalists are skeptical about the prospects for a theory of consciousness. This is not because they are new mysterians. It is because they think that 'consciousness' names a heterogeneous hodge-podge and because they do not believe that one can develop a theory for a hodge-podge (P. S. Churchland 1983, 1988; Wilkes 1988a, 1988b). Consciousness includes sensations, perceptions, moods, emotions, propositional-attitude states, and large narrative structures. Dreams are experienced, as are other altered states of consciousness, many psychotic states, and so on. At a fine-grained level we will want to individuate types within these larger types, so that, for example, there will be a different experiential type for each sensory modality (touch, olfaction, vision, and so on). And one can easily imagine the need to divide these subtypes into more fine-grained types, for example, seeing red versus seeing blue.

The claim that 'consciousness' names a heterogeneous set of phenomena is absolutely right. 'Consciousness' is a superordinate category term. But I don't see that the subcategories that constitute it, taken together or individually, show signs of being a hodge-podge, and therefore I don't share the conviction that the search for a theory of consciousness is an idle fantasy.

Wilkes (1988b, 33) thinks that "conscious phenomena" are more like the arbitrary set consisting of "all the words with 'g' as the fourth letter" than they are like a superordinate category ('metal', 'mammal', 'fish') or like a subcategory of such a superordinate category ('gold', 'whale', 'flounder'). Her argument turns on the conviction that for a superordinate category to be nonarbitrary, it must display a certain coherence, but that "conscious phenomena" fail to display the required coherence. "What sort of coherence? Well, even though most of the interesting laws may concern only the subclasses, there might be some laws at least that are interestingly—nontrivially—true of all the subclasses; or even if this is not so, the laws that concern the subclasses may have significant structural analogy or isomorphism" (Wilkes 1988b, 33–34).

Contrary to Wilkes, I think that the evidence suggests that conscious phenomena display coherence. First, despite the truth of the heterogeneity thesis, all conscious mental events share the property of being conscious, of being in awareness, of there being something it is like to be in one of the relevant states. Second, whereas the subsets that make up a hodge-podge make it up precisely because they lack any interesting systematic connection to each other, all conscious phenomena bear the interesting systematic relation of being phenomena of mind.

The shared phenomenological property and the fact that conscious phenomena are properties, states, and events of the mind suggest that conscious mental life constitutes a category suitable for marking a set of phenomena in need of scientific explanation. To be sure, the theory of consciousness will be an interest-relative subset of our overall science of the mind. In this respect, our theory of consciousness may well turn out like our theory of memory. 'Memory' is a superordinate category. It divides first into long-term and short-term memory. Long-term memory is usually divided into declarative or explicit memory and nondeclarative or implicit memory. Declarative memory is memory for facts and events; nondeclarative memory covers acquired skills and habits, priming effects, habituation, classical conditioning, and subliminal learning. The neural substrate differs for these different types of memory, as do the psychological generalizations that describe them (Squire and Zola-Morgan 1991). The theory of memory consists of a classification scheme and of all the well-founded psychological and neurophysiological generalizations about the events so classified. In terms of underlying neurophysiology, it might be that short-term memory has more in common with the semantic representation of single words than short-term memory does with declarative long-term memory. This interesting commonality would be revealed in the larger systematic structure of the general theory of mind. But it would not undermine the fact that for the theorist interested in memory, there exists a set of well-founded generalizations about different types of memory that does not include the well-founded generalizations about semantic representation. These will be part of a different theory, the theory of semantic representation. The point is that there is a clear and coherent sense in which there is a theory of memory, a theory of all the different types of memory. This is true despite the fact that this theory crosscuts in important ways our theories of perception, learning, and consciousness. For example, declarative memories are subject to conscious recall in a way that nondeclarative memories typically are not.

Like the superordinate categories of perception, memory, and learning, the category of consciousness might play a coherent, nonarbitrary role in the science of the mind. There are a variety of ways it could play such a role. Suppose that there is some underlying physical property P that is necessary and sufficient for all experiences. If this is so, then just as $E = mc^2$, so consciously experiencing = being in state P, and therefore, it is a truth of nature that if some organism is in state P, then that organism is consciously aware of something. New mysterianism actually frames things in this way, that is, as if from "the God's eye point of view" there is some property P (beyond our cognitive powers to discover) that subserves all experience.

Or, to imagine a somewhat weaker relation, it is possible that a single brain property P, say the 40-hertz oscillation patterns I've mentioned several times, plays the role for all experiences that the virus plays that subserves the variety of conditions, differing widely in severity and symptomatology, that we call the common cold. The cold virus is not sufficient for a cold—the body might beat back the virus—but it is necessary for a cold. Likewise, 40-hertz oscillation patterns might be necessary for conscious experiences. Not sufficient, but necessary. The point is that the property of conscious awareness could conceivably turn out to be type-identical with some neural feature or there could turn out to be necessary connections between certain neural properties and conscious states even if there are no strict type identities.

Genes provide an illuminating model of a superordinate type defined by certain shared properties whose subtypes nonetheless have heterogeneous realizations and causal powers. Genes hold in their DNA the key to life. The property of being alive is realized, as far as we know, only in systems with DNA (although there are RNA viruses). But different types of genes have distinctive structures and distinctive roles in the etiology of phenotypic traits. The idea that the neural properties subserving visual awareness might be different from those subserving consciously planned action is no more incoherent than the actual fact that the genes subserving eye color are different from those subserving cystic fibrosis or Huntington's disease. If we think in terms of the superordinate category of the gene, then the right thing to say is that a heterogeneous set of properties supervene on a common type of thing, genes. If we think in term of the subtypes, that is, in terms of specific kinds of genes, then we will say that heterogeneous phenotypic traits have their roots in heterogeneous gene types. Depending on the level of analysis we choose, heterogeneous properties can be legitimately viewed as subserved by the same superordinate type or by different subtypes.

In all probability there is a large set of neural connections capable of subserving different kinds of conscious experience. Perhaps they share some interesting and ubiquitous micro properties, such as the 40-hertz oscillation patterns. Perhaps they do not. No one yet knows one way or the other. But if there exists some single brain property P that is necessary and sufficient, or just necessary, for all conscious experience, then there exists a lawlike link between property P and all conscious experiences. Even if there is no ubiquitous property P subserving conscious states of every kind, there may be different property sets $\{P_1, P_2, \ldots, P_n\}$ that ground the type identity of certain kinds of experience, for example, color perception or sweet sensations or hearing a high note. If different sets of brain properties subserve different types of conscious experiences, then there exist generalizations linking the neural with the phenomenological. There may well be certain types of phenomenal experience that, despite being realized in the brain, do not map in remotely clean ways onto neural types, even for the same person over time. If so, this will be an important discovery.

There exists an important class of cases where phenomenal similarity is not subserved by similarity at the micro level. For example, the phenomenal property of wetness is multiply realized. After all, H_2O is wet, and heavy water D_2O is wet. Perhaps consciousness is such that at the phenomenal level there is the shared property but this shared property is subserved by all manner of different types of brain processes. I have already acknowledged this possibility. I don't see that it harms the prospects for a theory of consciousness as I have been conceiving it. But one might imagine cases where phenomenal similarity is unsupported by similarities at lower levels. If this is so, it might be used to argue that the shared property of being experienced may be superficial, even if it is nonarbitrary.

Patricia Churchland reminds us how the commonsense concept of fire has fared as science has progressed: "'Fire' was used to classify not only burning wood, but also the activity on the sun and various stars (actually fusion), lightning (actually electrically induced incandescence), the Northern lights (actually spectral emission), and fire-flies (actually phosphorescence). As we now understand matters, only some of these things involve oxidation, and some processes which do involve oxidation, namely rusting, tarnishing, and metabolism, are not on the 'Fire' list" (1988, 285). Churchland concludes that "the case of fire illustrates both how the intuitive classification can be re-drawn, and how the new classification can pull together superficially diverse phenomena once the underlying theory is available." This is true and important. Our commonsense concept of consciousness is open to revision, to being redrawn. Indeed, it would be very surprising if different kinds of consciousness were not realized in different ways. The individuation of conscious events at the neural level will undoubtedly entail tracing complex neural maps originating at different points on the sensory periphery and traversing all sorts of different neural terrain. This will be true even if all the events mapped share a physical property, such as having the same oscillatory frequency. We should also expect the neural underpinnings of certain kinds of conscious states to be essential components of certain nonconscious states but not of other kinds of conscious states. For example, it might be that the areas of the brain that light up during ordinary visual awareness or when we are solving problems in geometry also light up when we turn over during sleep but never light up when we are listening to music with our eyes closed. And perhaps there is a deep reason why the relevant area lights up in the conscious and nonconscious cases in which it lights up. Imagine that the area is a necessary component of all spatial analysis, so it is activated when one is wide awake and trying to prove the Pythagorean theorem and when one is sound asleep but computing information about edges and distances in order to keep from falling out of bed. In cases like this the theory of consciousness is interwoven, as it must be, with theories of unconscious processing.

But such results would in no way undermine the idea that conscious phenomena are legitimate explananda for which to build theory and are possibly legitimate explanantia with which to build theory. It is to be expected that the development of the science of the mind will reveal deep and surprising things about the phenomena with the shared property of being experienced. Such discoveries might include the discovery that there are greater similarities in certain respects between certain phenomena that possess the shared property and those which do not than among all those with the shared phenomenal property. The neural spatial analyzer would be such an example. But this could happen even as important generalizations are found among all or most of the disparate events that possess the shared property.

The critics suspect that 'conscious phenomena' names a hodge-podge or is too superficial to play a useful role in explanation or prediction. The evidence suggests otherwise. Indeed, the evidence suggests that conscious phenomena will not merely serve up phenomena to be explained by the science of the mind but may also play an explanatory role. There are credible grounds for believing that some interesting generalizations will implicate consciousness in causal roles. For example, there are important functional differences between people with phenomenal awareness in certain domains and those without. Suitably motivated individuals with normal sight naturally carry out voluntary actions toward seen things. When thirsty, we step over to the water fountain we see to our right. However, blindsighted individuals who are identically motivated and who process information about the very same things in the visual field do not naturally or efficiently carry out suitable actions toward the "seen" things. There are also the differential abilities of amnesiacs to form integrated self-concepts and to create and abide by a consistent narrative model of the self. And persons incapable of experiencing certain qualia, for example, color-blind people, show all sorts of functional differences from non-color-blind people. Check out their wardrobes.

This evidence suggests that there are true counterfactual generalizations in the domain of consciousness. Some of these generalizations will relate phenomena at the psychological level, for example, persons with qualia of kind q do x in circumstances c, but persons without qualia q (who are otherwise identical) fail to do x in c. Other generalizations will link psychological processes with brain processes. Here are three from a multitude of possible examples. (1) Persons with damage to the speech centers, and in particular to the left brain interpreter, will have trouble generating a narrative model of the self. (2) Persons with certain kinds of frontal-lobe damage will have trouble formulating plans and intentions; other kinds of frontal-lobe damage will obstruct links between consciously formulated action plans and actually carrying out the intentions. (3) Rats, cats, and humans all possess four types of taste receptors. In rats the pathway subserving bitter tastes "shows a narrower range of evocable activity (it is less discriminating) than it does in humans. In cats, it shows a wider range of activity (it is more discriminating)" (P. M. Churchland 1989, 105). This explains why rats eat anything and cats are finicky eaters. And as Paul Churchland says, it also gives us some insight into what it is like to be a rat (or a cat).

Since these sorts of generalizations already exist and have been corroborated, it follows that there are laws that conscious mental life answers to. To be sure, the laws are pitched to the heterogeneous multiplicity of events and processes that possess the shared property of being experienced. But I see no reason to say that they are not part of an emerging theory of consciousness, one basic insight of which is that consciousness is heterogeneous.

Physics deals with an extraordinary variety of heterogeneous entities and processes. But no one is tempted to think that there cannot be a physical theory. We do not infer the impossibility of a unified field theory from the heterogeneity of the known physical forces. We do not think celestial mechanics is suspect because of the heterogeneity of the composition, size, and gravitational force of bodies in our solar system. Nor do we think that the astronomical variety of subatomic particles, within the three main classes, forecloses the possibility of quantum theory. A theory of consciousness will in the end be part of a unified theory of the mind. This is compatible with the theory making generalizations suited to whatever deep local idiosyncrasies exist. Physics tells us that bodies at extremely far distances from each other traveling at close to the speed of light are subject to regularities very different from objects moving around our little spherelike home. It would be no more surprising and no more damaging to the success of the science of the mind if it tells us that visual consciousness obeys very different laws and is subserved by different neural mechanisms from conscious reflection on one's love life. In fact, this is exactly what we expect.

Some think that it is important to distinguish the question of whether there can be a scientific theory of some phenomena from the question of whether there can be a unified theory of those phenomena. I doubt that the distinction is especially clear, or even if it is, that it is especially important. It seems to me that there can be a scientific theory of conscious phenomena in a relatively straightforward sense. Conscious phenomena constitute legitimate explananda, and conscious events play explanatory roles in certain well-grounded generalizations. Gathering together whatever scientific truths there are about this set of phenomena will constitute the theory of consciousness. It will amount to gathering together all the interesting truths about the class of phenomena that possess the shared feature of being experienced. Such a theory will cut across our theories of perception, memory, and learning. It will be replete with information about the neural substrate upon which phenomenal experiences supervene and about various kinds of nonconscious processes that are essential components of conscious phenomena. The theory of consciousness will be part of the larger, more systematic theory of the mind as a whole, and it is capable of taking on whatever depth the facts require. This much will confer two sorts of unity. First, the theory of consciousness will be about a set of phenomena that we find interesting in its own right and that we can mark fairly perspicuously by the shared phenomenal property. Second, the theory and the uncovered generalizations have a unity conferred by the fact that they are truths about a unified biological system, the human mind. The products of a scavenger hunt constitute a heap, an arbitrary set, because they are gathered from locations that have no interesting intersystemic relations. But facts gathered about aspects of the mind are facts about a complex integrated system. The truths about perception or memory or consciousness have a unity that derives from there being truths about salient kinds of activity of a unified mental system that is the product of evolutionary processes. Things are different with fire. Gathering together all the now accepted truths about fire will produce a theory in one sense, but it will have less integrity than the theory of consciousness, for there is no single system, certainly not a biologically evolved one, in which the heterogeneous kinds of fire occur, unless it is the whole universe itself.

There is perhaps a stronger sort of theoretical unity. A theory or a science can be unified in this stronger sense if there are certain important laws that govern all the types in its domain. Physics is often said to be unified, or on its way to unity, in this sense. But it is unclear why one of the least mature sciences should be judged against our most mature science. It may be that all conscious phenomena are governed by a small set of laws, and more generally that mental phenomena are governed by an even smaller but more inclusive set of laws. It is too early to tell. But it seems to me a mistake to hold up an idealized model of physics and hold that there must be a small set of deep laws that govern a domain for the domain to be a coherent domain of scientific inquiry. And in any case, even if we operate with this ideal, there is no way of knowing in advance of long-term inquiry which domains might satisfy the ideal and which domains most likely cannot.

There must be truths about consciousness, since consciousness exists, is a natural phenomena, and is in need of explanation. So there can be a theory of consciousness. What sort of unity the theory will possess and what interrelations it will have to other theories within the overall science of the mind we do not yet know. The best strategy is to get on with the hard work of providing the right fine-grained analysis of conscious mental life and see where it leads. It will be our proudest achievement if we can demystify consciousness. Consciousness exists. It would be a mistake to eliminate talk of it because its semantic past is so bound up with ghostly fairy tales or because it names such a multiplicity of things. The right attitude, it seems to me, is to deliver the concept from its ghostly past and provide it with a credible naturalistic analysis. I have tried to say a bit about how this might be done, indeed, about how it is already being done.

2   A Brief Recapitulation

The constructive naturalistic theory I have sketched pictures consciousness as a name for a heterogeneous set of events and processes that share the property of being experienced. Consciousness is taken to name a set of processes, not a thing or a mental faculty. The theory is neo-Darwinian in that it is committed to the view that the capacity to experience things evolved via the processes responsible for the development of our nervous system: migration, mutation, genetic drift, natural selection, and free riding. The theory denies that consciousness is as consciousness seems at the surface. Consciousness has a complex structure. Getting at this complex structure requires coordination of phenomenological, psychological, and neural analyses. The theory is neurophilosophical in that it tries to mesh a naturalistic metaphysic of mind with our still sketchy but maturing understanding of how the brain works. The most plausible hypothesis is that the mind is the brain, a Darwin machine that is a massively well-connected system of parallel processors interacting with each other from above and below and every which way besides. It is no wonder that meaning holism is true, that we somehow solve the frame problem, and that my belief that snow is white is realized quite possibly in a somewhat different way in my brain than the same belief is realized in yours. Finally, the theory claims to provide an explanation of the gap between the first-person way in which conscious mental life reveals itself and the way it is, or can be described, from an objective point of view. Mind and brain are one and the same

* Then, can't reply to Jackson that color scientist
acquired new knowl. on seeing red.

A Unified Theory of Consciousness?   221

thing seen from two different perspectives. The gap between the subjective
and the objective is an epistemic gap, not an ontological gap. Indeed, it is
precisely the fact that individuals possess organismic integrity that explains
why subjectivity accrues first-personally.

Conscious inessentialism, the doctrine that consciousness is not essential
to the analysis of human mentality, can be set to one side when the task is,
as I have framed it, to sketch a naturalistic theory of consciousness consistent with our natures as biological creatures with nervous systems of a
certain kind. There are possible creatures that are identical to us at the level
of observable input-output relations but that lack inner lives altogether. We
are not like this. Consciousness is essential to human nature and to the
human mind.

The epiphenomenalist suspicion should be taken seriously, but it should
not overwhelm us. Some conscious processes are akin to the ineffectual
functionary who is always the last to know. But other conscious processes
and models, including the self that is the center of narrative gravity, figure
crucially in cognition and in the overall conduct of our lives.

New mysterianism, the doctrine that consciousness is part of the natural
order, though it nonetheless can never be understood as such, is belied by
the degree of understanding that constructive naturalism has already given
to us. Thinking that consciousness is terminally mysterious is easy to fall
for if we set impossibly high standards on explanation and intelligibility.
But if we require "perfect intelligibility" for the consciousness-brain problem, then we should require such standards before we declare a solution to
any interesting problem relating two seemingly disparate phenomena. The
trouble is that abiding by such high standards would mean that we know
nothing about any interesting natural process, for example, the origin and
nature of life, the existence of the subatomic world, and so on. If we
operate with more sensible standards of intelligibility, several credible
stories can already be told to explain how such things as sensory qualia
supervene on certain patterns of neural activity. Just as ordinary water
is H_2O and is *caused* by H_2O, so too are experiences of colors, tastes,
and smells identical to and caused by activity patterns in certain brain
pathways. Higher-level sorts of consciousness also supervene on brain
processes. But whether they do so by satisfying even roughly hewn type-
identity conditions is something we do not yet know.

The idea that a mind's "I" stands behind all experience as a very condition of its possibility is an illusion. My consciousness is mine; it is uniquely
personal. But this is not because some mind's "I" or some immutable
transcendental ego shadows my experience. It is because of my organic
nature, because of the way thoughts hang together in evolved human
beings. The self emerges. It is a complex construct that we are eventually
able to represent in language and in thought. The self that is the center of

narrative gravity provides grounds for identity and self-respect. Conscious representation of this self is one type of self-consciousness. Such self-consciousness is nothing mysterious. It is realized in the brain. But the narrative represented is the joint production of the organism and the complex social world in which she lives her life. Presumably, it would be idle labor to look for type-identical neural maps of the self-representations of different individuals. This is not because self-representation is not neurally realized. It is because the phenomenological particularity of self-represented identity suggests neural particularity. Self-representation is a good candidate for activity that, despite being realized in the brain, is probably realized in very complex and multifarious ways. Our theories of self-representation may therefore profitably proceed with a certain explanatory autonomy from the level of neural analysis.

Despite its extraordinary difficulty, the problem of consciousness is beginning to yield. One will not see the entry points if one plays ostrich and puts one's head in the sand, having declared the whole thing beyond us. But if one looks to naturalistically informed work in the philosophy of mind, to neuroscience and neuropsychology, and to certain segments of psychology and cognitive science, one will see the sort of work I have described here, and one will be less reticent about undertaking the project of making consciousness reveal its secrets. Understanding consciousness with the conscious mind is a wonderful, giddy idea, yet it is also a genuine possibility.

References

Adams, Robert M. 1987. "Flavors, Colors, and God." In *The Virtue of Faith and Other Essays in Philosophical Theology*. New York: Oxford University Press.

Baars, B. J. 1988. *A Cognitive Theory of Consciousness*. Cambridge: Cambridge University Press.

Bandura, A. 1986. *The Social Foundation of Thought and Action: A Social Cognitive Theory*. Englewood Cliffs, N.J.: Prentice-Hall.

Block, N., ed. 1980a. *Readings in Philosophy of Psychology*. 2 vols. Cambridge: Harvard University Press.

Block, N. 1980b. "Troubles with Functionalism." In Block 1980a.

Block, N. 1991. "What Does Neuropsychology Tell Us about a Function of Consciousness?" Unpub. ms.

Block, N. 1992. "Begging the Question against Phenomenal Consciousness." *Behavioral and Brain Sciences*. Comment on Dennett and Kinsbourne 1992.

Bradford, H. F. 1987. "Neurotransmitters and Neuromodulators." In Gregory 1987.

Bratman, M. 1987. *Intention, Plans, and Practical Reason*. Cambridge: Harvard University Press.

Bruner, J. S. 1983. *In Search of Mind: Essays in Autobiography*. New York: Harper and Row.

Bruner, J. S. 1986. *Actual Minds, Possible Worlds*. Cambridge: Harvard University Press.

Calvin, W. H. 1990. *The Cerebral Symphony: Seashore Reflections on the Structure of Consciousness*. New York: Bantam.

Calvin, W. H. 1991. *The Ascent of Mind: Ice Age Climate and the Evolution of Intelligence*. New York: Bantam.

Changeux, J. P. 1985. *Neuronal Man: The Biology of Mind*. Translated by L. Garey. Oxford: Oxford University Press.

Churchland, Patricia S. 1983. "Consciousness: The Transmutation of a Concept." *Pacific Philosophical Quarterly* 64:80–93.

Churchland, Patricia S. 1986. *Neurophilosophy*. Cambridge: MIT Press.

Churchland, Patricia S. 1988. "Reduction and the Neurobiological Basis of Consciousness." In Marcel and Bisiach 1988.

Churchland, Paul M. 1981. "Eliminative Materialism and the Propositional Attitudes." *Journal of Philosophy* 78:67–90.

Churchland, Paul M. 1988. *Matter and Consciousness*. Rev. ed. Cambridge: MIT Press.

Churchland, Paul M. 1989. *A Neurocomputational Perspective: The Nature of Mind and the Structure of Science*. Cambridge: MIT Press.

Churchland, Paul M., and Patricia S. Churchland. 1990. "Intertheoretic Reduction: A Neuroscientist's Field Guide." *Seminars in the Neurosciences* 2:249–256.

Craik, K. 1943. *The Nature of Explanation*. Cambridge: Cambridge University Press.

Crick, Francis, and Christof Koch. 1990. "Towards a Neurobiological Theory of Consciousness." *Seminars in the Neurosciences* 2:263–275.

Dawkins, R. 1976. *The Selfish Gene*. Oxford: Oxford University Press.

Dennett, D. 1969. *Content and Consciousness*. London: Routledge and Kegan Paul.

Dennett, D. 1971. "Intentional Systems." In Dennett 1978.

Dennett, D. 1978. *Brainstorms*. Cambridge: MIT Press.

Dennett, D. 1982. "How to Study Consciousness Empirically; or, Nothing Comes to Mind." *Synthese* 59:159–180.

Dennett, D. 1986. "Julian Jaynes's Software Archeology." *Canadian Psychology* 27, no. 2:149–154.

Dennett, D. 1988a. "Why Everyone Is a Novelist." *Times Literary Supplement* 4, no. 459 (September): 1016–1022.

Dennett, D. 1988b. "The Evolution of Consciousness." CCM-88-1. Center for Cognitive Studies, Tufts University.

Dennett, D. 1988c. "Quining Qualia." In Marcel and Bisiach 1988.

Dennett, D. 1989. "The Origins of Selves." *Cogito* 2:163–173.

Dennett, D. 1991a. *Consciousness Explained*. New York: Little Brown.

Dennett, D. 1991b. Review of Colin McGinn, *The Problem of Consciousness*. *Times Literary Supplement*, May 10.

Dennett, D. 1991c. "The Problem of Consciousness." *Times Literary Supplement*, Letter. June 14.

Dennett, D. 1991d. "Real Patterns." *Journal of Philosophy* 88:27–51.

Dennett, D., and M. Kinsbourne. 1992. "Time and the Observer: The Where and When of Consciousness in the Brain." *Behavioral and Brain Sciences* 15:183–247.

Dewey, John. 1922. *Human Nature and Conduct*. New York: Henry Holt, 1957.

Dixon, N. F. 1987. "Subliminal Perception." In Gregory 1987.

Edelman, G. M. 1987. *Neural Darwinism*. New York: Basic Books.

Edelman, G. M. 1989. *The Remembered Present: A Biological Theory of Consciousness*. New York: Basic Books.

Ekman, P., R. W. Levinson, W. V. Freisen. 1985. "Autonomic Nervous-System Activity Distinguishes among Emotions." *Science* 221:1208–1210.

Erikson, Erik H. 1968. *Identity: Youth and Crisis*. New York: W. W. Norton.

Eysenck, H. J. 1967. *The Biological Basis of Personality*. Springfield, Ill.: Charles C. Thomas.

Fehrer, E., and D. Raab. 1962. "Reaction Time to Stimuli Masked by Metacontrast." *Journal of Experimental Psychology* 63, no. 2:143–147.

Flanagan, O. 1991a. *Varieties of Moral Personality: Ethics and Psychological Realism*. Cambridge: Harvard University Press.

Flanagan, O. 1991b. *The Science of the Mind*. 2nd ed. MIT Press.

Fodor, J. 1975. *The Language of Thought*. New York: Crowell.

Fodor, J. 1981. "Special Sciences." In *Representations*. Cambridge: MIT Press.

Fodor, J. 1991a. "Too Hard for Our Kind of Mind?" Review of Colin McGinn, *The Problem of Consciousness*. *London Review of Books*, p. 12.

Fodor, J. 1991b. "The Problem of Consciousness." Letter. *Times Literary Supplement*, June 7.

Gardner, Howard. 1983. *Frames of Mind: The Theory of Multiple Intelligences*. New York: Basic Books.

Gazzaniga, M. S. 1988. *Mind Matters: How Mind and Brain Interact to Create Our Conscious Lives*. Boston: Houghton Mifflin.

Goldman, A. I. 1986. *Epistemology and Cognition*. Cambridge: Harvard University Press.

Goldman, A. I. 1991. "The Psychology of Folk Psychology." Paper given at the annual meetings of the Society for Philosophy and Psychology, San Francisco.

Gould, S. J., and R. Lewontin. 1979. "The Spandrels of San Marco and the Panglossian Paradigm: A Critique of the Adaptationist Programme." *Proceedings of the Royal Society of London*, series B, 205.

Gregory, R., ed. 1987. *The Oxford Companion to Mind*. Oxford: Oxford University Press.

Griffin, Donald R. 1981. *The Question of Animal Awareness: Evolutionary Continuity of Mental Experience*. Los Altos, Calif.: William Kaufmann.

Hacking, Ian. 1991. "Two Souls in One Body." *Critical Inquiry* 17, no. 4:838–867.

Hardin, C. L. 1988. *Color for Philosophers: Unweaving the Rainbow*. Indianapolis: Hackett.

Henriques, J. B., and R. J. Davidson. 1990. "Regional Brain Electrical Asymmetries Discriminate between Previously Depressed and Healthy Control Subjects." *Journal of Abnormal Psychology* 99, no.1: 22–31.

Hobson, J. Allan. 1988. *The Dreaming Brain*. New York: Basic Books.

Hume, David. 1777. *Enquiries Concerning Human Understanding and Concerning the Principles of Morals*. Ed. L. A. Selby-Bigge. Oxford: Oxford University Press, 1975.

Humphrey, N., and D. C. Dennett. 1989. "Speaking for Ourselves." *Raritan: A Quarterly Review* 9:69–98.

Hundert, E. 1989. *Philosophy, Psychiatry, and Neuroscience: Three Approaches to Mind*. New York: Oxford University Press.

Jackendoff, R. 1987. *Consciousness and the Computational Mind*. Cambridge: MIT Press.

Jackson, F. 1982. "Epiphenomenal Qualia." *Philosophical Quarterly* 32:127–136.

Jackson, F. 1986. "What Mary Didn't Know." *Journal of Philosophy* 83, no. 5:291–295. Reprinted in D. Rosenthal, ed., *The Nature of Mind*. New York: Oxford University Press, 1991.

James, William. 1890. *The Principles of Psychology*. 2 vols. New York: Dover, 1950.

James, William. 1892. *Psychology: The Briefer Course*. Ed. G. Allport. New York: Harper and Row, 1961.

Jaynes, J. 1976. *The Origin of Consciousness in the Breakdown of the Bicameral Mind*. Boston: Houghton Mifflin.

Johnson, Mark. 1987. *The Body in the Mind*. Chicago: University of Chicago Press.

Johnson-Laird, P. N. 1983. *Mental Models*. Cambridge: Harvard University Press.

Johnson-Laird, P. N. 1988. *The Computer and the Mind: An Invitation to Cognitive Science*. Cambridge: Harvard University Press.

Kagan, J. 1984. *The Nature of the Child*. New York: Basic Books.

Kagan, J. 1989. *Unstable Ideas: Temperament, Cognition, and Self*. Cambridge: Harvard University Press.

Kermode, Frank. 1967. *The Sense of an Ending: Studies in the Theory of Fiction*. New York: Oxford University Press.

Kim, Jaegwon. 1990. "Supervenience as a Philosophical Concept," C-3, no. 23, Research Group on Mind and Brain, University of Bielefeld.

Lackner, J., and M. Garrett. 1973. "Resolving Ambiguity: Effects of Biasing Context in the Unattended Ear." *Cognition* 1:359–372.

Lakoff, G. 1987. *Women, Fire, and Dangerous Things: What Categories Reveal about the Mind*. Chicago: University of Chicago Press.

Levine, J. 1983. "Materialism and Qualia: The Explanatory Gap." *Pacific Philosophical Quarterly* 64:354–361.

Lewis, David. 1980. "Mad Pain and Martian Pain." In Block 1980a.

Libet, B. 1985. "Unconscious Cerebral Initiative and the Role of Conscious Will in Voluntary Action." *Behavioral and Brain Sciences* 8:529–566.

Lloyd, Dan. 1989. *Simple Minds*. Cambridge: MIT Press.

Loar, Brian. 1990. "Phenomenal Properties." In *Philosophical Perspectives: Action Theory and Philosophy of Mind*. Atascerdo, Calif.: Ridgeview.

Locke, John. 1690. *An Essay Concerning Human Understanding*. Ed. P. H. Nidditch. 2nd ed., 1694. 5th ed., 1706. Oxford: Oxford University Press, 1975.

Logothetis, N., and J. D. Schall. 1989. "Neuronal Correlates of Subjective Visual Perception." *Science* 245:761–763.

Luria, A. R. 1972. *The Man with the Shattered World.* Cambridge: Harvard University Press, 1987.

Lycan, W. 1981. "Form, Function, and Feel." *Journal of Philosophy* 78:23–49.

Lycan, W. 1987. *Consciousness.* Cambridge: MIT Press.

McCauley, R. N. 1986. "Intertheoretic Reduction and the Future of Psychology." *Philosophy of Science* 53:179–199.

McCauley, R. N. In press. "Cross-Scientific Study and the Complexity of Psychology." *Annals of Theoretical Psychology*, vol. 8.

McGinn, C. 1989. "Can We Solve the Mind-Body Problem?" *Mind* 98:349–366. Reprinted in McGinn 1991.

McGinn, C. 1991. *The Problem of Consciousness.* Oxford: Blackwell.

MacIntyre, A. 1981. *After Virtue.* London: Duckworth.

Mandler, George. 1985. *Cognitive Psychology: An Essay in Cognitive Science.* New York: L. Erlbaum.

Marcel, A. J. 1988. "Phenomenal Experience and Functionalism." In Marcel and Bisiach 1988.

Marcel, A. J., and E. Bisiach, eds. 1988. *Consciousness in Contemporary Science.* Oxford: Oxford University Press.

Marr, David. 1982. *Vision.* San Francisco: Freeman.

Minsky, M. 1985. *The Society of Mind.* New York: Simon and Schuster.

Myers, Gerald E. 1986. *William James: His Life and Thought.* New Haven: Yale University Press.

Nagel, Thomas. 1974. "What Is It Like to Be a Bat?" In *Mortal Questions.* Cambridge: Cambridge University Press, 1979.

Nagel, Thomas. 1986. *The View from Nowhere.* New York: Oxford University Press.

Peirce, C. S. 1898. *Collected Papers.* Vol. 6, *Scientific Metaphysics.* Ed. C. Hartshorne and P. Weiss. Cambridge: Harvard University Press, 1935.

Phelps, M. E., and J. C. Mazziotta. 1985. Positron Emission Tomography: Human Brain Function and Biochemistry. *Science* 228:799–809.

Popper, K., and J. Eccles. 1977. *The Self and Its Brain.* New York. Springer-Verlag.

Quine, W. V. O. 1952. "On Mental Entities." In *The Ways of Paradox and Other Essays.* New York: Random House, 1966.

Quine, W. V. O. 1985. "States of Mind." *Journal of Philosophy* 82, no. 1:5–8.

Raichle, Marcus E. 1987. "Images of the Brain in Action." In Gregory 1987.

Rey, Georges. 1983. "A Reason for Doubting the Existence of Consciousness." In *Consciousness and Self-Regulation*, vol. 3, ed. R. J. Davidson, G. E. Schwartz, and D. Shapiro. New York: Plenum.

Rey, Georges. 1988. "A Question about Consciousness." In *Perspectives on Mind*, ed. H. R. Otto and J. A. Tuedio. Dordrecht: Reidel.

Rorty, R. 1982. *Consequences of Pragmatism.* Minneapolis: University of Minnesota Press.

Rosenthal, David. 1986. "Two Concepts of Consciousness." *Philosophical Studies* 49:329–359.

Rosenthal, David. 1989. "Thinking That One Thinks." ZIF report no. 11, Research Group on Mind and Brain, University of Bielefeld, Germany.

Rosenthal, David. 1990. "Why Are Verbally Expressed Thoughts Conscious?" ZIF report no. 32, Research Group on Mind and Brain, University of Bielefeld, Germany.

Rumelhart, D., J. McClelland, and the PDP Research Group. 1986. *Parallel Distributed Processing: Explorations in the Microstructure of Cognition.* 2 vols. Cambridge: MIT Press. Order of authors is McClelland and Rumelhart for vol. 2.

Ryle, Gilbert. 1949. *The Concept of Mind.* London: Hutchinson.

Sacks, Oliver. 1983. *Awakenings.* New York: Dutton.

Sacks, Oliver. 1985. *The Man Who Mistook His Wife for a Hat and Other Clinical Tales*. New York: Summit.

Sandel, M. 1982. *Liberalism and the Limits of Justice*. Cambridge: Cambridge University Press.

Schacter, D. 1989. "On the Relation between Memory and Consciousness: Dissociable Interactions and Conscious Experience." In *Varieties of Memory and Consciousness: Essays in Honour of Endel Tulving*, ed. Henry L. Roediger III and F. I. M. Craik. Hillsdale, N.J.: L. Erlbaum.

Searle, J. 1984. *Minds, Brains, and Science*. Cambridge: Harvard University Press.

Shallice, T. 1988. *From Neuropsychology to Mental Structure*. Cambridge: Cambridge University Press.

Shweder, Richard. 1991. *Thinking through Cultures*. Cambridge: Harvard University Press.

Smolensky, Paul. 1988. "On the Proper Treatment of Connectionism." *Behavioral and Brain Sciences* 11:1–23.

Spence, D. 1982. *Narrative Truth and Historical Truth: Meaning and Interpretation in Psychoanalysis*. New York: W. W. Norton.

Squire, L., and S. Zola-Morgan. 1991. "The Medial Temporal Lobe Memory System." *Science* 253:1380–1386.

Stern, D. N. 1985. *The Interpersonal World of the Infant*. New York: Basic Books.

Stich, S. 1978. "Autonomous Psychology and the Belief-Desire Thesis." *The Monist*, vol. 61.

Swinburne, R. 1984. "Personal Identity: The Dualist Theory." In *Personal Identity*, ed. S. Shoemaker and Richard Swinburne. Oxford: Blackwell.

Taylor, Charles. 1989. *Sources of the Self: The Making of the Modern Identity*. Cambridge: Harvard University Press.

Treisman, A. M., and H. Schmidt. 1982. Illusory Conjunctions in the Perceptions of Objects. *Cognitive Psychology* 14:107–141.

Van Gulick, R. 1988. "A Functionalist Plea for Self-Consciousness." *Philosophical Review* 97, no. 2: 149–181.

Van Gulick, R. 1990. "What Difference Does Consciousness Make?" *Philosophical Topics* 17:211–230.

Van Gulick, R. In press a. "Understanding the Phenomenal Mind: Are We All Just Armadillos?" In *Consciousness: A Mind and Language Reader*, ed. M. Davies and G. Humphrey Oxford: Blackwell.

Van Gulick, R. In press b. "Consciousness May Still Have a Processing Role to Play." *Brain and Behavioral Sciences*.

Varela, F. J., E. Thompson, E. Rosch. 1991. *The Embodied Mind: Cognitive Science and Human Experience*. Cambridge: MIT Press.

Velmans, M. In press. "Is Human Information Processing Conscious?" *Brain and Behavioral Sciences*.

Von der Heydt, R., E. Peterhans, and G. Baumgartner. 1984. "Illusory Contours and Cortical Neuron Response." *Science* 224:1260–1262.

Weiskrantz, L. 1988. "Some Contributions of Neuropsychology of Vision and Memory to the Problem of Consciousness." In Marcel and Bisiach 1988.

Weiss, Rick. 1990. "A Flight of Fancy Mathematics: Chaos Brings Harmony to a Birder's Puzzle." *Science News* 137:172.

Wellman, Henry M. 1990. *The Child's Theory of Mind*. Cambridge: MIT Press.

Wimsatt, W. 1976. "Reductionism, Levels of Organization, and the Mind-Body Problem." In *Consciousness and the Brain*, ed. G. Globus, G. Maxwell, and I. Savodnik. New York: Plenum.

Wilkes, K. V. 1988a. *Real People: Personal Identity without Thought Experiments*. Oxford: Oxford University Press.

Wilkes, K. V. 1988b. "_____, Yishi, Duh, Um, and Consciousness." In Marcel and Bisiach 1988.

Index